# A CONSUMER'S GUIDE
## TO THE
## PUBLIC SCHOOL

# A CONSUMER'S GUIDE TO THE PUBLIC SCHOOL

*Edited by*

## GARY M. MILLER, Ph.D.

*Associate Professor*
*College of Education*
*University of South Carolina*
*Columbia, South Carolina*

*and*

## GYURI NEMETH, Ph.D.

*Assistant Principal*
*Tucker High School*
*DeKalb County School System*
*Tucker, Georgia*

CHARLES C THOMAS • PUBLISHER
*Springfield • Illinois • U.S.A.*

*Published and Distributed Throughout the World by*
CHARLES C THOMAS • PUBLISHER
2600 South First Street
Springfield, Illinois, 62717, U.S.A.

© *1983, by* CHARLES C THOMAS • PUBLISHER

ISBN 0-398-04755-3

Library of Congress Catalog Card Number: 82-10628

*Printed in the United States of America*
*CU-R-1*

*Library of Congress Cataloging in Publication Data*
Main Entry under title:

A Consumer's guide to the public school.

Bibliography: p.
Includes index.
1. Public schools--United States--Addresses, essays,
lectures.    I. Miller, Gary M., 1941-        II. Nemeth,
Gyuri.
LA217.C63   1983        371'.01'0973        82-10628
ISBN 0-398-04755-3

# PREFACE

P UBLIC education is unique to the United States. Throughout the development of this educational adventure, numerous forces have influenced the development of public education. Combined with these influences has been an increased specialization of personnel who work in our schools.

This book examines the development of education and the numerous specialists who currently work with students and school personnel. It has been developed to assist the reader to acquire a better comprehension of public education and a clearer understanding of what one can anticipate in the way of services from professional educators.

We hope this book is helpful to you as a consumer of public education. We also hope reading it will encourage you to talk with your local educators about the programs and services they offer.

G.M.M.
G.N.

# CONTENTS

    *Page*

*Preface* ............................................................ v

*Chapter*

1. THE HISTORICAL DEVELOPMENT OF AMERICAN EDUCATION ....... 3
   *Josephine Walker Martin*
2. THE CHILDREN WE TEACH ............................. 40
   *Sandra Longfellow Robinson and Edward H. Robinson III*
3. WHAT TO LOOK FOR IN EARLY CHILDHOOD EDUCATION ......... 56
   *Kevin J. Swick and Pamela Kearce*
4. THE ROLE OF THE ELEMENTARY TEACHER IN THE
      PUBLIC SCHOOL ...................................... 71
   *John Van Hoose and Evelyn B. Dandy*
5. THE ROLE OF THE SECONDARY TEACHER IN THE
      PUBLIC SCHOOL ...................................... 87
   *Fredric L. Splittgerber and Richard H. Kherlopian*
6. THE ADMINISTRATIVE ASPECT OF PUBLIC SCHOOLS ............ 103
   *Gyuri Nemeth*
7. THE SCHOOL GUIDANCE COUNSELOR ....................... 116
   *Gary M. Miller*
8. THE SCHOOL PSYCHOLOGIST ............................ 135
   *Susan G. Forman and Ann W. Engin*
9. THE ROLE OF THE SPECIAL EDUCATOR ..................... 154
   *Dean K. McIntosh*
10. ROLES AND RESPONSIBILITIES OF THE READING SPECIALIST ...... 173
    *Richard E. Kemper*
11. VOCATIONAL AND CAREER EDUCATION ..................... 189
    *Leonard Maiden*
12. COMMUNITY-BASED, LIFELONG EDUCATION ................. 202
    *H. Larry Winecoff and W. Jackson Lyday*

13. CITIZEN PARTICIPATION IN EDUCATION....................226
*Mary C. Jackson and Mary House Kessler*

Appendix...............................................257
Name Index............................................263
Subject Index.........................................267

# A CONSUMER'S GUIDE
## TO THE
## PUBLIC SCHOOL

# Chapter 1

# THE HISTORICAL DEVELOPMENT
# OF AMERICAN EDUCATION

JOSEPHINE WALKER MARTIN

*JOSEPHINE W. MARTIN is an associate professor in the Department of Social Foundations, College of Education, University of South Carolina. She holds a master's degree from Columbia University/Union Theological Seminary, a master's degree in secondary education, and a doctorate in foundations of education from the University of South Carolina.*

*She is a former teacher of U.S. history, English, and French and a guidance counselor in public secondary schools in South Carolina. Her writings concerning the history of education include "I See the Need for Somebody to Be Here," University of South Carolina Education Report, 14, December 1971, "The Carolina Teacher: South Carolina's First State Education Journal," South Carolina Education Journal, 3, Spring 1972, and "Dear Sister" Letters written on Hilton Head Island 1867. Beaufort, South Carolina, Beaufort Book Company, 1977.*

---

Education in the United States has been developing from small beginnings, not without difficulty, since the time of the American Revolution, which necessitated the blessings of education along with the blessings of liberty. It would be of benefit, therefore, to understand the educational ideas of the English people who colonized the Atlantic coast of North America beginning in the early decades of the seventeenth century, as it will help us understand traditional ideas as well as the newer ideas of education in the development of our public school system. Both are attracting much attention from many segments within our society today.

## MEDIEVAL EDUCATION

The educational ideas brought to colonial America by the English colonists were to a great extent an inheritance from the cathedral schools of the Middle Ages. These schools were established by the church primarily for the education of boys who were to become priests, but sons of the nobility, who would hold secular positions in society, were also admitted to study in these schools.

The church exercised full control over the schools. The bishop of the diocese had the authority to license the headmaster and teachers for positions within the city and the diocese, specifying their duties in what would be considered a contract today. These schools were not free to all students; well-to-do boys paid tuition but the head-master was required to teach without charge bright but poor boys (Wieruszowski, 1966).

All the students studied Latin grammar, that is they learned to read, write, and speak Latin, the universal means of communication in the religious and intellectual life of the times. The readings were from the Holy Scriptures, the writings of the church fathers, and from classical Roman writers, who emphasized the importance of character and virtue. Enough arithmetic was taught to do basic com-putations, and music was learned for church services. The teaching method in these schools was memorization. Lapses in learning and in conduct were corrected with corporal punishment. While the cur-riculum was religious and literary, the primary goal was practical, for the ability to speak, read, and write Latin was essential for a career in the church or the state.

Girls were not admitted to the cathedral schools, but education was available to some in the convents. Nuns were taught to read and write, and were educated in religion; however, the convents were not noted intellectual centers.

During the twelfth century, noted cathedral schools were attract-ing students from all over Europe. These large schools were ad-ministered by the chancellor of the cathedral who was given the authority to issue the *licentia docendi,* a license to teach within the diocese, to men who passed a required examination. This examina-tion was an attempt to ensure the scholarship and orthodoxy of the teachers. No one was allowed to teach in any school or in private without the license. As these schools increased in size and in ex-cellence they acquired the title *studium generale,* a place of general study. In 1179 the pope, recognizing their importance to the entire church, granted their graduates a license to teach anywhere, *licentia docendi ubique* (Wieruszowksi, 1966).

By the end of the twelfth century, church schools with the title *studium generale* had evolved into universities. Students sought out a distinguished teacher with whom they wished to study, and the master and his students comprised a guild, a university (Barnes, 1971). The teacher was a master of the seven liberal arts, one who had served his apprenticeship of study in a way similar to a master in the craft guild and one who had been granted the universal teaching license.

The curriculum in the universities was grammar, rhetoric, logic (the Trivium), arithmetic, geometry, astronomy, and music (the Quadrivium); and the philosophy of Aristotle. To receive a bachelor of arts (an apprentice teacher) the student studied for three or four years and passed an examination of the Trivium. To receive a master of arts, he completed the study of the Quadrivium and studied Aristotle for another four or five years. Usually, he was required to defend a thesis as well. To become a doctor in theology, law, or medicine there were additional years of study, and at Paris no one less than thirty-five years of age could become a doctor (Thompson & Johnson, 1937).

Courses were taught by the lecture method, the master reading from his text, commenting and interpreting as he read. This method was necessary because the printing press had not been invented, texts — handwritten manuscripts — were too scarce and expensive for students to own, and there were no libraries in the early universities. Another learning method in the universities was the formal disputation or debate by students. Unlike the lecture, the debate gave the students an opportunity to use their intellectual skills, judgment, and training in logic. The disputation was also excellent preparation for the student's final challenge, the defense of his thesis.

Faculty prerogatives were an issue before the year 1200. The masters wished to control their own affairs as other guilds did, setting the curriculum, the standards for teaching, appointing new faculty members, and having a voice in the licensing of teachers. The faculty also wanted the master of arts degree recognized as the license to teach rather than having the chancellor of the university grant the license. By the end of the thirteenth century, the men awarded the master of arts were qualified to teach in any university (Downs, 1959).

Although the faculty were concerned with these practical matters, their aim was to produce Christian scholars. To achieve this they emphasized grammar and logic, believing that these two subjects strengthened the powers of reason and led, through knowledge of philosophical truth, to God, a mental attitude that, above all others, was suited to Christians (Wieruszowski, 1966).

## RENAISSANCE EDUCATION

Medieval ways of thinking and political and social patterns were changing as the Renaissance began in northern Italy in the late 1300s. Whereas medieval education had placed emphasis upon piety, humility, and obedience and had discouraged individualism, the education of Renaissance Italy was to emphasize personal excellence and individuality, the complete man of action in this world.

The Italian intellectuals of the fifteenth century felt themselves to be the direct inheritors of the ancient Roman empire, not just the Rome of St. Peter, the church fathers, and the popes. Francis Petrarch led a group of Florentine intellectuals to search the monastic libraries for long lost classical works, laboriously copied and preserved by monks centuries before. As the manuscripts were recovered, they were copied by scholars, studied, and compared with other manuscripts, thus initiating historical criticism as they learned classical Latin (Artz, 1966).

The study of the Latin works was the study of Roman history and culture. The old idea of the citizen as an educated man of action was the view held by the Italians of the Renaissance. The ideal of the *l'uomo universale*, the complete man, was one who had a knowledge of the classics, history, poetry, and moral philosophy and was also a master of rhetoric, "the art of graceful but forceful persuasion" (De Molen, 1974, p. 42). An appreciation of the arts was essential as well as physical vigor, grace, and skill in the martial arts. Above all, the complete man sought full self-realization, glory, and fame, at the same time not seeming to do so (Plumb, 1965).

When Cicero's *De Oratore* was discovered in 1422, what must have been the thoughts of the first Renaissance teacher when he read these lines? "My private opinion is, that no one can be real orator in the full sense of the word unless he first acquires a knowledge of all the great subjects of human study" (Hadas, 1951, p. 179). These subjects were the humanities (*humanitas*). The humanities were to be studied as a guide to an active, practical, and worthy life in society.

What education was needed to produce this new man? Who was to be educated and how? During the first half of the fifteenth century, several works on education besides Cicero's *De Oratore* were recovered. Plato's *Republic* and Aristotle's *Politics* were translated into Latin and had an impact upon Renaissance thought, but a complete copy of Quintilian's *Institutes of Oratory,* discovered in the year 1416, had the greatest effect upon education and his work influenced such Renaissance educators as Vittorino da Feltre, Erasmus, and Martin Luther (Wheelock, 1974).

Quintilian's educational classic, written at the request of friends after he had retired from twenty years of teaching, was completed about the year 95 A.D. His aim of education was to form the good man, the man of character, skilled in the art of speaking.

The education necessary to the task was in three stages: preschool or early childhood in the home, grammar school, and the rhetorical school. Quintilian, the only educator of antiquity who detailed his ideas of early childhood education, believed that most children are quick to reason and to learn. Their home environment should be such that they are ready and eager to attend school, the aim of public kindergartens today.

In the grammar school, equivalent to our upper elementary and secondary levels, the boys' schoolmaster was expected to adapt his teaching to the abilities and capacities of the students. Learning was encouraged by competition with classmates and praise and attention from the teacher. Quintilian strongly disapproved of whipping, the usual method of discipline, calling it "a disgraceful form of punishment . . . an insult" (Wheelock, 1974, p. 46).

The curriculum in the grammar school was writing and reading Latin literature and learning to speak and read Greek. This preparatory training of the orator, the "good man skilled in speaking" (Rusk, 1967, p. 40), also included music, arithmetic and geometry, and physical training for health and graceful bearing.

The school of rhetoric completed the education of the orator, the man of character as a citizen who is qualified for the management of "public and private business, the man who can guide a state by his counsels" (Wheelock, 1974, p. 24).

The pattern of the Renaissance schools in Italy was established by Vittorino da Feltre, the first and greatist humanist schoolmaster, who combined Quintilian's aims, classical curriculum, and methods of education with the moral and religious teaching of the church in the school he established in 1423 for the four sons and the daughter of the Marquis of Mantua. Other children were invited to attend the school, and Vittorino chose some poor boys of outstanding ability and character to attend the school free of charge. The students ranged in age from six to twenty for older student teachers.

Life in the school was natural and happy. After the young children had learned to read and write in Italian and had learned arithmetic through games, they began Latin, which the older students were required to speak in school. Religion was not taught directly, but the students attended daily mass, and morals were inculcated in the traditional way through stories and strict supervision of behavior.

At about age six, boys began their rhetorical studies, memorizing and reciting short passages from Latin classics, and by age ten some were composing and reciting their own compositions following Quintilian's models. Mathematics were studied as good training in orderly habits of mind. Instruction in Greek in order to read ancient philosophy and the New Testament was given in the advanced classes. Along with academic instruction, the knightly disciplines of fencing, wrestling, and riding were learned, the students acquiring grace of movement quite naturally. Vittorino's education was thus a practical discipline, preparing youth for a life of action by training mind, character, and body (Woodward, 1906; 1967).

The Graeco-Roman ideal of the Renaissance schools emphasized individual development and assertiveness in politics, the church, literature, and art. This was the education of the children of patrician families and also of the sons and daughters of the merchant middle class who were educated to be courtiers and ladies of distinction. The modern era had begun in Italy and a new kind of education was its hallmark.

The spread of the new classical learning into Northern Europe during the second half of the fifteenth century was greatly aided by the invention of printing making available the classics and the writings of Christian antiquity. Churchmen and scholars in the north became aware of the importance of a knowledge of Greek and Hebrew for the study of the Bible, early Christian literature, and church history. This study made it obvious that the church had lost its original simplicity and that many church practices had no scriptural or historical basis. The study of the Holy Scriptures thus added a new dimension to the religious life and to religion as a means of improving society. As contrasted with the Italian humanists, the northern or Christian humanists were more interested in religious matters, in improving public morality, and in encouraging a new piety, through which men and society could be reformed as a result of intellectual discipline and the new learning. Thus a new program of education was essential (Gilmore, 1962).

The new learning of the Renaissance was begun in England by John Colet, dean of St. Paul's Cathedral in London, when in 1509 he gave a large sum of money inherited from his father to establish a new grammar school for "education and bringing up children in good manners and literature and to increase knowledge and worshipping God" (Lupton, 1887; 1961, pp. 271 & 279). One hundred and fifty-three boys were to be taught free, until age fifteen or sixteen, an unusually large school for its day.

Colet gave careful thought and planning to the school and was aided by his close friend Erasmus, the most noted northern humanist scholar. Erasmus wrote a discourse for Colet on teaching methods and curriculum, *De Ratione Studii*, reflecting Quintilian's work, which was the basis for the school's curriculum. Recognizing the need for textbooks written for students, Erasmus prepared *De Copia* to give beginning students in Latin composition a thesaurus, a book of Latin words, idioms, and ideas from classic works. Colet wrote a Latin grammar for the schoolboys, in which he noted that "Latin speech was before the rules, not the rules before the Latin speech" (Lupton, 1887; 1961, p. 291).

The schoolboys had to be able to read and write English before they were admitted at age six or eight. The curriculum included for the first time in an English grammar school the study of the Greek language as well as Latin. Religious studies and daily worship were customary, and Colet wrote his own catechism for the boys. Colet had an unusual appreciation and understanding of the child's nature and, like Eramus, insisted upon kind and gentle teaching methods. Colet's *Statutes* for the school differed greatly from other schools. Recognizing that conditions would change, he did not lock the headmaster into a fully specified curriculum and textbooks.

During the mid-sixteenth and continuing into the seventeenth century, many of the old grammar schools adopted St. Paul's school curriculum, but not its teaching methods. By 1575 there were some 350 grammar schools in England. The education in these schools, while religious and literary, was also utilitarian in that young men were able to communicate in Latin with educated men of other countries, and the studies were preparation for Oxford, Cambridge, or any university in Europe. It was the means for the young man, whether his father was a gentleman, yeoman farmer, shopkeeper, or tradesman, who going on to Oxford or Cambridge would be considered a scholar and gentleman, educated for a position in law, medicine, the church, or other leadership in society (Notestein, 1962).

## THE REFORMATION

The element of reform, which had been inherent in northern humanism from its beginning, moved from the university into the world in 1517 when Martin Luther, a young German professor and priest at Wittenberg University, was drawn into the area of controversy and reform within the church by his objections to the sale of indulgences (De Molen, 1974). He posted his ninety-five propositions for debate to the door of the castle church, a common practice of disputation or debate in the universities. The debate did not take place, but because of the new printing presses, Luther's theses were published and within a few months were circulated throughout Germany and Europe.

Much controversy ensued during which time Luther clarified his position and his theology. In 1521, refusing to repudiate his writings and accepting only the Bible as the ultimate authority for church doctrines and practices, he came under the ban of the church. Luther had become, however reluctantly, the leader in reformation.

Other Christian humanists took their stand for reformation of the church, notably Zwingli and Calvin. Both men agreed with Luther that the Bible was the ultimate authority for church doctrine, practice, and guide for life; thus the teaching of reading to every child, male or female, became a religious necessity for the first time.

In Germany Luther urged the government to make elementary education in church schools compulsory. Calvin and his followers in Holland and in Scotland emphasized establishing schools not only in the cities and towns but also in the country so that all children would learn to read, learn the catechism and the Ten Commandments.

The Reformation came last to England. The reason for the break with Rome was political rather than doctrinal as had been the case with Luther and Calvin. In 1527 Henry VIII, having no son as heir to the English throne, requested and not unreasonably expected in view of the custom of the time an annulment of his marriage to Queen Catherine. Unfortunately for Henry, the Emperor Charles V, Catherine's nephew, gained control of Rome and the papacy. The annulment was not forthcoming. Henry continued to seek an annulment from the pope until 1533 when the Archbishop of Canterbury pronounced the marriage null and void (Bindoff, 1950). In 1534 Parliament passed the Act of Supremacy, declaring the king "the only supreme head in earth of the Church in England" (Bainton, 1956, p. 143). Parliament denied the authority of the pope in civil matters in England but church doctrine was not changed at this time.

Education in England, which continued the pattern of church schools, suffered a setback when Henry VIII seized the monasteries and confiscated their wealth. This took from many poor boys the opportunity of a Latin grammar school education. However, the royal injunctions of 1536 and 1538 ordered all priests to teach children the Creed, the Lord's Prayer, and the Ten Commandments in English instead of Latin. In order to achieve a better educated clergy for English churches, the injunction of 1538 required priests in wealthy parishes to give financial aid to needy Latin grammar school students and university students (De Molen, 1974, p. 242).

While many elementary schools were destroyed by the seizure of the monasteries, Henry VIII encouraged humanistic studies (Caspari, 1968). Many new grammar schools were founded and Henry himself reestablished eleven important cathedral grammar schools along humanist lines (Thompson, 1958).

An accomplished student of the classics, Henry encouraged the teaching of classical studies and the endowment of chairs of Greek and Hebrew in the universities. At Oxford, he founded Christ Church College, a center for humanist studies, and Trinity College at Cambridge (Caspari, 1968).

While there was no call from Henry or from the leadership of the Church of England to establish elementary schools to teach all children to read in order to read the Bible, there were some elementary schools called petty schools, taught by local clergymen or housewives, in which boys and girls usually at four years of age were taught to read English and the elements of arithmetic. The books used by the children were *The ABC with the Catechism* and the *Primer* which contained the Lord's Prayer, the Creed, the Ten Commandments, and the Psalms (Thompson, 1958). The children usually attended the petty school for three years. The boys were prepared to enter the Latin grammar school and the girls, if they were to be educated further, were educated at home.

The actual reformation of the Church of England did not begin until Henry VIII was succeeded by his nine-year-old son, Edward VI (1547-1553). The Edwardian Act of Uniformity in 1549 made the English *Book of Common Prayer* the only legal form of public worship in England. Together with the English Bible and the school primers of Henry's reign, an English form of Protestantism was being established. This was interrupted during the short reign of Queen Mary (1553-1558) who reinstated Catholicism. At that time many Protestant clergy and laymen went into exile in Calvinist Switzerland.

When Queen Elizabeth acceded to the throne in 1558, the *Book of Common Prayer* was restored as the only authorized liturgy and the 1559 Act of Supremacy made the queen the only "supreme governor" in all spiritual and temporal matters. The exiles returned to England, and, in their desire to reform the Church of England along the lines of Calvin's teachings, the Puritan movement was begun and soon came into conflict with the established church. Many Puritan clergymen and teachers refused to conform to the practices and ceremonies of the Church of England. An oath was imposed on all schoolmasters and public and private teachers to ensure that they recognized the supremacy of the queen in church matters before receiving from the bishop a license to teach (Armytage, 1970).

During Elizabeth's reign thirty-two new Latin grammar schools were founded by secular charitable trusts and by 1600 there were 542 of these schools throughout England where an able poor boy could receive a free education that would prepare him to enter Oxford or Cambridge (Armytage, 1970).

In 1601, two years before the death of Queen Elizabeth, an attempt was made to break the poverty cycle in England. The Act for the Relief of the Poor taxed property owners in every parish to provide for the poor and required the compulsory apprenticing of poor children (Knight, Vol 1, 1949).

The Puritan clergy looked forward with hope to the accession of King James I (1603-1625) who had been brought up in Scotland under John Knox's stern Calvinism. They expected a sympathetic hearing to their petition for changes in practices in the Church of England, but their hopes were short-lived for James told them to conform to the *Book of Common Prayer* or be removed from their churches. Relatively few refused to conform, but some Puritans left for Holland (Ashley, 1961).

## COLONIAL EDUCATION

In the first two decades of the seventeenth century English colonization in North America was quite slow, but with an economic depression and the persecution of Puritans after 1625, congregational groups considered the possibility of establishing the Lord's Society, the New Jerusalem, in America. In 1629 a group of Puritans secured from King Charles I a charter for the Massachusetts Bay Company and prepared to leave England for America (Morison, 1965).

The Puritans went to America in family groups for a religious purpose and they took with them the traditional humanist education of the Latin grammar school and the college, necessary for the education of clergy and secular leaders. In Massachusetts, however, by the Act of 1642, the teaching of reading to all children was required for the first time in the English speaking world. The law empowered the select men, town officials, to see that parents and masters of indentured children were teaching them "to read and understand the principles of religion and the capital laws of the country" and, reflecting the English Poor Law of 1601, the law also required the apprenticing of children who were not being taught a trade. This act placed direct responsibility for supervision of education upon secular authorities, rather than the church (Noll & Kelly, 1970).

In 1647 a second school act stipulated that every town of fifty householders appoint a teacher of reading and writing for any parents and masters wishing to send their children to him for instruction. His salary was to be paid by the parents or masters of the children or by the inhabitants in general. In small villages children were taught the ABCs from a primer, writing, and the rudiments of arithmetic in "Dame Schools," by a housewife, in much the same way as in the petty schools of England (Noll & Kelly, 1970).

Secondary and higher education were not neglected. The 1647 law required every town of 100 households to establish a Latin grammar school in order to give a good general education in the humanities to as many boys as possible. The grammar schools prepared boys to enter Harvard College, which had been founded in 1636 "to advance learning and perpetuate it to posterity" (Cremin, 1970, p. 210) and to provide clergyman.

The settlement of New England in compact townships, organized for religious, economic, and political purposes, made community action possible. Going beyond the requirements of the 1642 act, requiring parents or masters to teach children to read, towns established common schools open to all the children in the community. Parents able to do so paid tuition, but children of poor families were taught free. Education was thus recognized in colonial New England as benefiting both church and commonwealth.

Virginia, unlike Massachusetts, was not settled in family groups but for the purposes of trade and as a permanent settlement and military post against the Spanish. Religion, however, was not to be left behind in England. The Charter of Virginia in 1606 specifically mentions bringing the Christian religion to people (the native Americans) "ignorant of the true knowledge and worship of God" (Knight, Vol. 1, 1949, p. 5). In December 1606, the Virginia Company of London, a joint stock company, sent 120 men and boys including an Anglican clergyman to establish a colony, Jamestown, in the southern region of Chesapeake Bay. The company recognized that more than men and supplies were required to make a successful colony. Families were needed, a guarantee of basic rights, and English common law rather than company rule. Authorized by the Virginia Company, the first representative assembly in America met in Jamestown in 1619. This first assembly established the Church of England in Virginia, required all clergy to teach children the catechism every Sunday afternoon, and required everyone to attend church services on Sundays (Greene, 1970).

The Virginia Company granted land of 1250 or more acres to

anyone bringing settlers to Virginia. The population was thus dispersed and children necessarily were educated by their parents or tutors on the plantation or received no education. The compulsory education in Virginia during the colonial period was that required in the laws regulating the apprenticing of pauper children and orphans. An act in 1642 required poor children to be taught an honest and profitable trade and to avoid sloth and idleness (Knight, Vol. 1, 1949). Like the English Poor Law of 1601, no requirement was made for the teaching of reading to the children. Since the people in Virginia were not building a new social order, but were attempting to transfer the old, there was no great religious need to teach all children to read. The people in authority generally saw no need to provide education other than apprentice training for children who would otherwise become paupers. The upper class educated their children either at home or in private schools.

Attempts had been made to establish a college in the 1660s, but it was not until 1693 that the College of William and Mary was founded "that the Church of Virginia may be furnished with a Seminary of the Ministers of the Gospel . . . and that the Christian Faith may be propagated amongst the Western Indians. . . ." (Knight, Vol. 1, 1949, p. 401). The religious intent in the charter of 1606 was not forgotten.

The English ideas of education and the pattern of social classes were transplanted to the Carolina colony when the first settlers arrived in 1670. The Lords Proprietors of Carolina had received a charter from King Charles II that required the laws of the colony to conform to English law and guaranteed religious toleration with the intent of attracting settlers. The constitution of the colony, drawn up by Anthony Ashley Cooper, with the help of the philosopher John Locke, established a type of nobility for the colony based upon the amount of land owned (Wallace, 1951).

The first settlers to Carolina entered Charleston harbor in April 1670 with their governor and his three slaves from Bermuda aboard, thus introducing from the beginning a class within the English social order for which there were no social or legal precedents (Wallace, 1951). The institution of slavery and the development of the plantation aristocracy were to affect every aspect of life in the southern colonies — social, economic, political, and educational.

Although there was religious toleration in the Carolinas, an Act of the Assembly in 1698 established the Church of England, allowing only that church to receive public funds to build churches and pay the salaries of the clergy. An important aid to the Anglican churches and to education in America, particularly in South Carolina where it began its work, was the Society for the Propagation of the Gospel in Foreign Parts, established in 1701 to supply ministers and teachers for the American colonies. The Bishop of London, responsible for the Anglican churches and for licensing all teachers in the colonies, was a charter member of the SPG. To accomplish its mission, the SPG established fellowships at Oxford to train clergy who would be sent to the colonies as ministers and teachers. Thus, those men going to the American mission field took with them the traditional curriculum of the Latin grammar schools and Oxford University. The 1706 instructions to SPG teachers required them to teach children to read for the purpose of reading the Holy Scriptures, to write a legible hand, and to learn as much arithmetic as was necessary for useful employment. The teachers were also to supervise the conduct of the students and, reminiscent of John Colet's teaching, "use all kind and gentle Methods . . . that they may be loved as well as feared by them" (Knight, Vol. 1, 1949, p. 76). When they had the opportunity the teachers were expected to teach and give religious instruction to Indians and Africans and their children (Knight, Vol. 1, 1949). This was done by the Rev. Benjamin Dennis, SPG schoolmaster at St. James' Church, Goose Creek, who had for several years prior to 1710 conducted a school for twenty-seven white boys, two Indians, and one Negro. At this time the separation of the races was evidently not so strict as it later became (Wallace, 1951).

Prior to 1710, "several charitable and well disposed Christians" had left money for the establishment of a free school in Charleston, but the school was not begun until the passage of the Free School Act of December 12, 1712. In colonial America, a free school was a tuition school with a certain number of places for poor boys who would be taught free. The Charleston Free School was established to instruct youth in the Latin and Greek languages and other arts and sciences and useful learning as well as in the principles of the Christian religion as professed in the Church of England.

The school commissioners, appointed by the General Assembly, were given the authority to write school policies, to visit the school to see that they were carried out, and to suspend teachers and students for cause — powers held by school boards to this day.

The headmaster had to conform to the Church of England, teach Latin, Greek, and religion, and was required also to teach a number of free students. He was allowed an assistant teacher, and a teacher was hired for the vocational subjects, which included the teaching of reading, writing, merchants' accounts, navigation, surveying, and practical mathematics, all needed for the growth of the colony. The free school was thus a combination of the Latin grammar school and the more practical academy that had developed in England after 1662.

In Charleston there were also numerous private schools offering the elementary subjects of reading, writing, and arithmetic as well as dancing for young ladies and gentlemen; vocational subjects; modern foreign languages; and, for young ladies, drawing and needlework (Knight, Vol. 1, 1949). On the plantations outside of Charleston, the children were usually taught by a private tutor, following the kind of education advocated by John Locke (Ulich, 1965). This pattern of private education at home and limited free elementary instruction for poor white boys attending tuition paying schools suited the stratified social structure of Charleston and the coastal regions of South Carolina, Georgia, North Carolina, and Virginia and continued until the Civil War.

In colonial New Netherland, New York, and Pennsylvania, the diversity of the population and the lack of a common inheritance of language and of religious and political beliefs resulted in a type of education that reflected the heterogenous composition of the people. New York and Pennsylvania differed from New England and the southern colonies and from each other.

New Netherland, founded in 1626 by the Dutch West India Company to engage in the fur trade, actively sought settlers in Holland and any Protestants who were persecuted in Europe or in New England to come to New Netherland with the promise of religious freedom and land. Following the Calvinist tradition of church and state cooperation in providing schools to teach reading and religion, the company established the first school in New Amsterdam in 1638. The company licensed the teachers and paid part of their salaries but tuition fees were paid by parents. As in the other colonies, the most important qualification for teaching was religious orthodoxy. In 1659 a Latin grammar school was established in New Amsterdam, and elementary schools had been provided in nearly all of the Dutch villages prior to the English takeover of the colony in 1664 (Cremin, 1970).

New Amsterdam surrendered to the English without bloodshed, and the English governor was given full authority to govern the former Dutch colony without an elected assembly. Land grants made to Dutch families were honored, and the policy of religious toleration was continued. In 1664 an attempt was made to establish the Church of England, but this succeeded in only four counties. In a society as heterogeneous as New York's, the establishment of state schools was not possible. The Dutch Latin grammar school in the city of New York continued and a similar school under a Church of England schoolmaster was begun about 1700. The various religious groups conducted elementary schools for their children. The English government did little in the way of aiding education beyond providing charity schools for poor children and supervising the apprenticing of orphans.

The Society for the Propagation of the Gospel supported several schools in New York City as well as schoolmasters in each of the parishes served by a SPG missionary. In New York City, the society's charity school, because of distinguished schoolmasters, attracted as many as eighty to ninety students (Cremin, 1970). Tuition paying schools were also established by the SPG outside the city, but they were not supported by the well-to-do English who preferred to educate their children at home under private tutors.

Private teachers in New York, as in other cities, provided the vocational education needed for the continued economic growth of the city and colony. These schools were numerous and offered a variety of subjects for middle- and upper-class students. Some were open to girls as well as boys and some were exclusively for young ladies, offering in addition to reading, writing, and arithmetic, music, history, and Latin.

Provision for higher education in New York was made near the end of the colonial period when a group of Anglicans obtained a charter for King's College in 1754. This was to have been an Anglican college, but viewing the college as benefiting the whole commonwealth, it was chartered as a private institution rather than a church-supported school (Smith, 1973). In addition to the traditional classical curriculum medicine was added in 1767, and a professorship of law, the first in America, was instituted in 1773. Closed during the American Revolution, it reopened as Columbia College after the war.

Pennsylvania, established in 1682 as a refuge for English Quakers, granted complete freedom of religion to all people persecuted for their religious beliefs in Europe, in England, or in America. William Penn, the founder of the colony, believed that education was essential to the well-being of the government and of the individual. In his second Frame of Government, passed by the General Assembly in 1683, all parents and guardians of orphans were required to teach their children reading and writing by the time they were twelve-years-old and then a useful trade "that the poor may work to live, and the rich if they become poor may not want" (Cubberley, 1920, p. 307). Penn and the council hired a schoolmaster to teach reading, writing, and accounts to students paying tuition. The Friends' Public School was opened in 1689, and while admitting children of all denominations, it was a private Quaker school. The council provided for the establishment of other schools as they became necessary (Cubberley, 1920).

Penn's educational ideas could not be realized in Pennsylvania with its population representing numerous religions, nationalities, languages, and cultures. Religious freedom in a heterogenous society at a time when education was associated with teaching religion became a barrier to state-supported schools.

In 1749 Benjamin Franklin wrote his proposal for an academy emphasizing practical and vocational subjects rather than the traditional Latin and Greek studies of the Renaissance-Reformation (Ulich, 1965). This school was not the first to teach practical subjects in America. The Charleston Free School in 1712 had taught "useful learning" as had private schools in the colonial cities, but Franklin's academy was highly influential. Four years after it was established it became the College of Philadelphia, a private institution free from any religious connection or control, and as a college the curriculum included, in addition to the classics, such subjects as advanced mathematics, philosophy, politics, natural history, chemistry, and physics (Smith, 1973). In this sense, it was a new educational institution reflecting a practical emphasis that marks American higher education today.

The educational pattern established in the diverse culture of the middle colonies developed a system of private and parochial schools, free from governmental control, that prevailed well into the nineteenth century. In the late 1700s private schools, free from religious control, led the way to a new education incorporating scientific studies, which indicated order in the natural world, laws that could be discovered by reason and used to serve the needs of man. Natural law also included the revolutionary idea of the natural rights of man, the idea of human progress, the belief that man by exercising his powers of reason could reform his institutions — political, social, economic, and educational — and promote the general welfare. Such were the ideas leading to revolution.

## THE PUSH FOR PUBLIC EDUCATION: A REVOLUTION

After the Revolutionary War nearly all American statesmen and leaders recognized that the new republican form of representative government required a new kind of education, democratic and nonsectarian, to promote national unity and to provide educated men dedicated to public service. Above all this education was to be used for the improvement of society and to keep the people free.

Even before the American Revolution was won, Thomas Jefferson, believing that education was needed for orderly government, to provide wise and honest leaders in government and to protect individuals in the free exercise of their natural rights, proposed a bill in the Virginia Legislature in 1779 to create a secular, statewide system of elementary and secondary schools and a state college. The elementary schools were to be established in districts in every county, tuition free, and open to all white children, male and female, for three years. This proposal, far ahead of its time, was the first to suggest the teaching of all free children at state expense. The children were to be taught reading, writing, and arithmetic. The books used to teach reading were the means to teach Greek, Roman, English, and American history. Being state schools, neither the Bible nor religion was to be taught (Smith, 1973).

The proposed Latin grammar schools were to charge tuition for boys able to pay, but ten poor boys "whom nature hath endowed with genius and virtue" were to be taught at state expense for one or two years. The curriculum included the study of Latin and Greek,

English grammar, geography, and higher mathematics, the traditional and practical studies that enabled young men to enter William and Mary College (Smith, 1973).

Jefferson's bill was not enacted into law, but it was widely circulated throughout the nation. His ideas, which would have made elementary education available to many boys and girls who otherwise would have received no education, were opposed by many Federalists, political conservatives, and sectarian groups. But Jefferson's ideas on free elementary education at state expense would be reflected in state educational programs beginning in the 1830s.

Other national leaders who, like Jefferson, believed that the common man, if educated, would exercise the powers of reason, contribute to social progress, and be guardians of freedom, also took up the cause of state-supported public education. Doctor Benjamin Rush of Philadelphia believed that the independence of the United States necessarily changed the traditional education. Because of the diversity of the population in Pennsylvania, in 1786 he urged the establishment of public schools, which would provide one general and uniform system of education, to "render the mass of the people more homogeneous, and thereby fit them more easily for uniform and peaceable government" (Vassar, Vol. 1, 1965, p. 122).

Doctor Rush also addressed himself to the proper education for women in a republic (Knox, 1965). He recognized that the first impressions on the minds of children came generally from women, and he thought that the conduct of men was often regulated by them. Therefore, he proposed that young women should be taught the principles of liberty and government and the obligation of patriotism in addition to the usual branches of female education — reading, writing, needlework, and drawing (Vassar, Vol. 1, 1965).

Unlike Jefferson, however, Rush believed that the only foundation for a useful education in a republic was in religion. He disagreed with Jefferson's objections to having the Bible used as a schoolbook, believing that there was no book in the world containing "half so much useful knowledge for the government of states" (Knox, 1965, p. 13). Rush's view of nonsectarian Christianity was common in the public schools in the United States until 1963 and is still an issue in parts of the country today.

Congress, acting under the Articles of Confederation, was not unmindful of the new nation's need for education, and two ordinances supportive of education were passed. The Land Ordinance of 1785 provided for the surveying of the lands northwest of the Ohio River and divided the territory into townships. The center lot in every township was "for the maintenance of public schools within the said township" (Noll & Kelly, 1970, p. 165).

The Ordinance of 1787, passed while the Constitutional Convention was assembled, set up the government for the Northwest Territory, guaranteed the rights of the people, and recognized the importance of religion and education: "Religion, morality, and knowledge being necessary to good government and the happiness of mankind, schools and the means of education shall be forever encouraged" (Noll & Kelly, 1970, p. 165). Public education, while not mandated, was viewed as a proper function of the local or state government.

When the U.S. Constitution was ratified in 1789, however, education was not mentioned in it. This should not be understood as a lack of interest in education among the framers of the Constitution, but rather as a reflection of the times. When the Bill of Rights was added to the Constitution in 1791, the Tenth Amendment, which reserved to the states all powers not delegated by the Constitution to the federal government, was interpreted to mean that the states, not the federal government, had the right to establish and maintain public schools.

By 1810 ten new states had been added to the Union and most had constitutions that encouraged or made some provision for education. Even with these provisions, little was done to implement the establishment of public schools in the sense of public schools today, entirely free and open to all children and youth from kindergarten through high school. The free state education provided was confined to elementary schools where children, usually poor, were taught the three Rs and religion.

During the period from 1781 to 1828, however, many leaders in the cities agreed with Jefferson that the major purpose of education was to provide men able to guard the rights and liberties of their fellow citizens and were thus not content to wait for the establishment of public schools at state expense. They recognized that pauper and charity schools had no place in a republic and that free schools were necessary to the growth and good order in society and to prepare children of immigrants and poor Americans for citizenship in a free society. Thus, leaders in the cities organized and worked to replace the pauper schools with free schools sponsored by civic and patriotic groups.

One innovative idea was the Sunday school begun in England in 1780 by Robert Raikes, an individual who was concerned about the condition of the child factory workers who labored from morning to night six days a week and on Sundays disturbed the peace with their noisy and wild behavior. These children received no education and no religious instruction. Adapting the old church practice of religious instruction for children on Sunday afternoons, Raikes hired four women to teach children from six to fourteen years of age reading, writing, arithmetic, and catechism in the neighborhood church Sunday afternoons. Many children who otherwise would have remained illiterate and "a set of little heathens" received instruction in the basics and religion (Cubberley, 1920, pp. 514-16).

Raikes' plan for the school and its successful results were widely publicized and gained the support of people who recognized the need for social and educational reform in England and in America.

Sunday schools were established in cities in the United States beginning in the late 1780s. These schools for working children were not viewed as pauper schools, but as free schools, and thus did not carry the stigma of pauper education. They served a useful purpose in teaching several thousand young people who, in the absence of public schools, had no other opportunity for schooling.

Foremost among the educational organizations providing free schools in the cities was the Free School Society of the City of New York, organized by DeWitt Clinton in 1805 for the aid of poor children who, "living in total neglect of the religious and moral instruction, and unacquainted with the common rudiments of learning . . ." would become the "burden and pests of Society" (Smith 1973, p. 342). The society's first school adopted the monitorial school system of Joseph Lancaster, another innovative English plan. The chief feature of this plan was the use of the brightest students to be monitors, students teaching other students the lesson taught them by the school master. Each monitor "taught" ten students, that is he heard each recite what he had memorized in the same schoolbook, and the monitor was responsible also for their discipline. One schoolmaster teaching 100 monitors would provide instruction to 1,000 students, conducted under a strict military-type discipline.

The monitorial school was a successful and inexpensive way to provide instruction in the basics to large numbers of poor children. In New York several free schools supported by churches and a school for free blacks adopted the monitorial plan. In Philadelphia the plan was introduced into two schools for female students, and other monitorial schools were established in cities throughout the nation (Smith, 1973).

The free education provided by philanthropic societies met a need in the cities, but was far from Jefferson's belief that children had a right to state-supported elementary education, which would contribute to the common good, thereby making *E pluribus unum,* the motto for the society in the new republic, a reality (Nye, 1963).

In the towns and rural areas the problems were not so acute as in the cities, but thinking citizens everywhere recognized that knowledge was essential for the people to retain the power given to them by the Constitution. Education, therefore, was seen as "the grand safeguard of our liberties . . . of all our rights and privileges" (Benton, Vol. 5, 1968, p. 157).

While the traditional curriculum in the schools continued, a change came by way of new schoolbooks written for American children. The old primers and English schoolbooks were replaced by Noah Webster's *American Spelling Book* (1783), which combined spelling and reading; McGuffey's *First* and *Second* Readers (1836), highly didactic, nationalistic, and graded to the pupils' age; Warren Colburn's *First Lessons in Arithmetic in the Plan of Pestalozzi* (1821), using a new teaching method; and Jedidiah Morse's *American Universal Geography,* which introduced geography in the elementary schools. The authors believed that the books used in public schools were important for the future of the republic and must inculcate "American principles" (Elson, 1964, p. 2).

In the period from 1789 to 1830, public schools in the United States were still viewed as schools for the poor and nowhere reflected the educational ideas of the Founding Fathers. However, Massachusetts and Connecticut, because of the tradition of local support for schools stemming from the Massachusetts School Laws of 1642 and 1647, were in a better position to promote public education than was the South, where education in the nineteenth century was still seen as a parental responsibility. The states of the old Northwest Territory followed the pattern of New England in the idea of common schools, but the schools were not sufficiently funded.

In the North, where slavery was abolished by 1830, free blacks were educated separately in private schools or free schools sponsored by societies. In the South where slaves comprised approximately 50 percent of the population, the teaching of reading and writing to slaves was prohibited by law. As for the Indians, the native Americans, the state governments were not concerned with their education.

The work to establish state school systems along Jeffersonian lines began in earnest in the Northern states after 1825 primarily with the work of James G. Carter and Horace Mann in Massachusetts and Henry Barnard in Connecticut and Rhode Island. In 1821 Carter wrote a series of letters to the Boston *Transcript* calling attention to the poor condition of the public schools in Massachusetts. He blamed the teachers and the textbooks for the lack of quality: "The success of our schools depends as much on the principles, by which they are governed, and the school books, as on the personal and literary qualifications of the instructor" (Chambliss, 1971, p. 153). To Carter the object of education was not so much to give knowledge as to develop the powers of the mind. He argued for the inductive method, noting that "the mind does not perceive a general truth, till it has perceived the particular truths, from which it has been derived" (Chambliss, 1971, p. 157). Teachers must be competent in the inductive method and new texts written to aid the student in disciplined thinking. To accomplish this, Carter urged the establishment of a new state school, a normal school, to train teachers. The normal school would emphasize not only knowledge but the ability to communicate knowledge (Johanningmeier, 1980). Carter's writings on educational reform were widely read and helped prepare the way for the work taken up by Horace Mann. In 1837 Carter, then a member of the Massachusetts legislature and chairman of the committee on education, drafted a bill creating a state board of education.

Horace Mann was appointed secretary of the board, a position that was, in fact, the state superintendent of education. His first task was to gather information about the actual condition of the schools, information about successful plans and methods elsewhere, and publicize the information to gain support for the schools in Massachusetts. This he did in his annual reports to the board of education from 1837 to 1848. The reports were widely read and were extremely influential in furthering the cause of public education in Massachusetts and in other parts of the country.

Mann considered the most pressing need to be well-trained teachers, for without them no parents would choose to send their children to public schools. A public minded citizen agreed with him, and in 1838, offered $10,000 for state normal school education if the legislature would match his funds. The legislature agreed and the first three state normal schools in the United States were opened in less than two years. The subjects studied in these schools for the first year, the minimum amount of study, were the subjects taught in the common schools. For the young men and women able to study longer, additional courses were offered and the science and art of teaching was required (Cubberley, 1920).

Mann's twelve annual reports clearly indicate his commitment to the education of all children and proclaim his educational credo. He believed that education was "the *absolute right* of every human being," would save children from poverty and vice, and enable every child "to perform all domestic, social, civil, and moral duties" (Chambliss, 1971, pp. 36-37). Education was thus "the great equalizer of the condition of men" (Rippa, 1969, p. 199).

As a result of Mann's labors, the common schools in Massachusetts were greatly improved. The curriculum was expanded and teaching methods and school discipline were based upon Pestalozzi's theories of education (Cremin, 1957). Financial support for the schools increased, public high schools were established, and the public school system was accepted and supported by the people.

Another outstanding leader in the cause of public education was Henry Barnard, who in 1835-37 visited European schools that were using Pestalozzi's new educational methods. In 1838 he sponsored and helped pass a bill in the Connecticut legislature that created a board of education and the office of secretary to the board, a position which he was persuaded to undertake. His work as secretary was similar to that of Horace Mann, but more difficult because the Connecticut schools were even worse than those in Massachusetts. To remedy the situation and to promote the cause of public education, Barnard visited schools and teachers, addressed educational conventions and public meetings, and founded an educational journal for the common schools of the state. He emphasized the need for teacher training, recommended Pestalozzi's method, and established the first teachers' institutes in the United States (Monroe, 1907; 1969). To spread the knowledge of the art of teaching to as many teachers as possible, Barnard sent a travelling model classroom to the counties to give demonstration lessons. Barnard thus exceeded the letter of the law to promote the schools by taking what was needed to the teachers.

Barnard continued his active career in public education as secretary of the state board in Rhode Island, as first principal of the new State Normal School in Connecticut, and when the United States Government in 1867 created the Department of Education, Barnard was named the first U.S. commissioner of education. From 1856 to 1881, Barnard edited and published the *American Journal of Education,* which gives the most complete history of American education during those years. Barnard's lifelong service to the cause of public education was immeasurable.

The work of Carter, Mann, and Barnard set the pattern for the course of American public education to be followed by other regions in the United States for the remainder of the nineteenth century and their belief in the absolute right of every child to an education continues to the present. This is not to say that every child had an opportunity for free public education at local or state expense. Indeed, even in the states having constitutional provisions for education, schools were slow to be established, public schools were opposed by those favoring church or private schools, and there was general opposition to local taxation for schools. Nevertheless, recognition of the need for public education was spreading throughout the nation, aided by the press, school organizations, and leaders in the several states.

The message of the school reformers was heard by educators and some public leaders in the South, but due to the social pattern and the aristocratic control of state governments, the voices speaking in behalf of the education of all white children were not heeded. Attempts were made by state legislatures to establish free schools, but, considered by the people to be pauper schools, parents kept their children at home, and many remained untaught.

The first major effort to educate blacks in the South was begun during the Civil War when the U.S. Army occupied several South Carolina sea islands. In 1862 teachers were sent by northern

Freedmen's Aid Societies to teach the blacks abandoned on the plantations when the Confederate troops withdrew. Schools established for children and for adults were highly successful in teaching people eager to learn to read. Reports of the success of these schools and a call for aid were widely circulated in the North, resulting in financial support and additional volunteer teachers for the educational work. When the Civil War was over, more teachers went to the South to establish schools for black children and night schools for adults.

In 1865 Congress created the Freedmen's Bureau to aid the former slaves in their transition from bondage to freedom, and, recognizing that education was essential to their rights as citizens, required the bureau to provide school buildings and protection for the teachers and students. This federal aid was given to black schools in the South until 1870 when the work of the bureau ended, but many schools continued their efforts to eliminate the illiteracy imposed by slavery.

In 1868 Congress, as a part of the reconstruction of the former Confederate states, required them to draft new state constitutions. All contained provisions for state public school systems, and four states required the public schools to be free and open to all children without regard to race. In actual practice, however, a dual school system of separate schools for whites and for blacks was established — the same pattern as generally existed in the nation at that time. Though all the Southern states had constitutional provisions for education in 1868, they had yet to build the base upon which the New Englanders had started their work in the 1830s. The South, impoverished and 100 years behind Massachusetts in terms of public education, was just commencing its public school system.

Throughout the nation in the post-Civil War period, states continued to expand opportunities for free public elementary schools, and educational leaders, receptive to new ideas and new educational needs, took the lead to expand the system to include public kindergartens, high schools, and teacher training institutions. Progress toward the establishment and improvement of public schools systems was made in all states. The pace was not equal, however, and the school systems established were at varying degrees of development in the 1880s.

The kindergarten was brought to the United States by German immigrants after 1848, but it was not until 1873 that the first public kindergarten was established in St. Louis — the result of the work of William T. Harris, superintendent of public schools. Harris was concerned with the condition of children living in the slums with no proper adult supervision from about age three to six when they entered school, unprepared for the classroom, generally dropping out of school after three years (Johanningmeier, 1980). Harris saw the kindergarten as a means to remedy the situation by giving the children a headstart and a chance for success, the same purposes as those of today's federal program. He enlisted the aid of a trained teacher who taught the first public kindergarten using the methods of Froebel. Contrary to the common belief that children were clay to be molded by the teacher, Froebel believed that children learned through self-activity and play, learning to think in an environment adapted to their stage of development. Many citizens supported the kindergarten believing that it not only benefited the child, but also society, agreeing with Froebel that "the child that has been led to think will . . . be led to industry, diligence — to all domestic and civic virtues" (Ulich, 1965).

The American high school, first established in Massachusetts in 1821, did not become a regular part of the state school systems in the nation until after the Civil War. People favoring public high schools stressed the importance of equality of educational opportunity and the benefit to society in educating youth together as in elementary schools (Katz, 1971). In the cities separate high schools were established for males and for females, the curriculum including such practical subjects as mathematics, the sciences, history, and geography, as well as the classical college preparatory courses. Some public high schools for women included an additional two-year normal course for training teachers for the elementary schools.

In Kalamazoo, Michigan, in 1872 citizens challenged the taxes levied for the support of its public high school. The chief justice of the Michigan Supreme Court concluded that the state, in providing free elementary schools and a state university, had intended to provide the means whereby all young people desiring to do so might be prepared to take advantage of the state university (Calhoun, 1969). The Kalamazoo decision clearly established the legality of the American public high school.

The normal school movement expanded rapidly after the Civil War to keep pace with the need for trained teachers in the public schools. The purpose was to produce better teachers, teachers who understood the nature of children, the stages of child development, and the natural development of young minds in order to teach what the child could most readily understand, first through the senses, then through reason (Borrowman, 1965). The art of teaching was practiced in actual classrooms. By the end of the century recognition of the need for trained teachers had led to the establishment of four-year normal colleges awarding degrees in pedagogy.

## THE PROGRESSIVE MOVEMENT IN EDUCATION

The modern era had begun in the 1890s with the growth of cities, the increase of immigration, industrialization, and the labor movement. All had an impact on society and on education. The public schools in the cities were seen as the means to "Americanization," making citizens of the children of immigrants. The expansion of the public school systems made efficiency in operations and teaching essential, but with this went uniformity and conformity in methods and curriculum. A reform of school curriculum and of teacher education to meet the needs of a pluralistic society was begun with the establishment of teachers' colleges granting the bachelor of arts degree.

These needs were recognized by the Progressives, a loosely knit group of social critics, professionals in education, law, business, industry, and government, people committed to social reform. They believed that social ills, such as poverty and ignorance, should and could be reformed by professionals with appropriate specialized academic training. In the cause of public education, they worked for the passage of compulsory school attendance laws and child labor laws (Butts, 1978).

The leader of the Progressive wing in education was John Dewey who in 1896 established the Laboratory School, an experimental school at the University of Chicago, "to discover in administration, election of subject matter, methods of learning, teaching, and discipline, how a school could become a cooperative community while developing in individuals their own capacities and satisfying their own needs" (Cremin, 1961, p. 136). Dewey's experimental school required teachers having a knowledge not only of the subjects taught but also of child growth and development, child psychology, and an understanding of how the child's experiences could be utilized in the acquisition of knowledge in the classroom.

It was important to Dewey that learning be related to a child's interests, for interests show the teacher the state of development the child has reached, and related to the child's experience — acting, trying, experiencing, and undergoing of consequences — learning something. Thus Dewey's learning theory, the scientific method, required active learning, encountering real problems, formulating hypotheses to solve the problems, then testing them until a solution was found. The teacher's job was to present real problems that the child at his or her level of development and experience could solve. This was how the child could best learn how to learn, that is to think (Dewey, 1916; 1966). This was Dewey's child-centered education. The children learned the academic subjects, as well as the industrial and domestic arts, fine arts, and music. In addition, the children learned to work together cooperatively, still a principal aim today in the public schools.

When Dewey moved to Columbia University in 1904 as a professor of philosophy, he continued his interest in educational philosophy and theory, and his progressive educational work was taken up by William Heard Kilpatrick at Teachers College, a former student of Dewey's and in the 1920s Dewey's foremost interpreter (Cremin, 1961). Dewey's and Kilpatrick's progressive education was education in its fullest sense, for the good of society, for the development of the individual eager and able to contribute to the democratic society that provided the education. This education was a working model of the principle, recognized in ancient Athens, Rome, and in the Northern Renaissance, that it was the educated person who could and would, as a result of this education, most benefit society. To Dewey, education was "the fundamental method of social progress and reform" (Ulich, 1965), by giving the individual the kind of education that allows him or her to participate in and have a personal stake in our democratic society.

The Progressive Movement in education from the 1890s to World War I, in its spirit of educational reform, could claim as a forerunner, the Land Grant College Act of 1862. Proposed by Senator Justin Morrill to meet the national need to improve agricultural practices, the act granted federal lands to the states to establish state colleges in which the science of agriculture, the mechanical arts, and military science would be taught in addition to the traditional curriculum (Rippa, 1969). Congress viewed this act as a proper function of its power to "promote the general welfare" clause in Article I, Sec. 8, of the Constitution and continued the encouragement of education given in the ordinances of 1785 and 1787.

In 1867 Congress created the U. S. Department of Education with an appointed commissioner of education whose major function was to promote the cause of education throughout the country by collecting and disseminating information about all aspects of education. This was exactly what Mann and Barnard had been instructed to do in Massachusetts and Connecticut in the 1830s and, because of his experience, Henry Barnard was appointed first U. S. commissioner, serving until 1870. Since 1887, in addition to its original function, the department has been assigned and performed various administrative tasks connected with federal educational programs (Krug, 1966).

In 1917, backed by progressive education reformers, industry, labor, and the National Education Association, Congress passed the Smith-Hughes Vocational Educational Act, doing for the public high school what the Morrill Act of 1862 had done for the colleges: attempting to meet the national need for trained workers for economic growth. The federal government provided funds to be matched by the states to train and to pay the salaries of high school teachers of agriculture, home economics, and trade and vocational education, thus broadening the high school curriculum from college preparatory courses to provide equality of educational opportunity to young people from all classes in society and to prepare them for gainful employment.

Prior to World War I progressive education had been a part of the general progressive movement in the United States and public education was believed essential to the renewal and reform inherent in a democratic society. After the war the social reform element was less evident and in education a new emphasis upon individual development appeared in 1919 when the Progressive Education Association was organized. The aim of the society was "the freest and fullest development of the individual. . . ." (Cremin, 1961, p. 241). They held that this development could not take place in the schools as they were organized with large classes without regard for differences in ability, all studying the same lesson in the same book.

What was needed, it was felt, was a flexible curriculum with the teacher serving as a guide and facilitator, utilizing interest as the motive of all work (Krug, 1965). These "new" experimental schools, private for the most part, included kindergarten, elementary, and some secondary schools, but the latter were restricted by college entrance requirements.

In the 1930s the association created a commission on the relation of school and society, which sponsored the eight-year study of college entrance requirements and experimental high schools' curricula. The commission persuaded 300 colleges and universities to waive their admissions requirements to recommended graduates of thirty experimental high schools redesigning their curricula to achieve mastery learning, understanding of contemporary problems, better teaching and teaching materials, and a type of education responsive to changing needs and based upon an understanding of the qualities needed in adult life. "We are," the commission declared, "trying to develop students who regard education as an enduring quest for meanings rather than credit accumulation. . . ." (Cremin, 1961, p. 253). The graduates of the progressive schools were compared with graduates of traditional schools with the prescribed college preparatory curriculum. The evaluation team found that the students from the experimental schools did as well in college as those from the traditional schools, and they demonstrated more resourcefulness, participated in more student organizations, and showed more concern with national and international affairs (Cremin, 1961). Progressive education had met the test, but the public was not aware of it and during the war and afterwards blamed what they perceived to be the inadequacies in American education on progressive education; however, many of its principles, such as equality of educational opportunity, the learning and application of ideas in the classroom and in society, and creative inquiry, are goals in education today.

After World War II the U. S. Office of Education, Congress, and the Supreme Court played an increasingly important role in American education. In 1945 the Office of Education invited a number of educational leaders to a conference to plan for vocational education for the high school students neither college-bound nor trained for skilled jobs whose educational needs were not being met and as a result dropped out of school at age sixteen or earlier where compulsory attendance was not enforced. This large group, approx-imately 60 percent of the students, was targeted for "life adjustment" education designed to prepare "all American youth to live democratically with satisfaction to themselves and profit to society as home members, workers, and citizens" (Krug, 1966, p. 132). By the 1950s the American public believed the fundamental skills were be-ing neglected in the schools, and when the Soviet Union orbited the first space satellite in 1957, Congress joined the public in blaming life adjustment education for the nation's having fallen behind.

To remedy the situation, Congress in 1958 passed the National Defense Education Act (NDEA) declaring that the security of the nation required "the fullest development of the mental resources and technical skills of its young men and women. . . ." (Krug, 1966, p. 140). Institutes were established to train guidance counselors and modern foreign language teachers, funds were offered the states on a matching basis to purchase instructional materials and equipment to strengthen the teaching of science, mathematics, and foreign languages, and low interest loans were offered to superior students intending to teach these subjects.

## EQUAL OPPORTUNITY BECOMES LAW

Equality of educational opportunity, an ideal and a goal of many national leaders beginning in the early days of the republic, became a part of the body of Constitutional Law in 1954 in *Brown v. the Board of Education* when the Supreme Court ruled that segregation by law, *de jure* segregation, of whites and blacks in separate public schools was unconstitutional on the grounds that separate schools for blacks violated the equal protection of the laws guaranteed by the Four-teenth Amendment and that separate schools were inherently un-equal. Many states resisted the decision, but by 1970 desegregated schools were a fact where *de jure* segregation had existed. *De facto* segregated schools, segregated by patterns of living but not by law, still exist primarily in large urban communities and constitute one of the many issues confronting public schools today.

Like the Supreme Court in the school desegregation cases, Con-gress took a step toward promoting equality of educational oppor-tunity in an amendment to the NDEA in 1964 when it established institutes for training teachers of disadvantaged young people who were culturally, economically, socially, and educationally handicapped. This group was equivalent to the high school group the life adjustment educators had been concerned with twenty years before. But by far the greatest effort toward providing equality of educational opportunity came when Congress passed the Elementary and Secondary Education Act of 1965 (ESEA). Title I, the first section of the act, provided funds for compensatory education for students from low-income families preschool through college, and included Project Head Start, designed to prepare disadvantaged children for elementary school — the same idea that W. T. Harris advocated in establishing the first public kindergarten in St. Louis in 1873.

Title II of the ESEA provided instructional materials, such as library books, resource materials, and textbooks, for private and parochial schools as well as public schools as long as none of the materials was used for religious instruction. In doing this, Congress recognized the child benefit theory, established by the Supreme Court in 1930 in the *Cochran* case, which allows public funds to be used to pay for textbooks, school lunches, and bus transportation for students in parochial schools as direct aid to the child, not to the church school.

Religious practices in the public schools, however, were quite a different matter. The time honored practice of daily Bible reading and recitation of the Lord's Prayer was challenged by citizens, and in 1963 the Supreme Court in the *Schempp* and *Murray* cases declared that state laws or school board policies requiring prayer and Bible reading in the public schools constituted establishment of religion prohibited by the First Amendment. This was and continues to be a controversial issue for many Americans, and the court's decision reflected an attitude far removed from the colonial idea that the teaching of reading was essential in order to read the Bible and the laws of the colony.

Congress officially declared it to be the policy of the United States to provide every person an equal opportunity to receive an education of high quality when it passed the act creating the National Institute of Education in 1972, and in 1975 with the passage of the Education for All Handicapped Children Act (P. L. 94-142), providing for individualized instruction for all physically, mentally, and emotionally handicapped children to be mainstreamed in regular public school classrooms, equal opportunity was mandated for all.

The ESEA programs caused the states to look at their state and local funding for the state systems of education required by the state constitutions with respect to equality of educational opportunity and the rights of children to receive equal opportunity regardless of the tax base of their school district. Fair school finance acts calling for a reassessment of property and establishing a state minimum amount of per pupil expenditure for each public school student regardless of where he or she lives have been passed by the states. This is more than a matter of simple justice. It is the "equal protection of the laws" of the fourteenth Amendment, the Constitution's requirement to "promote the general welfare," and Horace Mann's belief in the absolute right of every child to an education.

## EVALUATION OF THE EDUCATIONAL SYSTEM

With the massive federal aid to the states since the mid-60s for compensatory education, how successful have the programs of the ESEA been? In 1965 U. S. Commissioner of Education Francis Keppel took seriously his responsiblity to make annual reports to Congress on the condition of education. He discussed with John Gardner, Ralph Tyler, and other leaders in education the best means of gathering accurate information to report to Congress. Tyler took the lead in developing a project, which in 1969 became the National Assessment of Educational Progress (NAEP), funded by the federal government, administered by the Education Commission of the States, and authorized by the NIE. The subjects to be assessed every five years were reading, writing, and arithmetic. Other subjects including science, literature, civics, and social studies were to be assessed at less frequent intervals (Shane, 1981). By 1976 the NAEP reported that the compensatory education programs were working, that reading skills of nine-years-olds had improved significantly from 1971 to 1975, and that the thirteen- and seventeen-year-olds were holding their own. Most significantly, black nine-year-olds in compensatory programs made the greatest increase in reading tests (Butts, 1978). The school programs were making a difference.

As a nation we are currently concerned with "back to basics," accountability, educational standards, minimum competency, and how well our educational programs are working. We must remember that education, in trying to meet new needs of society, inevitably runs into conflict with established patterns that are known and accepted and therefore slow to change. Education must not merely attempt to meet changes but must take the lead in providing the education needed. The view that education is the means to reform people and society has had a long history, and when we see the gains we have made it should not discourage us that we still have problems. Although we still debate what education is of most worth, do we not finally agree with William Heard Kilpatrick (1931) that —

> At the present time, when change is more rapid, more pervasive than ever before; when a larger proportion of people than ever existed before on this earth are unsettled on what they think to be fundamental matters . . . then is responsible thinking more needed. . . . Education must try to meet this need. Education must help the rising generation to become better able to take care of the more rapid changes in affairs. The future of civilization is uncertain. It rests with those who are able to think, and that is our task. . . . If education is to change the world and the individual into something better than they would otherwise be, we must consider the individual. . . . If we are teachers or parents, then we ask with regard to each child: What kind of world am I helping this child to build? What kind of self am I helping him to build?

## REFERENCES

Armytage, W.H.G.: *Four Hundred Years of English Education,* 2nd ed. London, Cambridge University Press, 1970.

Artz, F.B.: *Renaissance Humanism 1300-1550.* Oberlin, Ohio, Kent State University Press, 1966.

Ashley, M.: *England in the 17th Century.* Baltimore, Penguin Books, 1961 (orginally published, 1952).

Bainton, R.H.: *The Age of the Reformation:* New York, Van Nostrand Reinhold, 1956.

Barnes, D.R.: *For Court, Manor, and Church: Education in Medieval Europe.* Minneapolis, Burgess Publishing, 1971.

Benton, W. (Ed.): *Steps Toward Equalitarianism, 1821-1832,* The Annals of America, Vol. 5. Chicago, Encyclopaedia Brittannica, 1968.

Bindoff, S. T.: *Tudor England.* Baltimore, Penguin Books, 1950.

Borrowman, M.L.: *Teacher Education in America: A Documentary History.* New York, Teachers College Press, 1965.

Butts, R.F.: *Public Education in the United States from Revolution to Reform.* New York, Holt, Rinehart & Winston, 1978.

Calhoun, D. (Ed.): *The Education of Americans: A Documentary History.* Boston, Houghton-Mifflin, 1969.

Caspari, F.: *Humanism and the Social Order in Tudor England.* New York, Teachers College Press, 1968 (originally published, 1954).

Chambliss, J.E. (Ed.): *Enlightenment and Social Progress Education in the Nineteenth Century.* Minneapolis, Burgess Publishing, 1971.

Cremin, L.A.: *American Education in Colonial Experience, 1607-1783.* New York, Harper & Row, 1970.

Cremin, L.A. (Ed): *The Republic and the School: Horace Mann on the Education of Free Men.* New York, Bureau of Publications, Teachers College, 1957.

Cremin, L.A.: *The Transformation of the School: Progressivism in American Education, 1876-1957.* New York, Knopf, 1961.

Cubberley, E.P.: *Readings in the History of Education.* Boston, Houghton-Mifflin, 1920.

De Molen, R.L. (Ed.): *The Meaning of the Renaissance and Reformation.* Boston, Houghton-Mifflin, 1974.

Dewey, J.: *Democracy and Education.* New York, Free Press, 1966 (originally published, 1916).

Downs, N. (Ed.): *Basic Documents in Medieval History.* Princeton, New Jersey, Van Nostrand, 1959.

Elson, R.M.: *Guardians of Tradition: American Schoolbooks of the Nineteenth Century.* Lincoln, Nebraska, University of Nebraska Press, 1964.

Gilmore, M.P.: *The World of Humanism, 1453-1517.* New York, Harper & Row, 1962 (originally published, 1952).

Greene, J.P. (Ed.): *Great Britain and the American Colonies, 1606-1762.* Columbia, South Carolina, University of South Carolina Press, 1970.

Hadas, M. (Ed.): *The Basic Works of Cicero.* New York, Modern Library, 1951.

Johanningmeier, E.V.: *Americans and Their Schools.* Chicago, Rand McNally College Publishing Co., 1980.

Katz, M.E. (Ed.): *School Reform: Past and Present.* Boston, Little, Brown, 1971.

Kilpatrick, W.H.: A theory of progressive education to fit the times. *Progressive Education, 8,* April 1931.

Knight, E.W. (Ed.): A Documentary History of Education in the South before 1860. *European Inheritances,* Vol. 1. Chapel Hill, North Carolina, University of North Carolina Press, 1949.

Knox, Samuel (Ed.): *Essays on Education in the Early Republic.* Cambridge, Belknap Press, 1965.

Krug, E.A.: *Salient Dates in American Education, 1635-1964.* New York, Harper & Rowe, 1966.

Lupton, J.H.: *A Life of John Colet, D.D.* Hamden, Connecticut, The Shoestring Press, 1961 (originally published, 1887).

Monroe, W.S.: *History of the Pestalozzian Movement in the United States.* New York, Arno Press, 1969 (originally published, 1907).

Morison, S.E.: *The Oxford History of the American People.* New York, Oxford University Press, 1965.

Noll, J.W., and Kelly, S.P. (Eds.): *Foundations of Education in America: An Anthology of Major Thoughts and Significant Actions* New York, Harper and Row Publishers, 1970.

Notestein, W.: *The English People on the Eve of Colonization, 1603-1620.* New York, Harper & Rowe, 1962 (originally published, 1954).

Nye, R.B.: *The Cultural Life of the New Nation, 1776-1830.* New York, Harper & Rowe, 1963 (originally published, 1960).

Plumb, J.B.: *The Italian Renaissance.* New York, Harper & Rowe, 1965 (originally published, 1961).

Rippa, S.A. (Ed.): *Educational Ideas in America: A Documentary History.* New York, David McKay, 1969.

Rusk, R.R.: *Doctrines of the Great Educators,* rev. ed. New York, St. Martin's Press, 1967.

Shane, H.G.: Measuring Educational Quality. *Phi Delta Kappan, 63,* December 1981.

Smith, W. (Ed.): *Theories of Education in Early America. 1655-1819.* New York, Bobbs-Merrill, 1973.

Thompson, C.R.: *Schools in Tudor England.* Washington, The Folger Shakespeare Library, 1958.

Thompson, J.W., and Johnson, E.N.: *An Introduction to Medieval Europe.* New York, W.W. Norton, 1937.

Ulich, R. (Ed.): *Three Thousand Years of Educational Wisdom,* 2nd ed. Cambridge, Harvard University Press, 1965.

Vassar, R.E. (Ed.): *Social History of American Education, Colonial Times to 1860,* Vol. 1. Chicago, Rand McNally, 1965.

Wallace, D.D.: *South Carolina: A Short History.* Chapel Hill, North Carolina, University of North Carolina Press, 1951.

Wheelock, F.M.: *Quintilian as Educator.* New York, Twayne Publishers, 1974.

Wieruszowksi, H. (Ed.): *The Medieval University.* Princeton, New Jersey, Van Nostrand, 1966.

Woodward, W.H.: *Studies of Education During the Age of the Renaissance, 1400-1600.* New York, Teachers College Press, 1967 (originally published, 1906).

*Chapter 2*

# THE CHILDREN WE TEACH

SANDRA LONGFELLOW ROBINSON AND EDWARD H. ROBINSON III

*S*ANDRA LONGFELLOW ROBINSON *is the mother of two children, a son and a daughter. She is currently assistant professor of education at the University of South Carolina in Columbia, South Carolina. She has lived in West Virginia, where she received her early education and was graduated from Marshall University. She has taught in the public schools in Maryland and North Carolina and received her master of education degree and doctorate from Duke University. She has been a supervisor and coordinator of primary grades and established and directed a learning center for three to five-year-olds. She has been assistant director of the Duke University Reading Center and an instructor at Duke University. Her publications have appeared in such journals as* The Phi Delta Kappan, Reading Horizons, Reading Improvement *and the* Kappa Delta Pi Record.

*Edward H. Robinson III is the father of two children. He is currently assistant professor of education at the University of South Carolina in Columbia, South Carolina. His early education was in the public schools in Harford County, Maryland. After he received his bachelor of arts from Marshall University, he returned to Maryland to teach at Aberdeen High School. He received his master of education from Johns Hopkins University and his doctorate from Duke University. He has been a counselor, assistant director of admissions, and director of pupil support services in North Carolina. He was formerly assistant professor of education at Marquette University. He has recently edited special issues of* The Journal for Specialists in Group Work *and the* Humanist Educator *and has published works in the* Journal of Learning Disabilities, Counseling and Values, *and* Journal of Educational Research.

---

The education of children and the practice of child rearing consumes a great deal of time and energy in our society today. This has not always been so. "The history of childhood is a nightmare from which we have only recently begun to awaken. The further back in history one goes, the lower the level of child care, and the more likely children are to be killed, abandoned, beaten, terrorized, and sexually abused" (de Mause, 1974, p. 1).

It has only been in the last century that children have found protection under the law. In New York in the early 1900s the first child abuse case was heard. Since there was a lack of appropriate laws pertaining to the children, the case was adjudicated under the prevention of cruelty to animals statutes.

Perhaps because children have only recently been the focus of increasing time and interest, our understanding of childhood and child growth and development is itself in the infancy stage. Our technological society has cured dreaded disease, put men into space, and created powerful forces that have the potential to rival nature, but we have done little to meaningfully alter the occurrences of unwanted and unneeded human behavior and to consistently promote constructive behavior. Only time will tell if we can understand the nature of the human condition; this will occur only if the resources are available to study and understand the individual from birth to death.

The purpose of this chapter is to provide the reader with an overview of child development as we currently interpret it. This is offered with the hope that even in the beginning stages of our knowledge we can be more effective in promoting the positive growth of the child if we understand the nature of that growth and the implications that this has for educating and rearing the child.

## DEVELOPMENTAL THEORY

The theory of development deals with sequential changes that occur in the individual at different age levels. Developmental theory is concerned with both the internal processes (heredity) and external forces (environment) that combine in the total growth, learning, and maturation of the individual. Much of developmental theory is based on the epigenetic principle: As organs of the body appear at specified times during fetal development of the embryo, they eventually combine to form the whole child. Thus in later physical, cognitive, social, and emotional development, certain elements appear at specified times and eventually allow the formation of the system and the person as a whole.

## Principles of Development

A number of authors have provided a framework for examining the theory of development. Lefrancois (1979) has integrated several ideas into eleven key principles. We have summarized these for the reader here because we feel they offer the student of developmental theory a guide for examining and understanding the general nature of developmental concerns:

1. *Both* heredity and environment are important contributors to development. For years, the nature vs. nurture controversy raged and theorists felt obliged to support one and refute the other. Today, it is much more common to find experts who stress the importance of a child's genetic makeup *and* that child's experiences in the growing-up process. Some debate still centers around the question of which skills are inherited and which are obtained through experience (environment).

2. Different parts of the organism mature and develop at different rates. This principle can be graphically demonstrated by lining up a class of kindergarten students and observing the differences in height, weight, and facial features. Asking this group to skip across the playground will highlight a wide variance in motor skills of children of approximately the same age. That this principle is true across age spans can be demonstrated by performing the same observations with groups of sixth, eighth, or eleventh graders.

3. Changes in the child's experience (environment) have the most effect upon the child if they occur during a peak period of change. Likewise, any changes that occur during a slow period in the child's mental or physical growth will have lesser effects upon the child's development. As Lefrancois explains, "This principle is most clearly illustrated in the area of physical growth. It is evident, for example, that changes in environment are not likely to affect the height of subjects over twenty. On the other hand, dietary changes for children under one could conceivably have a very significant effect on future height" (1979, p. 207).

4. From the time of conception, a child's development proceeds through a series of stages. These progressions follow each other in a predictable order. Some theorists (*see* the charts explaining the ideas of Piaget, Kohlberg, and Erickson) have

studied and attempted to identify these stages by descriptive names and to provide approximate ages at which each stage will emerge.

5. One stage of development blends so discretely into the next that transitions are rarely observable. It is possible for a child to operate in two different stages for a time as he proceeds from lower to higher stages.

6. Each person acts, grows, behaves, and thinks in a unique fashion. Thus, there can be no truly homogeneous group of nine-year-olds. Lefrancois goes so far as to say, "There is no normal, average child, the average child is a myth invented by grandmothers and investigated by psychologists" (1979, p. 209). There are, however, enough characteristics that nine-year-olds have in common to generalize and expect certain observable behaviors within certain age groups.

7. Once a child begins his journey upon his life course, environmental factors are the cause of any changes in his development. These changes can be of a positive, enriching nature or of a negative, depriving nature. Bloom (1964) emphasized the importance of the first four years of life and many studies have been, are being, and will be conducted to determine the effects of stimulation and deprivation of a child's environment during these formative years. Nutrition has been cited as an important influence upon a child's development from the prenatal period. Bronfenbrenner (1981) stresses the importance of a totally, unalterably caring person in fostering the development of a child. Through such studies we have hypothesized that given a fostering environment, a child's development can be accelerated. Conversely, being with a negative environment can have adverse effects on the child's development.

8. Advanced or retarded development seems to be a consistent quality in an individual. Contrary to a typical sterotype, athletes are not typically stupid. Lefrancois cites the studies of Terman in 1925 to support his contention, "The person who excels in one area is likely to excel in others." (1979, p. 211). Likewise, the person who is below average in one area tends to perform on a similar level in other areas. In regard to this principle (as in all others), it is important to remember that there are exceptions to all rules and that these principles are

in reality not rules but generalizations or guidelines.

9. Principle 9 reinforces Principle 4 — development proceeds through a series of orderly stages and clarifies Principle 5. These stages are continuous and overlapping but, nonetheless, identifiable.

10. Adults of high intelligence began life as precocious infants. This is indeed a generalization based upon little quantitative data but supported by a survey conducted by Bloom (1964) and suggesting that human characteristics are indeed stable.

11. "Development is directional" (1979, p. 213). Lefrancois explains this principle in two senses. First, development proceeds from the general or undifferentiated to the specific or differentiated. As we walk into a crowded room, we first get a general overall view of people, sounds, and activity. After a few moments of observation, we can identify specific groups and/or individuals. In the study of careers, young children learn about policemen, doctors, and teachers. Older children study the particular job responsibilities of criminologists, detectives, internalists, obstetricians, flight instructors, and professors. Secondly, development occurs in proximodistal (near to far) and cephalocaudal (head to tail) fashions. Fetal growth and early physical control follow the pattern described, for example children learn to throw a ball before they learn to print their names.

## AREAS OF CHILD DEVELOPMENT

Because developmental theory is focused on discovering and unlocking the process of growth of the individual as a whole person, there are as many areas of child development under study as there are systems of growth and maturation. Examples are psychosexual (Freud, 1949), psychosocial (Erickson, 1950), cognitive (Piaget, 1963), physical sexual (Gesell, 1956; 1946), vocational (Super, 1957), moral (Kohlberg, 1976), ego (Loveinger, 1978), and social (Dupont, 1981) areas but perhaps to add clarity we classify development in three general catagories:

1. Developmental models arising from physical maturation
2. Developmental models arising from the cultural pressure of society

3. Developmental models arising from the internal focus of the individual personality

Although this classification may help the reader to visualize three broad areas of developmental study, it must be stated that development in each area interacts with that in all other areas. The primitive nature of our measurement devices and observational techniques has not allowed for the total isolation of any one area of development nor is this likely to occur. We have selected four developmental models for illustration and for illustration purposes. It is hoped that through a brief examination of these four, the reader will gain an appreciation for developmental theory in its present state.

### Erickson's Stages of Psychosocial Development

Erickson's theory of psychosocial development is based on the epigenetic principle. He hypothesized that all the subsystems necessary for the personality development of the child are present in the individual but that each in turn is the focus of a period of development and subsequently becomes interrelated to future development. This view is apparent in his writings concerning epigenetic development. "In this development each organ has its time of origin and this time factor is as important as the place of origin. If the eye, for example, does not arise at the appointed time it will never be able to express itself fully, since the moment for the rapid outgrowth of some other part will have arrived, and this will tend to dominate the less active region, and suppress the belated tendency for eye expression" (Erickson, 1950 pp. 61-62). Thus, as noted in Figure 2-1, the time for autonomy is approximately two to three years of age. If not developed at this time, the subsystem of autonomy loses it preeminence as a focal point of the developing child and will interact throughout the process with future development.

As can also be noted in Figure 2-1, Erickson views psychosocial development as series of focal points described in terms of dichotomies. This is not to suggest that a child will get all of one side of the dichotomy and none of the other but rather that the ration that emerges should favor the positive side for the child to development in a positive mode.

*Childhood Birth to Six Years*

1. Trust vs. Mistrust                                          0 - 18 months

   Nurturances providing consistency and continuity lead to trust. Lack of nurturance through neglect and inconsistency leads to mistrust.

2. Autonomy vs. Shame                                          1½ - 3 years

   Experiencing the environment through independence and differentiating self from others through skills that allow independence levels to autonomy. Overprotection or lack of support for independent behaviors leads to personal shame and doubt in self.

3. Initiative vs. Guilt                                          3 - 6 years

   Freedom to search for sexual identity and to initiate questions concerning identity leads to initiative. Lack of response and restriction of activities by parents leads to questions of guilt.

*Juvenile*

Mastery vs. Inferiority                                          6 - 12 years

Praise for making and doing and rewards for accomplishments lead to feelings of mastery. Criticism and strict limitations lead to feelings of inferiority.

*Adolescence*

Identity vs. Identity Diffusion                                          12 - 18 years

Increasing amounts of independence and responsibility with consistence allows for continued identity. A lack of independence and responsibility in a time of great personal change leads to confusion and identity diffusion.

*Young Adulthood*

Intimacy vs. Isolation

Establishment of close interpersonal relationships leads to intimacy. A competitive and counterproductive relationship leads to feelings of personal isolation.

*Middle Age*

Generalization vs. Stagnation

Involvement with rearing and guiding future generations leads to a sense of general activity. Concerns with self needs lead to stagnation.

*Older Adulthood*

Ego Integrity vs. Despair

Acceptance of one's life, accomplishments, and failures leads to a sense of integrity. Denial of one's life or feelings of lost time leads to despair.

Figure 2-1. Erickson's Stages of Psychosocial Development

I. *Sensorimotor Stage*                                    0 - 2 years

Focuses on the importance of both the child's use of sight, hearing, smell, touch, and taste to gain knowledge and the child's development of mobility to explore the world.

During this period the child develops a sense of object permanence — the realization that a ball covered by a handkerchief does not disappear just because it is out of sight.

II. *Preoperational Stage*                                 2 - 7 years

A. Preconceptual Phase                                     2 - 4 years

May call a cow, a pig, and a horse by the same name — "dog"; does not realize that objects can have similar characteristics but individual identities.

B. Intuitive Phase                                         4 - 7 years

Nine pebbles spread over a table are judged to be "more" than nine pebbles arranged in a pile.

III. *Concrete Operational Stage*                          7 - 11 years

Child can solve problems by physically manipulating concrete objects or by recalling specific past experiences.

IV. *Formal Operational Stage*                             11 - 16 years

Child can deal with mental abstractions; can propose hypotheses and test them without the use of concrete models.

Figure 2-2. Piaget's Stages of Cognitive Development

## Piaget's Stages of Cognitive Development

Figure 2-2 outlines Piaget's stages of cognitive development. He believed that the child's development flows from one stage to another. That is to say that the stages of cognitive development are not absolute in the sense of having concrete boundaries. While a child is in the preoperational stage, he or she may exhibit behavior common to both the sensorimotor stage and the concrete operational stage. The child's developmental stage is classified as that stage in which the majority of behaviors are observed. Piaget believed that although the rate of a given child's progression through the developmental stages might vary, the sequence is the same for all children.

*Level I*

Preconventional or Premoral                              0 - 9 years of age

Moral values are seen as external phenomena not residing in standards or within an individual.

Stage I:   Obedience vs. Punishment. This stage is characterized by egocentric deference to power. Moral decisions are based primarily on avoiding punishment.

Stage II:  Naive Egalitarian. Reciprocity as it serves self-interests. Moral issues are decided based on satisfaction of one's own needs and occasional others as they serve self-interest.

*Level II*

Conventional                                            9 - 15 years of age

Moral values are seen as a part of the conventional order of things. Emphasis is on doing right or good by the rules and meeting the expectations of others.

Stage III:  Approval and Pleasing. Moral judgment is based on pleasing others and seeking approval from others. Overt attention is given to maintaining relationships.

Stage IV:  Law and Order. Orientation is toward doing one's duty and maintaining the social order for its and one's own sake. Respect is given for authority, and virtuous acts deserve rewards.

*Level III*

Postconventional                                        16 years and up

Standards of morality are self-accepted. Moral decisions are based on principles that are universally applicable. Judgments are complex.

Stage V:   Democratically Contractual — Legalistic. Moral decisions are based on right and wrong as defined in terms of contracts. Avoidance of violations of the rights of others and the will of the majority that takes precedence over individual needs. Rules are seen as arbitrary but accepted for sake of agreement.

Stage VI:  Principles of Conscience. Consideration is given to laws and regulations but an emphasis is placed on universal logic and consistency. Conscience thus examined provides the directing agent for decision, and mutual trust and respect become important factors.

Figure 2-3. Kohlberg's Stages of Moral Development

| | |
|---|---|
| *Growth* | Birth – 4 years |
| | Self-exploration and self-definition with an integration of the world of work and an understanding of work. |
| *Fantasy* | 4 – 10 years |
| | Role playing and fantasying about different life tasks and work roles. |
| *Interest* | 11 – 12 years |
| | Development of patterns of like and dislike provides major determinant of activities and career aspirations. |
| *Capacity* | 13 – 14 years |
| | Identification of abilities begins to merge with interest as determinant of career aspirations. Career and job requirements are given some considerations. |
| *Exploration* | 14 – 24 years |
| | Process of formal selection and implementation of career choice. |
| *Tentative* | 15 – 17 years |
| | Integration of abilities, interests, and values and opportunities are fostered, and choices are made. These are explored through fantasy, discussion, and experiential activities, including work. |
| *Transition* | 18 – 21 years |
| | Generalized perceptions of work roles are given more concrete avenues to specific choices with the press of reality in the form of market considerations, opportunity, and training. |
| *Trial* | 22 – 24 years |
| | With the advent of work role in the first job original commitment is verified or rejected. The search for a vocational preference crystallizes and begins to take on commitment, or the person may reinstitute the process of implementing a vocational preference. |
| *Establishment* | 24 – 44 years |
| | The individual endeavors to establish himself or herself in the chosen occupation. Changes are of type, location, and responsibility not of a substantive occupational nature. |
| *Stabilization* | 25 – 30 years |
| *Advancement* | 31 – 40 years |
| *Maintenance* | 44 – 65 years |
| | Holding one's own is the focus; little innovation or real change is typically sought. |
| *Decline* | 65 years |
| | New roles based on nonoccupational factors must be explored and accepted. |
| *Deceleration* | 65 – 70 years |
| *Retirement* | 71 + |

Figure 2-4. Super's Stages of Career Development

## Kohlberg's Stages of Moral Development

Basing his theory on a long series of studies with children and adults, Kohlberg found that moral development occurs in a sequential manner of developmental stages (Figure 2-3). The level of development of the individual may in part depend on the interaction of the child with those adults surrounding the child but will nonetheless be sequential in nature. Kohlberg has hypothesized that children generally understand moral judgments at their own stages of development as well as one stage above that stage at which they are currently operating. Thus, in Stage 2-3, a child is primarily assessing moral decisions based on seeking approval and pleasing others, but he might understand and, in some instances, base his decisions on elementary social order and respect for authority.

## Super's Stages of Vocational Development

Donald E. Super has postulated that vocational choice can also best be understood by a developmental framework (Figure 2-4). He suggests that certain behaviors that begin during the child's school years, such as school achievement, athletic achievement, peer relationships, and work role responsibilities, help to develop a sense of success or failure, which relates to occupational selection. As in Erickson's model, there is a prime time for the development of certain orientations. Super also hypothesizes that the process is sequential, but, as Piaget has suggested with regard to cognitive development, the process of vocational development flows at an individual rate with the potential for overlap.

## DEVELOPMENTAL CHARACTERISTICS OF CHILDREN

To further illustrate the developmental perspective, it may be helpful to look at the general characteristics of children at a number of different age levels. Muro and Dinkmeyer (1977) have provided a general description, which has been adapted here:

## Some Generalizations Concerning Five- To Nine-Year-Olds

At about five years of age a child —

seldom attempts more than he can manage.

is generally described as good.

usually responds to others.

likes to play with children of his own age.

enjoys being helpful.

needs and wants immediate adult attention; waiting is difficult.

may interrupt frequently.

has a need to show and share, to perform before an audience.

likes structure.

enjoys directed activities of 20-25 minutes.

when asked what he does best, responds, "play."

thrives on praise.

does not like to be called bad or told that he is wrong.

At about six years of age a child —

is egocentric.

swings to opposite behaviors.

is extremely energetic.

tires easily.

swings legs, wiggles, bites his nails, makes noises.

cries easily and may be prone to tantrums.

thrives on praise.

finds it difficult to share, take turns, or lose.

may cheat.

feels that the teacher's word is law.

is beginning to develop a sense of time: past and future.

enjoys fantasy.

At about seven years of age, a child —

is more organized and quiet.

can concentrate and reflect.

may begin to withdraw and to be very critical of himself.

may worry about school, health, and death.

can sit longer periods of time.

may have crush on the teacher.

may have a sense of self-confidence that is easily disturbed.

At about eight years of age, a child —

can be very inquisitive.

may undertake more than he can perform.

shows a lot of enthusiasm.
is very curious.
may have a very short interest span.
tends to be impatient.
exaggerates.
is very critical of himself.
feels that peer relationships are very important.
will take more responsibility for actions.
needs praise.
develops an ability to express himself more clearly.

At about nine years of age, a child —

may exhibit a confusing array of characteristics.
might become more placid; may seem to live within a world of his own.
tends to become more independent.
places more importance upon the views of his peer group.
experiences periods of high levels of activity.
thinks independently and critically.
is interested in his community and other cultures.
is "here and now" oriented but is interested in history also.
develops an increasing sense of truthfulness.
is not self-confident.
rebels against authority.

At about ten years of age, a child —

will display more positive attitudes toward friends and family.
has a better developed sense of time (minutes, years, centuries).
is a television authority; knows many characters and understands most themes in shows.
tends to be obedient.
can display bursts of temper but is routinely cooperative and well adjusted.
usually prefers to talk or read than to write.
can usually be depended upon to complete tasks or errands independently.

At about eleven years of age, a child —

may become a social being; very interested in being with friends and engaging in adult conversations.

experiences a wide range of emotions, from happiness to desolation, in a short span of time.

becomes silly at frequent intervals; giggles; teases.

enjoys competition in sports and school work.

is curious.

has difficulty remaining immobile or moderately inactive for periods of time.

At about twelve years of age, a child —

is neither a child, an adolescent, or an adult but may exhibit characteristics of all three groups.

can sit and concentrate for longer periods of time than eleven-year-olds.

talks about what career to pursue but has no real concept of what prerequisite tasks are involved.

may require more privacy.

develops insight and is better able to judge the emotional reactions of others.

is increasingly self-reliant.

displays fewer incidents of emotionalism or moodiness.

tends to possess a good sense of humor.

during the period of adolescence, young people experience many changes in a relatively short period of time.

may switch from a same sex to an opposite sex orientation in terms of friendships.

search for identities.

seek purposes in life for themselves and those around them.

are capable of forming hypotheses and of generalizing and may find making decisions to be a major chore.

begin to consider abstract thoughts and may be fascinated with this new ability to the extent that they are filled with "profound" thoughts.

respect individual rights and, thus, favor moral decisions based upon social contracts rather than fixed laws and universal values.

explore and begin to develop specific interests, hobbies, and career orientations.

realize their abilities and limitations.

experience internal and external pressures, which may lead to changing or confused view points of career choices or which may direct them upon a career pathway from an early age.

## DEVELOPMENT AND EDUCATION

"Living in a modern society is a long series of tasks to learn, where learning well brings satisfaction and reward, while learning poorly brings unhappiness and social disapproval" (Havighurst, 1972, p. 2). The purpose of examining development of the child here is to suggest a key for facilitating the education of the child. Knowing certain general characteristics of children and the progression of their development is helpful in developing those experiences that will help the child learn, grow, and mature into a fully functioning adult. The developmental models examined here have all implied that certain life tasks common to all individuals will present themselves to the individual in a more or less sequential manner. Although different children will face these tasks at different times based on the interaction of each developmental system with the inherent nature of the child's general characteristics, the developmental elements will appear in roughly the same time setting. Havighurst (1972) has suggested that *successful achievement* of developmental tasks will lead to further success while *failure* will lead to difficulty with later tasks and perhaps to failure as an adult. Thus it behooves those adults in the child's life to utilize the current level of knowledge in fostering maximum task efficiency for *each* child at *each* level in *each* area of development.

## SUMMARY

With the gradual changes that have occurred over the past century, the status of children in our society has also changed. With the recognition of the importance of the child, more time and energy has been devoted to understanding children with the hope of ensuring the maximum potential of each child. Developmental theory has sought to examine both the hereditary and environmental factors that combine in the total growth, learning, and maturation of the child in order to better understand the child.

Through an understanding of how children develop in areas such as psychosexual, psychosocial, cognitive, physical sexual, vocational, moral, ego, and social areas, parents, teachers, and others dealing with children may increase their ability to assist the child in moving toward maximum potential. Knowing that certain general characteristics of children will progress in sequence and emerge at certain times in the child's life allows those dealing with children to plan corresponding events that facilitate successful acquisition and promote future development.

## REFERENCES

Bloom, B.S.: *Stability and Change in Human Characteristics.* New York, Wiley, 1964.

Bronfenbrenner, U.: *Two Worlds of Childhood.* New York, Russell Sage Foundation, 1970.

de Mause, L. (Ed.): *The History of Childhood.* New York, Psychohistory Press, 1974.

Dupont, H.: Affective development: Stage and sequence. In Mosher, R.L. (Ed.): *Adolescent Development in Education.* In Press.

Erickson, E.H.: *Childhood and Society.* New York, Norton, 1950.

Freud, S.: *An Outline of Psycho-analysis.* New York, Norton, 1949.

Gesell, A., Ilg, F.L., and Ames, L.B.: *The Years from Ten to Sixteen.* New York, Harper, 1956.

Gesell, A., Ilg, F.L., Ames, L.B., and Bulls, G.E.: *The Child from Five to Ten.* New York, Harper, 1946.

Havighurst, R.J.: *Developmental Tasks and Education,* 3rd. ed. New York, David McKay, 1972.

Kohlberg, L., and Turiel, P.: Moral development and moral education. In Lesser, G. (Ed.): *Psychology and Educational Practice.* New York, Scott Foresman, 1971.

Lefrancois, G.: *Psychology for Teaching.* Belmont, California, Wadsworth Publishing Company, 1979.

Loveinger, J.: *Ego Development.* San Francisco, Jossey-Bass, 1976.

Muro, J.A., and Dinkmeyer, D.: *Elementary and Middle School Counseling: A Pragmatic Approach.* Dubuque, Iowa, William C. Brown, 1977.

Piaget, J.: *The Psychology of Intelligence.* Patterson, New Jersey, Littlefield Adams, 1963.

Super, D.E., Drites, J., Hummel, R., Mosher, H., Overstreet, P. and Warnath, C.: *Vocational Development: A Framework for Research.* New York, Teachers College Press, Columbia, 1957.

# Chapter 3

# WHAT TO LOOK FOR IN
# EARLY CHILDHOOD EDUCATION

Kevin J. Swick and Pamela Kearce

*K EVIN J. SWICK is professor and chairman of the Early Childhood Education Department at the University of South Carolina, Columbia. Swick is currently involved in researching the relationships between home support behaviors of parents and children's social and academic performance. In addition, his research and writing have focused on parent involvement, parent education, and other areas of early childhood education.*

*Pamela Kearce received her undergraduate degree in education from Southwest Texas State University and a master's degree in early childhood education from the University of Texas. She is currently the coordinator for the laboratory school at the University of South Carolina and working on her doctorate in early childhood education.*

---

Parents and citizens are asking many questions regarding the entire field of early childhood education. What should a good day-care center look like? How soon should I put my child in a preschool center? Should I send my child to kindergarten? What is early childhood education? These are some of the frequently asked questions. Of course, one of the most important parts of any quality program is the personnel. This is especially so in early childhood programs because young children are learning more during this period of life than they will ever again. It is this area of concern (the role of the early childhood educator) that is the focus of this chapter. Before examining the complexities of what makes up a good early childhood education staff, however, the scope and purposes of programs need to be briefly described.

Early childhood education is generally defined as organized programs for children from three years of age to around seven or eight years of age. Quality programs have attempted to meet the social, physical, psychological, and educational needs of young children and their parents. By meeting these comprehensive child and family needs, it is believed that young children will be more capable of functioning effectively in their current roles and, later, as adult members of the community. In recent years, for example, research on child development has found that many learning and developmental problems can be prevented by providing children with quality experiences during the early years. The roles of today's early childhood educator, however, have their origins in a meaningful historical context.

## HISTORICAL OVERVIEW

Until recent times parents have been the primary adults in the lives of young children. For example in 1657 Comenius advocated a mothers' school for parents by which they would be instructed on how to care for their children. Other writers and thinkers of the seventeenth and eighteenth centuries stressed the importance of providing very young children with special attention so they would develop into functional adults (Comenius, 1657). While Rousseau focused on the natural development of the child, Froebel stressed the need for attending to the spiritual development of the child. It was Froebel who outlined the basic components of the kindergarten and established priorities for teachers of young children (Froebel, 1903). The beginning of the American kindergarten movement took it's initiative from European influence. The first kindergarten in America (1855) was a German-speaking school. Soon the idea spread throughout the United States, and the foundation for much of what we now consider to be early childhood education was under development (Cubberley, 1922).

The first English-speaking kindergarten was started in Boston (1860) by Miss Elizabeth Peabody. The first public school kindergarten was started in St. Louis (1873) by Susan Blow. These early teachers of young children recognized the need for a comprehensive approach to child development and used the school as a place for introducing children and parents to the benefits of early learning. During this same time span, the works of Sigmund Freud and John Dewey influenced the thinking of educators on the value of early childhood education. Freud stressed the significance of early environmental influences on the child's total development. In 1907,

Maria Montessori showed how a responsive learning setting could be of value in helping young disadvantaged learners to overcome environmental deficits. Through the efforts of people like Froebel, Peabody, Blow, Dewey, and Montessori, both a curriculum for the early years emerged and the basis for training teachers of young children was established (Osborn, 1980).

With the advent of the twentieth century the scope and depth of educational and social concerns for young children are broadened to include almost every facet of human development and learning. For example when the first White House Conference on Children was held in 1909, the list of topics included concerns on abuses of child labor, educational deprivation, neglect and abuse of children, lack of family stability, and many other concerns (Osborn, 1980).

Several significant events took place from 1910-1930 that further expanded the influence of early childhood educators. Industrialization of the society changed previously established rural-oriented living patterns. Children (especially the urban disadvantaged) were now in need of out-of-home care at early ages. As family needs became more complex, the need for social services to these families increased. These social changes coupled with the emergence of scientific research on child development and more public awareness of early childhood education enhanced the image of teachers (as well as other helping professionals) and made their role more culturally significant.

With this expansion of the roles of early childhood educators, the International Kindergarten Union (originally started in 1982) expanded the membership, broadened it's functions, and changed the name to Association for Childhood Education in 1930. The professionalization of early childhood education provided the framework for the development of sophisticated teacher-training curricula as well as fostering an interdisciplinary, child-oriented philosophy (Osborn, 1980).

Ironically, the Great Depression was a boon to early childhood education. Unemployed teachers were trained (of sorts) in child development and day-care operations and were employed through federal relief acts. A similar process was used during World War II to enable working women to build war machinery while their children were safely cared for in centers such as the Kaiser Center (Hymes, 1972). These emergency care centers served a social purpose and also provided an experimental setting in which teachers practiced the child development and curriculum theories they had studied. The experience and knowledge acquired during these times was later refined and used by teachers in Head Start, Home Start, and many other early childhood programs.

The 1950s, 60s, and 70s have been decades of expansion for all facets of early childhood. The role of the teacher is now a comprehensive one, placing emphasis on facilitating healthy development in children rather than simply intervening to correct problems. New issues have emerged and historical problems have surfaced in cyclical fashion, thus making the job of human service professionals a complex one. The remaining sections of this chapter focus on the varied and challenging tasks confronting today's teachers of young children.

## PROFESSIONAL PREPARATION

The professional preparation of early childhood educators has been diverse, out of necessity. Since those who work with young children have various roles to perform, their preparation and certification standards have never had the uniformity that is more common to other professions. In addition, the historical misnomer that "anyone can teach young children" has not helped develop public support for the professional preparation of early childhood educators. A good starting point is to examine the characteristics of a quality early childhood educator.

An effective teacher of young children must be a caring and sensitive person. Since young children are so malleable and responsive to the people in their environment, their role models must be extremely humane in their relationships with children. While the mature adult usually has an ordered sense of values, the young child is in search of experience he can use to form such a value structure. Thus the teacher who is conscious of providing children with multicultural experiences involves them in caring roles, assures that children's developmental needs are met, and is both proactive and reactive to their individual situations is providing the kind of adult guidance and direction so vital to the progress of young children (Seefeldt, 1980).

As we enter the 1980s and beyond, early childhood educators will find themselves a part of a new extended family in the sense of both helping and being helped by other adult care givers. Thus a reaching out quality should be an integral part of this professional group. Teachers who relate their classroom planning to the family as well as to the child are exhibiting the qualities desirable in early childhood educators (Swick & Duff, 1978).

The certification of early childhood educators is a relatively recent event. It was with the emergence of state-supported kindergarten programs that the proper certification of this professional group was even given minimal attention. Even today most state certification standards for teachers of young children are inadequate in terms of the desired qualities discussed previously in this chapter. Most states, for example, allow elementary education majors to become certified in early childhood education by taking one or two courses in methodology and child development. An educational program that leads to a high quality of certification is in existence at the University of South Carolina.

At the University of South Carolina (Columbia campus) the early childhood education student is involved in acquiring both a general education and professional training. Course work in the humanities, sciences, social studies, art, music, literature, drama, and related fields assure this future teacher has been exposed to general literacy components. A well designed professional program of studies, practica, and internships (commonly known as student teaching) are logically organized so the student is knowledgeable about children, methods of teaching, curricula designs, parental and family needs and has an adequate experiential base for initial entrance into the profession (Leeper, Skipper, & Witherspoon, 1979).

Beginning in the freshman year, the early childhood education major at the University of South Carolina is required to have practical experience in a variety of early learning settings (including the home) and with children and parents of different developmental and socio-economic backgrounds. The university maintains both an on-campus laboratory school (The Children's Center) and a community center for children and families (The Anna Boyd Child Development Center). The Anna Boyd Child Development Center is cooperatively managed by the university and a local public school system. These laboratory settings are supplemented by the use of many other early childhood programs as field placement centers for the teachers in training. Upon graduation (and formal certification) the "new" early childhood educator is capable of functioning in classroom settings and in various other capacities such as working in family-centered programs, child development programs in hospitals, prisons, and other institutions as well as in day care and other settings for young children.

Good certification programs are designed to provide continuing professional developmental experiences for early childhood educators. Most universities offer advanced degrees in specialty teaching methods, research, and other areas, such as school leadership and content dealing with specific facets of home-school development and programs for exceptional children.

With the need for preschool programs increasing more rapidly than available personnel, two rather unique certification programs have emerged to help meet this critical need. One program, known as the *career ladder* approach was developed within Head Start to enable promising volunteers and paraprofessionals to use a progressive training and educational arrangement to achieve eventual certification. In this way many capable adults could work and study at the same time. Actually this approach is simply a creative use of the apprentice system that had to be used in the early days of the teaching profession.

During the 1970s a system for certifying early childhood people to work in various programs with children but not be fully certified was developed. It was developed because of the urgent need to assure that young children would have adults who had minimal skills for handling the complex tasks of child development. The Child Development Associate program provided as method of assuring that trained personnel would be available to work in preschool programs that previously lacked this type of person. While this concept is still in the experimental stages, it certainly has many promising features and should be examined by those concerned with quality care for young children.

## PROFESSIONAL RESPONSIBILITIES

The teacher of young children has a variety of professional duties that concerned parents and citizens should be aware of when selecting quality places for children to learn and develop. A major responsibility of the teacher is to assure that the comprehensive needs of young children are the basis upon which a good program is developed. The effective early childhood educator views the child as part of a total social system including the family, school, and community (Swick & Hobson, 1979). This comprehensive perspective is also used in viewing physical, social, psychological, and intellectual development of the child. The effective teacher examines the curriculum, learning setting, and her own teaching approach to be sure that the following are functions that can be nurtured in young children:

1. *The Development of Independence.* Teachers have an important role in fostering appropriate independence in children. Is the instructional process designed so children are given assistance in selecting experiences but not unnecessarily screened from growth opportunities? This responsibility often goes unmet because many teachers opt for a highly structured and efficient classroom or center design. Children, however, will never learn to self-manage themselves without controlled but flexible opportunities to do so.

2. *The Development of a Positive Self-Image.* In watching how teachers relate to young children, see if they pay attention to the *child* rather than simply to a preordained curriculum. Does the teacher listen to each child? Does she praise children when appropriate? Children formulate a self-image through their many interactions with significant people, such as parents and teachers. When children are treated positively and given appropriate (and challenging) learning tasks, they generally respond in productive modes.

3. *The Development of Intellectual Curiosity.* Doctor Burton White has found that parents and teachers who stimulate the child's curiosity are effective teachers. Responsible early childhood educators use daily life experiences of the child as well as providing the child with materials that he can manipulate, explore, and design in intellectually formative ways. Curious learners ask questions, enjoy looking for new ways to do things, get involved in concrete manipulation of ideas, verbalize their feelings and insights to others, and initiate many of their own learning activities. As we examine early childhood settings we should ask ourselves if the environment is helping

the child develop intellectual curiosity.

4. *The Development of Creative Talents.* Young children enjoy using the imaginary to create new worlds of their own. Creative teachers organize the classroom so each child can be unique in using various art, music, literary, drama, and leadership experiences to develop their skills and talents. One of the most important things to look for in the teacher is how he responds to the differences among children. Capable teachers capitalize on these differences by incorporating each child's talents into the makeup of the curriculum.

5. *The Development of Social Skills.* Good schools for young children are based upon the premise that social interaction is a significant part of the learning process. Learning activities where children are encouraged to interact with each other promote the development of social skills they will use all of their lives. Good teachers recognize that problem-solving skills, group functioning, and personal self-confidence for relating to peers are developed within classrooms that encourage proactive social development.

6. *The Development of Physical Well-being.* The young child is in a formative stage of life, especially in terms of developing his physical well-being. The formation of physical activities that promote a sense of body control and total wellness are (or should be) an integral part of the early childhood program. Teachers who emphasize proper eating habits, provide movement experiences, and ensure that some part of each day is devoted to integrated learning (where children use body and spirit) are fostering in young children a wholesome approach to life.

7. *The Development of Emotional Well-being.* Today's young children are experiencing many events that can lead to emotional instability. By listening to children, observing their daily behavior, taking an interest in their personal concerns, and by providing a caring environment, the teacher is meeting the most important need of all children: a sense of personal integrity. Effective teachers model good emotional behavior by handling problems in a logical manner and through constructive expression of their ideas and feelings.

8. *The Responsible Teacher: A Final Comment.* It is obvious that

teachers of young children have multiple roles to perform. They are, in a most literal sense, guides and counselors to young children and their families. Far too often we look at the mechanical aspects of teaching or the physical presentation of the classroom. Yet it is the teacher and other people who relate to the children that make the difference in having a good or poor early childhood program. Teachers who continually renew themselves through professional development and by maintaining their personal well-being are usually most effective in meeting the criteria set forth in this section of the chapter. (For additional information on the professional responsibilities of the early childhood educator *see* Leeper, Skipper, & Witherspoon, 1979; & Seefeldt, 1980.)

## ISSUES AND TRENDS

The early childhood educator is confronted with a myriad of issues and trends that are directly effecting their relationships with children and families. It is impossible to give adequate treatment to all the issues and trends in a single chapter. Thus the most critical areas of concern are examined and discussed. For a more elaborate discussion of issues presented here and for information on other issues see the references suggested at the end of the chapter.

One of the major issues in early childhood education today deals with the demand for quality programs for young children at earlier and earlier ages. The number of mothers of preschool age children that are entering the labor force continues to increase and it is now believed that by 1985 two-thirds of all children will need some type of out-of-home care during the preschool years (Urban Task Force Report, 1980). The issue is whether there will be enough quality learning and care centers to meet this demand. Today there exists a shortage thus compounding the problem further. There are various questions related to this issue:

1. How accurate are the predictions that a critical shortage of early childhood programs already exists?
2. Whose responsibility is it to assure quality preschool programs for all children?
3. How can the need for quality preschool programs be met in an economical and yet humane way?

The answers to these questions are, of course, varied and depend upon the source consulted. Most early childhood educators, however, agree that the current need for quality preschool programs is great. It was only within the past decade that private and public educational and social agencies began to develop programs for preschool age children on a large scale (Masnick & Bane, 1980). While the quantity of programs has increased, the issue of quality is a critical one and has not been adequately met.

The issue of who should be responsible for the development of good programs for young children is certainly rhetorical as all of society has that responsibility. To place the burden on any one group is not only detrimental to the goal of having community programs but also a very narrow view of the life cycle process. Indeed, quality programs have emerged within many contexts, such as through federally sponsored projects and through the private efforts of innovative industrial systems. It is worth noting that during World War II our best programs were comprehensive in nature and involved all facets of the community. It is also worth noting that recent research on the persistence of preschool effects on children's learning and development had documented that when parents are involved in the programs, their children gain more in all facets of development, behavior, and academic success (Lazar, Hubbell, Murray, Rosche, & Royce, 1977).

How can we best meet the need for having good programs for children and families? Diversity has been a major strength in the field of early childhood education and this strength should be used to foster various approaches to meeting the needs of children and their families. While we must have national purpose to meet the total needs of all children, we must avoid any panacea as the way to accomplish our purpose. A more reasonable and, in the long term, more functional approach is to capitalize on the interests and skills of public school people, religious leaders, social agencies, private business firms, and lay citizens to forge community based programs. In this way the programs are more likely to succeed and to reflect the desires of the citizenry.

An issue that is with us and needs immediate attention is that of involving and educating parents relative to their role in the education of young children. The past decade has been characterized as one of increasing child abuse and neglect, decreasing involvement of parents with their children, and an increase in the number and percentage of children under six who spend a significant part of their time in some form of preschool educational setting outside the home. At issue is whether this phenomenon of home-school isolation has a negative effect on the child's development and learning. Perhaps the question can be answered in the positive sense: When parents are involved with their children and with their children's schools, both parents and children benefit. A recent research study indicated that preschool education programs had the most positive effect on children when the parents were directly involved in planning, implementing, or assisting in the program. Evaluation of children who participated in these parent-oriented programs indicates they were less apt to have special learning problems, more likely to find school as a positive experience, and were judged to be academically and socially successful by the their teachers (Lazar, Hubbell, Murray, Rosche, & Royce, 1977).

A predominant trend in the education of young children relates to what various people consider basic skills or fundamental knowledges. While it is encouraging that people are concerned about what children are learning, it is disturbing to see many programs focus on the narrow facets of academic readiness instead of giving credence to the total development of children. Research indicates very clearly that a balanced curriculum that is based upon the developmental needs of young children will provide a better arrangement for all children than a program that sacrifices social learning to academic exercises (Seefeldt, 1980). The recognition by consumers (those who select schools and centers for their children to attend) of the individuality of each child and the concrete manner by which children learn should provide them with a guide on what to look for in a good early childhood program.

A promising trend in the field of early childhood education is the emphasis now being placed on the prevention of learning and behavioral problems. Many of the recent innovations in early childhood education have focused on the use of methods and approaches that can lead to early diagnosis and correction of physical, social, and/or intellectual defects, which otherwise would impede the young child's progress. Many public and private schools have developed programs for three- and four-year-old children with one purpose being to prevent learning disabilities. Doctor Burton White has advocated that these efforts be extended downward to infancy, as three years of age is too late. Some states (through their education or social service departments) have developed parent-oriented education programs, which involve parents of infants and toddlers in learning activities where they can form effective parenting skills. The saying "Kindergarten is too late" is, according to research, accurate and indicative of the need for more focus on preschool education (Swick & Duff, 1979).

A growing number of early childhood education programs are mainstreaming handicapped and other exceptional children into their classrooms. With this trend comes a new challenge for teachers of young children as well as for parents and citizens. If the mainstreaming of children with special problems or unique talents is to be a success, three basic things must happen. First, and of utmost importance, is the training or retraining of teachers to deal with children who have exceptional situations. Attitudes, skills, and knowledges for teaching and relating to special needs children must become a part of the professional's collection of teaching behaviors. Second, parents and citizens need to be involved in shaping positive attitudes among children and adults toward the idea of mainstreaming. Third, the classrooms and learning centers of many schools need to be adjusted to meet the needs of handicapped children. Ramps, special toilet facilities, and additional teacher assistance are requisites if we expect the children to have a positive learning experience in the classroom. In selecting learning centers and schools for young children, parents of exceptional children should observe the classroom teacher and examine the facilities to see if they are realistically designed and oriented to accommodate the special needs student (Baruth & Duff, 1980).

The various questions being asked about early childhood education inevitably are related to some form of assessment of the effects of early education on children and families. For example many parents wonder aloud about the orientation of specific preschool programs. In the same respect various educators are examining the immediate and long-term effects of exemplary programs. More questions are being asked than answers being provided to the consumer. There are, however, some answers that have been put forth for parents, educators, and citizens to consider. The most observable results of early education are in the immediate detection and correction of simple health and learning problems. Recent studies have shown clearly that infants and young children who have the benefits of supervised adult attention are able to function better than their less fortunate peers in school-oriented activities. These studies are also valuable in that they point toward the need for a balanced approach to preschool and early education rather than the narrowly developed programs. While the examination of specific child development facets are worthwhile, the total functioning of young children must continue to be our primary objective in the designing and implementing of programs.

In the final analysis, the combination of historical wisdom and current research in early childhood education provides important insights into the quality of programs we need to develop. This knowledge base indicates that safe, secure, and stimulating but balanced learning environments are best suited to promote the total development of young children. Parents and teachers should be cautious in viewing programs and practices that promise quick solutions to problems that are inherent in the development of human beings. As the most recent research findings of Doctor Urie Bronfenbrenner (1979) indicate the making of human beings is complex and a long-term process that, if it is to be successful, must have the support of the total community.

## PROFESSIONAL ORGANIZATIONS

There are various professional associations that have a direct impact on early childhood education. The following list provides interested persons with places they can acquire information and assistance in terms of better understanding and helping young children and families:

Association for Childhood Education International (ACEI)
3615 Wisconsin Avenue, N.W.
Washington, D.C. 20016

National Association for the
Education of Young Children (NAEYC)
1834 Connecticut Avenue, N.W.
Washington, D.C. 20009

Southern Association for Children Under Six (SACUS)
Box 5403, Brady Station
Little Rock, Arkansas 72215

Council for Exceptional Children
Reston, Virginia 22070

Day Care and Child Development Council of America, Inc.
1426 H Street, N.W.
Washington, D.C. 20005

National Association for Mental Health
10 Columbus Circle
New York, New York 10019

Association for Children with Learning Disabilities
2200 Brownsville Road
Pittsburgh, Pennsylvania 15210

National Association for Retarded Children (NARC)
2709 Avenue E., East
Arlington, Texas 76011

Association for Education of the Visually Handicapped
711 14th Street, N.W.
Washington, D.C. 20005

National Easter Seal Society
2123 West Ogden Avenue
Chicago, Illinois 60612

## REFERENCES

Baruth, L., and Duff, E.: *Readings in Early Childhood Education*. Guilford Court, Special Learning Corporation, 1980.

Bronfenbrenner, U.: *The Ecology of Human Development*. Cambridge, Harvard University Press, 1979.

Comenius, J.A.: *The Great Didactic*. 1657.

Cubberley, E.: *A Brief History of Education*. Boston, Houghton Mifflin, 1922.

Froebel, F.: *The Education of Man*. New York, Appleton-Crofts, 1903.

Hymes, J.: *Living History of Early Childhood Education*. Washington, Childhood Resources, 1972.

Lazar, I., Hubbell, V., Murray, H., Rosche, M., and Royce, J.: *Summary Report: The Persistence of Preschool Effects*. Washington, Department of Health, Education and Welfare, 1977.

Leeper, S., Skipper, D., and Witherspoon, R.: *Good Schools for Young Children*. New York, Macmillan, 1979.

Masnick, G., and Bane, M.: *The Nation's Families: 1960-1990*. Cambridge, Joint Center for Urban Studies of MIT and Harvard, 1980.

Osborn, D.K.: *Early Childhood Education in Historical Perspective*. Athens, Georgia, Education Associates, 1980.

Seefeldt, C.: *A Curriculum for Preschools*. Columbus, Merrill, 1980.

Swick, K., and Duff, E.: *The Parent-Teacher Bond: Relating, Responding, Rewarding*. Dubuque, Kendall-Hunt, 1978.

Swick, K., and Duff, E.: *Parenting*. Washington, National Education Association, 1979.

Swick, K., and Hobson, C.: Child-Family-School Relations, *Education Report, 22:* 5, 1979.

# Chapter 4

# THE ROLE OF THE ELEMENTARY TEACHER IN THE PUBLIC SCHOOL

JOHN VAN HOOSE AND EVELYN B. DANDY

*JOHN VAN HOOSE is associate professor of Education, Department of Teacher Education, in the College of Education at the University of South Carolina. He has had teaching, counseling, and administrative experience in first through twelfth grades. He has taught undergraduate and graduate courses at Marian College in Indianapolis, Indiana University in Bloomington, and University of South Carolina. He has published articles in a number of national journals, including Phi Delta Kappan, Journal of Teacher Education, Middle School Journal, and the High School Journal, and has presented at numerous national, state, and regional conferences.*

*Evelyn B. Dandy is an assistant professor of reading at Armstrong State College in Savannah, Georgia. She completed undergraduate work at Millersville State College and earned a graduate degree at Temple University. She has taught in elementary schools and has served as a Title II reading teacher and a reading coordinator in Pennsylvania. She has taught graduate courses for teachers and has led numerous in-service workshops in reading and study skills for elementary and secondary teachers. She completed her doctorate at the University of South Carolina.*

## HISTORICAL OVERVIEW

The traditional role of teachers in the first public schools in the country was grounded in religious instruction. Early school masters were required to teach the Bible. Little else mattered. The belief by many that schools should allow prayers to be said and that teachers should be involved in moral education can be traced back to these first efforts in schooling in our country more than 300 years ago (Cubberley, 1934).

Regional differences in educational thinking during the colonial period brought about differences in methods of selecting early school teachers and deciding how they would fulfill their role (Cressman and Benda, 1956). In the middle colonies where schools were financially supported by the local government, masters were selected and certified by church authorities and appointed by civil authorities. Teachers of these parochial schools performed many types of services: "teacher, chorister, bell-ringer, sexton, and janitor at times being combined in one person — and for a small amount of pay that was difficult to collect" (Cubberley, 1934, p. 53).

In the New England colonies the Old Deluder Act of 1647 required that since the Old Deluder Satan's chief project was keeping men from knowledge of the scriptures, every township with fifty families must appoint someone within the community to teach children to read and write. The teacher's wages were to be paid either by children's parents or the citizens of the town. The "dame schools," founded in Connecticut during that period, were established to provide the fundamentals to children and were taught by women who did not have too many of their own children so that they were able to teach as well as get their own housework done (Cressman and Benda, 1966).

In the sparsely settled rural southern colonies education was generally thought of as a special privilege. Children were tutored in their homes by a teacher who had been selected by the parents. Charity or pauper schools were set up for a limited number of poor children. Indeed, some literate blacks on plantations were assigned the task of teaching children who lived on the plantation (Cubberley, 1934; Donley, 1976). These writers believe that the beginnings of the dual school system, based on race, is rooted in this tradition of the colonial era.

Teachers of the colonial period were for the most part humble and quiet. Their role was dictated by the community, which established strict rules of conduct regarding every aspect of their lives. Rules requiring church attendance, prohibiting smoking and drinking were enforced. Early teachers were evaluated by the town fathers who could enter the classroom at any time to see if pupils were learning.

Social and political forces during the eighteenth and nineteenth century brought about changes in the educational system of this country and therefore modified the role of the teacher.

The Northwest Ordinance of 1787 promised to forever encourage education by requiring that every township reserve a lot for the maintenance of public schools (Cressman and Benda, 1966). This act established a very important principle that would have a far-reaching effect on the teaching profession: federal aid to education. Subsequently, aid to schools through land grants was provided by every new state admitted to the union (Brodinsky, 1976). The national Constitution ratified in 1791 guaranteed the exercise of religious faith to everyone and also laid the foundations for this country's free, public, tax-supported, nonsectarian schools (Cubberley, 1934). This document also left, by implication, the primary responsibility for education to each individual state.

In 1821 a college education for women became a reality with the funding of Troy Seminary in New York. Horace Mann established the first state teacher training institution in America in 1839 (Cubberley, 1934). It was his dream to make schools public, tax-supported, free, and compulsory for every American child. When Massachusetts passed the first law compelling children to attend public school, other states followed. President Lincoln's signature on the Morrill Land Grant Acts opened the door to the setting up of state-supported institutions of higher learning for both men and women (Brodinsky, 1976). As the basic elements of the public school system were established, control of the schools shifted from church to state and much less emphasis was placed on religion.

The elementary school curriculum of the late 1800s and early 1900s included new methods for teaching reading and literature, arithmetic, oral language, history, geography, nature study, and music. Massive, foreign immigration and the industrial revolution of the period combined to produce sweeping social changes in this country. Educators were forced to broaden their activities and increase their efficiency to train the youth of a nation for democratic citizenship (Cubberley, 1934). Teachers were forced to adjust their role to changes in the school population, the physical plant, and curriculum.

Numerous legislative enactments of the twentieth century brought about changes in the complexion and financial provisions for the schools. In 1954 the U.S. Supreme Court ruled that segregation of black and white students in public education was unconstitutional.

Perhaps the most significant legislative commitment to education made by a government was enacted by Congress in the Elementary and Secondary Education Act of 1965. This act made provisions for new school opportunities for children of the poor, encouraged use of new teaching methods and materials, expanded library facilities, promoted research, and strengthened state departments of education (Brodinsky, 1976).

One other force that has shaped the work environment of the elementary and secondary teacher is the consolidation of schools and school systems. For many decades, schools were community agencies and an integral part of the life of the town or area they served. The one-room school house was a typical model. As the population that the school served expanded rapidly and as the nation changed from being predominantly rural in 1900 to predominantly urban by the 1950s and 1960s, schools became bigger. It was concluded that there was so much overlap and duplication of effort between small school districts that school systems should merge. This occurred first in urban areas and later in rural areas. This shift from the small community-based school to the consolidated multischool district led to greater efficiency. The facilities were improved and the resources for teaching were increased and less duplication of expensive facilities occurred. At the same time, teachers have been expected to cope with greater diversity, respond to more diverse expectations, complete more paperwork, and respond to more supervisors. It can be asserted that the impact of this consolidation process, still occurring today, has been a mixed blessing for elementary teachers.

The schools are a microcosm of the greater society, reflecting societal attitudes and concerns. For this reason the social, political, and economic forces in operation in our society throughout our history have had a profound effect upon the elementary schools. As the societal pendulum swings back and forth between a more liberating and a more conserving posture, elementary educators typically respond by making adjustments in emphasis. At the same time that these movements have occurred, steady progress in the preparation, competency, and status of elementary teachers has occurred. This once obedient public servant has become a trained professional who is relatively well paid, has job security and work benefits, and still plays an active role in molding the lives of the citizens of the future.

## PROFESSIONAL PREPARATION

In the 1800s, the typical elementary teacher had little preparation for teaching. Though some college experience was common, this did not involve coursework in education. However, in the early 1900s, departments of education were soon included in many colleges. Separate institutions called normal schools were also established for teacher training. After teachers graduated from a higher education institution and started teaching, in-service training was provided for them. This was necessary to help teachers learn how to use state-adopted textbooks and audiovisual materials that were being produced.

The pattern of preparation of elementary teachers that evolved included coursework in the history and philosophy of education, educational psychology, curriculum design, and methods of instruction. Practice teaching in laboratory schools was a common component of teacher training. There was also a heavy emphasis on the liberal arts and the sciences, such as academic coursework in English, philosophy, mathematics, and history. Some institutions did not allow elementary education students to earn a degree without majoring in an academic area along with their major in Elementary Education.

Though vestiges of this type of preparation program exist in most institutions today, some important shifts have occurred. While the liberal arts emphasis continues, it is no longer common to require elementary education majors to have an additional major. While student teaching is a part of virtually all preparation programs, most of this practice teaching is done in a public school classroom. This student teaching is a much more carefully monitored and carefully structured process.

A new addition to teacher education programs is the requirement that students take several practica courses early in their college career. Each practica typically requires a student to spend several hours a week in a public school classroom working as a teacher or as a tutor to small groups of students.

State legislatures and state departments of education have added specific requirements that must be embedded in teacher preparation programs. This may involve specific coursework in subjects such as mathematics or specific methods experiences such as coursework in the teaching of reading. Some states have mandated that students wishing to enter a teacher education program must pass a screening examination to demonstrate adult proficiency in reading, writing, and mathematics. Other states have prescribed a probationary period after graduation in which the new teacher is evaluated on the job.

The overall pattern of teacher preparation is one of expansion in the number of experiences and courses required. Some institutions have developed very structured programs with a series of competencies or skills that must be mastered. The emphasis in these institutions is on the mastery of these discrete skills that can be measured. Other institutions have developed a more flexible, loosely organized program with primary emphasis on the developmental needs of the learner. In this type of program, it is the perspective of the teacher that is important rather than discrete skills. Most programs can be placed along a continuum between these two extremes. One element is common to the majority of the teacher education programs in the country. This is a heavy emphasis on extensive experiences in public school classrooms. That trend is most likely to continue.

## PROFESSIONAL RESPONSIBILITY

Over the years, a teachers' primary responsibility has essentially remained the same: They impart knowledge. However, the methods used by teachers to carry out this responsibility have changed. These changes have been brought about by social, political, and economic forces, which are seen in the population being taught, the materials for teaching, and the teachers' own view of what education is.

The National Education Association (NEA) has conducted a vast amount of research about teachers in this country. The information it has compiled can be used to draw some general conclusions about teachers and their responsibilities as they can be seen over the past thirty years. The brief profiles that follow will give an overview of the "typical" teacher of three decades, the 1950s, 1960s, and 1970s.

The "average" teacher of the fifties was a  forty-five-year-old female who held a bachelor's degree and brought home about $4,575 a year. She was one of the short supply of teachers who had not been lured away from her career by the offer of higher pay. She lived in the community of the school in which she taught and took an active part in community affairs. She began her school day with morning devotions, which probably included a hymn and a reading from the Bible (NEA Research Bulletin, 1957). Her class of thirty-one pupils was assigned at random, so she was required to teach children from all ability levels. About 59 percent of her time was spent in class instruction, 25 percent preparing materials and grading papers, and 16 percent keeping records, talking with parents, and attending meetings (Cressman and Benda, 1956). This teacher relied heavily upon the textbook as she sought to prepare children for democratic citizenship (Stiles, 1957). One daily activity might have included taking children to the meagerly stocked library that had been converted from a classroom (Cressman and Benda, 1956). According to a poll taken by the NEA, teachers of the 1950s reported their greatest strengths were knowledge of the subject matter and ability to maintain control of their classroom (NEA Research Bulletin, 1957).

In sharp contrast, the more vocal teacher of the 1960s complained of problems such as large class size, lack of public support of education, inadequate salary, and growing problems with discipline (NEA Research Bulletin, 1971). In 1954 the U.S. Supreme Court ruled that segregation was unconstitutional, opening the doors to vast amounts of black children who were often mislabeled as disadvantaged. The influence of Sputnik and the Cold War with Russia along with increased government spending in education triggered many innovations, such as nongrading, programmed instruction, team teaching, and educational television. Classroom walls were knocked down to provide open space areas so that children could move about freely. Multipurpose media centers housed library books as well as teaching machines and individual packets of instruction. It was the responsibility of the teacher to integrate changes in population, buildings, and materials into her classroom instruction and to make certain that children learned mathematics, English, and especially the sciences (Goodlad, 1966). Other educators strongly urged this teacher to act as a catalyst to stimulate children to want to learn by discovery so that they could become independent productive citizens. The teacher of the 1960s, who received an average salary of 5,500 dollars, spent slightly more time (60.8 percent) in classroom instruction and slightly less time (14.6 percent) in monitorial duties than her counterpart of the 1950s. She spent the entire day with her pupils, supervising them at lunch and on the playground (Cressman and Benda, 1966).

Although there was a sharp increase in the number of males entering elementary education, the "typical" teacher of the 1970s was a thirty-seven-year-old female who may or may not be married. She had earned a bachelor's degree and was probably taking Saturday or evening courses to complete her certification requirements as well as an advanced degree (Campbell, 1975). Another variation on the typical day might be portrayed in this manner. The teacher began the day with a brief homeroom period in which attendance was taken and announcements were made. After this period, the students would have gone to the room in which the language arts block was taught. This included reading, writing, grammar, and spelling. The children were grouped by ability for instruction. Following language arts, mathematics also was taught to students who were grouped by ability. If the classroom did not have bathrooms adjoining it, the teacher may have taken the entire class to the bathrooms, especially in the primary grades. A recess period may have been provided and the teachers would have monitored the play period. The teacher may have been required to monitor the cafeteria while he or she ate with the children. After lunch, science, social studies as well as health, art, and music may have been scheduled. The students probably were not ability-grouped for these subjects. This "average" day might have included the administration of a standardized test or a state-wide assessment designed to diagnose the learner's strengths and weaknesses. Another part of the day could have involved "pull out" during which students would have left the classroom for additional help in math, reading, or other instructional programs and services. The teacher was expected to monitor the behavior of students as they boarded buses or got into cars to go home. As the teacher left school it would not have been uncommon for him or her to take home papers to grade.

The teacher's classroom contained enough open space to allow for large group, small group, or individualized instruction (Hansen, 1978). Since the 1970s brought a push for equality for the multicultural child, females, and the handicapped, materials and classroom facilities reflected these efforts. The day probably ended with the teacher attending an in-service workshop on mainstreaming, assessment procedures, or career education. The lack of public support complained about by the teacher of the 1960s had changed considerably. Local politicians, parents, and even students focused their attention on the schools, and more specifically on the teacher. Instructional goals had to be set, assessment had to be made, and evaluation and reassessment had to be provided. In light of this public attention, teachers also became more vocal, using collective bargaining, political action, and strikes to achieve rights they felt belonged to them.

The professional responsibilities of the teacher of the future will continue to be modified. Teachers will be responsible for teaching a variety of subjects and processes to students who come from a multiplicity of cultures. Since teachers of the next decade will essentially be better prepared, they should be able to draw upon the most carefully tested methods and choose from a variety of the most recent equipment and facilities to assure that they impart knowledge to their students.

The elementary teacher today faces an array of concerns that are almost overwhelming in intensity. These problems are by and large the result of changes in the greater society of which schools are a part. Many critics of education have called for a return to the way things were — the way school used to be. That is virtually impossible unless society itself returns to the way it was in the 1950s and earlier. That is highly unlikely! To underscore this critical point, observations about the ways schools were will be included in the analysis of current issues.

## CRISIS IN BEHAVIOR MANAGEMENT

In the 1980 poll of parents conducted by George Gallup (Gallup, 1981), parents listed discipline as the most serious problem facing schools. Many elementary teachers would agree. These teachers can't teach because the students are so disruptive. This problem is widespread, rearing its head in suburban and rural schools as well as inner-city schools. Of equal importance many students are refusing to apply themselves to the academic tasks they are assigned.

Many parents blame the lack of responsible behavior on the schools. Elementary teachers typically blame parents and administrators for the problem. Basically, the burden must be shared by all three. Society has encouraged adults to "do your own thing," "be your own person," and "live life with gusto." This message is widespread and has had its impact. Many adults have become more liberated and in some cases are more concerned about their needs before everyone else's. An extension of this self-serving mentality is being more permissive with children. If parents get to do their own thing, so should their children. It only seems fair, as some rather astute children will point out. Besides, it is easier to be more permissive with children and give into their demands when they report that all of their friends get to do *it*, whatever *it* is.

There is a pervasive catalyst and backup system to this mentality. It is the media in all its forms. Television, cinema, and popular magazines constantly bombard the modern mind with a myriad of self-serving messages. The heroes on television programs and in movies are self-indulgent, doing their own thing; the advertisements and commercials tell us how to be our own person, that is use this toothpaste or that deodorant; and the messages in programs or in the popular magazine articles encourage a self-centeredness mentality. When adults or children think only of themselves, the self-discipline to do something that is not fun causes a breakdown in respect for the rights of others. One dimension of this is a dilution of the traditional respect for those in positions of authority.

In our judgment, the elementary teacher is caught in a cross fire in this area. Some parents do not require their children to do their academic work or to be respectful of others at home, nor do some parents support and encourage respectful behavior at school. Some principals, fearful of parental reaction and board of education reaction to the strict enforcement of proper behavior policies, sometimes vacillate and are less supportive when teachers need their support in enforcing academic standards and discipline policies. Teachers maintain that the lack of support from the home and from administrators diminishes the likelihood of having a class of students who will behave properly and apply themselves to the tasks at hand. For some elementary teachers, it is almost impossible to teach the basics or anything else in some schools due to lack of control.

Qualifications must be made to this set of concerns. It is our contention that the vast majority of parents do care about their children and want them to have a good education. Many, perhaps most, want and expect their children to be respectful toward adults, including teachers. But the message of society that bombards parents through the media makes that task extremely difficult, even for the best parents. The point is that the greater societal norms run counter to good parenting.

While many parents are trying to raise their children properly, it must also be added that some parents are not doing what they should with their children. It is also our contention that this number has increased so that there are more students being disruptive in the classroom. Though these students may be the exception, the elementary teacher spends more and more time with these children who are exceptionally disruptive.

Investing an inordinate amount of time and energy with a few disruptive or indifferent children is not fair to the majority of students in a class nor is it fair to the teacher. The key to many of these concerns is to revive and underscore the critical importance of joining responsibility between educators and parents for the education and behavior of the children with whom they are charged. The difficulty in accomplishing this revival of the way things were is that the impact of many societal norms have to be neutralized in the process.

## THE LAW AND THE SCHOOLS

The result of legislative mandates and court orders has been to drastically expand the demands on the elementary teacher. While we applaud the basic sentiment behind laws that have been passed and court decisions that have been rendered, we must also stress that the practical implementation of some of these ideal mandates has been extremely difficult. The end result in many cases has been rather disappointing and very debilitating for elementary teachers. The most critical mandates will be discussed at this time.

*Desegregation* — In 1954, the Supreme Court ruled the separate but equal school is inherently unequal. This and subsequent decisions led to the elimination of dual school systems established by law (the technical term for this reality is *de jure* or *by law*) and to the judicial intervention in school systems that had most black students in one set of schools and most white students in another set of schools, even though these schools were part of the same system (the technical term for this reality is *de facto;* segregation clearly exists from the facts available). This court decision laid the foundation for numerous other decisions that had and still have a substantial impact on American schools. Basically, it created a set of extremely difficult challenges for teachers in two ways. The social challenge of nurturing and maintaining a positive learning environment when frictions between students existed was extremely difficult and is still a problem today. The academic challenge of helping children who had been denied access to quality schooling experiences made it most difficult to work with the "typical" students effectively and help the large number of disadvantaged students who entered many teachers' classrooms for the first time.

*Mainstreaming* — In 1975 Congress passed the Education for All Handicapped Act, P.L. 94-142. This law requires that all children receive the best possible education in the least restrictive environment. It also includes a provision for individualized schooling for 5 to 7 million physically, mentally, and emotionally handicapped students. The thrust of the legislature was noble. Its intent was to abolish the segregation of exceptional children into separate classes when it is not necessary, thus eliminating the stigma attached to these children who were clearly labeled as atypical. This intent is certainly worthwhile but the implementation of this law has had mixed results.

This federal statute did not mandate systematic in-service training for teachers to work with exceptional children, nor has special training in teacher preparation programs been required (Sarason et al., 1981). In practice a teacher may have twenty-five typical students, one educable mentally handicapped child, two emotionally disturbed children, one visually impaired child, and one child who is hard of hearing or some other configuration. He/she is expected to work with all children assigned to the class with no special preparation to do so. This is another example of a disservice to all students in the class as well as the teacher.

*The New Immigration* — While the courts and Congress are dealing with many concerns, another development is occurring that could have a profound impact on both our schools and our economy. This is the illegal immigration of millions of Mexican Americans into the United States. Harold Shane predicts that Hispanics will be the largest minority population in the country by the end of this decade: in excess of 20 million (Shane, 1979). These children must be assimilated into our schools. In some cases, bilingual education will be essential. In fact, the state of Texas is under court order to expand its bilingual education programs. The impact on the elementary teacher of this influx will be extensive. It will require the classroom teacher to deal with one additional population simultaneously with the other populations already in the school. And this population may not understand standard English at all.

*The New ABCs for Public Schools* — Accountability, Basics Education, and Competency-Based Education (Van Hoose, 1979) have emerged as the great triumvirate to solve our educational problems. The argument for this movement goes something like this. Educators are hired to do a job: help students learn. The degree of progress that a student makes should be the way to measure teacher effectiveness. We can hold teachers accountable for student progress. One problem is that teachers aren't focusing enough on the same kinds of things: the basics such as reading, etc. We should focus on these basic areas and measure the performance or competency of students through the use of standardized tests. A quest for greater accountability and a public outcry for heavier emphasis on the basics led to competency based education. The form of testing that was selected and refined to monitor this approach is criterion-reference testing, assessments that compare a student performance to a desirable standard or level of performance instead of a comparison to other students.

It is certainly appropriate to hold teachers accountable and it is imperative that schools teach the basics. Furthermore, standardized tests can be very useful tools in gathering a lot of data about student performance quickly. However, this thrust is based on an unrealistic premise — that schools can counter and overpower the forces in operation in the greater society and in the home. Elementary teachers are not the only individuals who should be held accountable. Parents are accountable in that they must see to it that their children apply themselves at school, do homework, and behave properly. Students are accountable for themselves in that they must be willing to try and should do their best. Teachers must have the skills, knowledge, and desire to work with and help children grow. When we talk about growth, we are referring to social and psychological development as well as academic growth. These three dimensions are inseparable.

The problem with the basics thrust and the competency testing is that they create one more set of pressures for elementary teachers. Elementary teachers are asked to deal with student populations more diverse than ever and are also expected to demonstrate tangibly — through test scores — that all of their students are progressing at the desirable rate determined by legislatures and state departments. They are also expected to provide remedial activities for those students who fall below the stated criterion level. All of this could be done with more resources and staff. However, many states are passing this type of legislation without providing any additional funds to remediate.

## SUMMARY

It should not be claimed that all legal mandates are having a negative impact on school. The federally subsidized lunch and breakfast programs and the various provisions of the Elementary and Secondary Education Act are examples of legislation that have had a rather positive impact. However, many pieces of legislation and court orders have been directed at resolving major societal concerns and moral issues through the schools. That simply cannot be done. Elementary teachers are being asked to do more and more with a more diverse population and to demonstrate their success with all children assigned to them in a tangible manner; this is a very simplistic set of expectations.

In a recent article in a popular news magazine, Will Rogers was quoted as saying over fifty years ago that "the schools aren't as good as they used to be, but they never were." We have had an unrealistic belief as a society that schools can do anything. That belief, as naive, as it is, is being replaced by a rather sinister attitude that schools now have the capacity to make even smart kids stupid. One additional burden that all educators must shoulder is to undo that conviction.

## ORGANIZATIONS

American Federation of Teachers
11 Dupont Circle, N.W.
Washington, D.C. 20036

Association for Individually Guided Education
318 North Center
4319 Covington Highway
Decatur, Georgia 30035

International Reading Association
800 Barksdale Road
P.O. Box 8139
Newark, Delaware 19771

National Association for Supervision and Curriculum Development
225 North Washington Street
Alexandria, Virginia 22314

National Association of Elementary School Principals
1801 North Moore Street
Arlington, Virginia 22209

National Education Association
1201 16th Street, N.W.
Washington, D.C. 20036

National Society for the Study of Education
5835 Kimbark Avenue
Chicago, Illinois 60637

## REFERENCES

A statistical picture of our schools. *NEA Research Bulletin, 35*(3):22-41, April 1957.

Brodinsky, B.: 12 major events that shaped America's schools. *Phi Delta Kappan, 58* (1):68-77, September 1976.

Campbell, R.F., Cummingham, L., Nystrand, R., and Usdan, M.: *The Organization and Control of American Schools,* 3rd ed. Columbus, Ohio, Charles E. Merrill, 1975.

Cressman, R., and Benda, H.W.: *Public Education in America.* New York, Appleton-Century-Crofts, Inc., 1966.

Cressman, R., and Benda, H.W.: *Public Education in America.* New York, Appleton-Century-Crofts, Inc., 1956.

Cubberley, E.P.: *Public Education in the United States.* Boston, Houghton Mifflin Company, 1934.

Donley, M.O.: The American schoolteacher: from obedient servant to militant professional. *Phi Delta Kappan, 58*(1): 112-117, September 1976.

Gallup, G.H.: The twelfth annual gallup poll of the public's attitudes toward the public schools. *Phi Delta Kappan, 62*(1):33-47, September 1980.

Goodlad, J. (Ed.): *The Changing American School.* Sixty-fifth Yearbook of the National Society for the Study of Education. Chicago, University of Chicago Press, 1966.

Hansen, H.: *Public Education in American Society,* 2nd ed. Englewood Cliffs, New Jersey, Prentice-Hall, Inc., 1963.

Hansen, T.: The changing role of the classroom teacher. *NASSP Bulletin, 62*(417):20-23, April, 1978.

Sarason, S., and Dorris, J.: Mainstreaming: dilemmas, opposition, opportunities. *Education 80/81.* Guilford, Connecticut, Dushkin Publishing Company, 1981, pp. 169-171.

Shane, H.: *Video Interview on Educational Futures.* University of South Carolina, Columbia, South Carolina, 1980.

Stiles, L. (Ed.): *The Teacher's Role in American Society.* New York, Harper and Brothers Publishers, 1957.

The American public-school teacher, 1970-71. *NEA Research Bulletin, 49*(4):101-108, December 1971.

Van Hoose, J.: The new ABC's for public schools. *The Imperative for Contemporary Education.* South Carolina Association for Supervision and Curriculum Development, 1979, pp. 9-13.

# Chapter 5

# THE ROLE OF THE SECONDARY TEACHER IN THE PUBLIC SCHOOL

FREDRIC L. SPLITTGERBER AND RICHARD H. KHERLOPIAN

*F*REDRIC SPLITTGERBER *is an associate professor of education at the University of South Carolina, Columbia, South Carolina. He completed his baccalaureate and master's degrees at the University of Omaha, Omaha, Nebraska. His doctorate was completed at the University of Nebraska. His teaching experience includes public schools in Kansas, Purdue University, and Ft. Wayne, and currently he is teaching undergraduate and graduate courses in secondary education, curriculum, middle school, and social studies at the University of South Carolina. Previously, he has been a department chairman of Education at Purdue University and Ft. Wayne and also department head of secondary education and curriculum and instruction at the University of South Carolina. He currently holds membership and is an active participant in Phi Delta Kappa, Association for Supervision and Curriculum Development, National Council for the Social Studies, and National Middle School Association.*

*Richard H. Kherlopian received the doctor of education degree from the University of North Carolina at Chapel Hill. He is currently serving as chairman of the Department of Curriculum and Secondary Education at the University of South Carolina. He has had extensive experience as a high school teacher, education teacher, and curriculum development specialist.*

## HISTORICAL PERSPECTIVE

The first public high school was established in Boston, Massachusetts, in 1821. Other public high schools quickly followed, and by 1840, the idea of tax-supported, publically controlled secondary schools had taken root. There were over 300 public high schools in the nation by 1860, but for the most part these were small preparatory schools located in the larger cities with highly selective admission requirements (Raubinger, 1969).

The established high schools at the turn of the century enrolled and catered to a fraction of the youth who were of school age. Approximately 298,000 students out of 3,000,000 eligible students were attending public high schools (French, 1967).

The early decades of the twentieth century witnessed a major shift in the role of the high school. The prevailing view that secondary schools were a place for students to prepare for entrance into college and that the same classical curriculum was necessary for all the students was in direct conflict with current economic, social, and political developments. The nation was moving from a predominantly rural agrarian society to a mechanized agrarian and urban industrial society. Legislation was enacted that restricted child labor and required mandatory attendance in schools.

With the entry of the United States into World War I the nation had become a great world power and was hesitantly drawn into the international arena. In 1918, the Commission on the Reorganization of Secondary Education, composed of principals, superintendents and professional educators, joined together to study the issues of the secondary school. The committee stated that secondary education should be based on the needs of society, characteristics of the individuals to be educated, and on the knowledge of educational theory and practice available. While the previous report of the Committee of Ten, 1892, focused on academic subjects, this report produced the Seven Cardinal Principles as the purposes and objectives of education listing: (1) health, (2) command of the fundamental processes, (3) worthy home membership, (4) vocation, (5) civic education, (6) worthy use of leisure time, and (7) ethical character (French, 1967).

The secondary schools were the center of tremendous progress and expansion. School enrollments doubled every decade from 1900-1930, rising from 630,000 students in 1900 to 4,427,000 students in 1930 (French, 1967). Schools could not be built fast enough to house secondary students. There was little time for anyone to stand aside and reflect on what type of educational opportunity should be provided for the millions of newcomers to secondary education.

Less than a score of years after the appearance of the Seven Cardinal Principles, the United States was in the midst of a world-wide economic depression. Although enrollments continued to increase during the depression, this was a period when education was in ferment over the purposes and curriculum of public high schools. Even though the purposes were firmly established by the Seven Cardinal Principles, the search for clarification continued. Several committees, Eight Year Study, American Youth Commission, Regents' Inquiry, and Educational Policies Committee, represented attempts to state coherent purposes, to clarify goals, and to provide statements of objectives to guide high schools. Most of the studies revealed gaps between what the high schools professed to believe and do and what they were doing (Holton, 1969).

The depression caused many youth to be unemployed or in need of work to help support their families. The federal government did not believe education was able by itself to resolve unemployment, and even educators who were more aware of the problems of unemployed youth did not have financial resources readily available to cope with unemployment. The president and Congress did not choose to work through the high schools but established separate agencies, Civilian Conservation Corps and National Youth Administration. Both agencies clearly demonstrated that the federal government could actually provide educational opportunities.

In 1942, the first Federal Aid to Education Act was passed. The act contained two major provisions: (1) the federal government should allot funds to states for the purpose of reducing extreme educational inequalities in education that existed in certain states and (2) the establishment of a complete and adequate educational program for all youth at the national level. The act also established the United States Office of Education (USOE), which was to grow into the cabinet post of Health, Education and Welfare and, finally, into its own cabinet post of Education.

At the same time state educational agencies were being established as the chief state school authorities. These agencies have continued to expand and take on additional responsibilities, which have made a significant contribution to fostering educational opportunities in the various states.

At the end of World War II the Harvard Report pointed out that secondary schools were failing to provide a meaningful education for persons who could not succeed either in the conventional college preparatory programs as then constituted nor in high school job skills offered in vocational education. The report proposed that general education should be provided to all focused on life adjustment. The recommendations called for a practical approach to the curriculum employing every day problems centered around such objectives as citizenship, home and family life, wise use of leisure time, health, consumer education, and basic skills of reading, mathematics, and writing, which had been expressed earlier in the Seven Cardinal Principles (Raubinger, 1969).

During the fifties, schools came under attack for the term *life adjustment*, implying that the program lacked academic excellence. Furthermore, there was concern expressed that the academically talented college-bound youth should be challenged, but at the same time it was impossible to ignore the unemployed youth and the increase in school dropouts. The debates and issues of the 1950s were best represented by the White House Conference on Education called by the president in 1954. The conference report reiterated the need to recognize intellectual achievement, determine and develop each child's talent to its fullest potential, and develop useful and practical skills in all learners. Furthermore, because scholars had not worked with teachers and the curricula of secondary schools, concern was expressed that public high schools had not developed sound mathematics, science, English, and social science programs. The National Science Foundation began to sponsor in-service programs to improve mathematics, science, and foreign languages.

In 1957, with the launching of Sputnik by Russia, the public schools were blamed for our nation failing to be first in space. Congress quickly passed the National Defense Education Act to improve the science, mathematics, and foreign language programs. High schools were criticized for failing to effectively train scientists and mathematicians. Admiral Rickover, who was in charge of the recruitment for the Nuclear Power Division of the Navy, was highly critical of the lack of specialized training among high school graduates recruited for the nuclear and space programs and blamed this failure on American high schools. He proposed selective and specialized secondary schools for the academically talented youth similar to those found in Europe (Raubinger, 1969). Near the end of the decade, Doctor James Conant, after studying 103 schools in twenty-six states, outlined twenty-one recommendations, such as how to provide effective counseling programs, individualized programs, improved reading programs, academically talented programs, curricular changes in social studies, and foreign languages for a comprehensive program (Conant, 1959).

The sixties saw a flourish of federal aid to education within the short span of five years. Project English and social studies grants were enacted to improve the curricula of language arts and social studies. The Vocational Education Act provided improved vocational preparation and area vocational schools. The National Defense Education Act, 1964, broadened the areas of emphasis in the 1958 act from science, mathematics, and foreign languages to include English, reading, history, geography, and civics. The Job Corps and Neighborhood Youth Corps provided employment for out-of-school youth, drop-out prone, and young people determined to be poor job risks. The Elementary and Secondary Act, 1965, provided grants to improve the quality of education for the poor through improved coordination and federal aid and established regional education centers to research educational problems. At the end of the decade there was still a great deal of unrest among the youth resulting in riots, personal injuries, death, and destruction of property.

During the seventies it was time again to question the curriculum of the high schools and to review the role and purposes of the public high schools. The holding power of the high schools increased even further from 70 percent to 80 percent while high school enrollments were declining due to a lower birth rate (Cawelti, 1974). Four major committees met again to review the role and purposes of the high school. these were the Panel on Youth of President's Science Advisory Committee, Carnegie Commission on Higher Education, National Commission on the Reform of Secondary Education, and National Panel on High Schools and Adolescent Education. The reports and recommendations included more programs centered in the community for public work, social service, and educational opportunities; more flexibility in programs for students entering and leaving formal school settings for work, service, or travel; broadened opportunity for students to test out of subjects and promotion of earlier entrance into higher education institutions; more incentives for larger school systems to develop alternative programs; and development of minimum competencies for graduation (Cawelti, 1974). Finally, in the later part of the decade less grant money was available for innovations in high school programs and at the start of the eighties the Reagan administration has begun a program to further reduce federal aid and spending in education.

In summary, the high school curriculum dominated by the classical college preparation course of study did not change appreciably until the early decades of the twentieth century. Although subjects such as modern history, geography, chemistry, physics, biology, algebra, geometry, modern foreign languages, and English were slowly added over the years and as they became requirements for entrance into college, the thrust remained the same. The "preparation-for-life" curriculum, or vocational education as it was known, continued to be an inferior option that was viewed as not leading to highly paid white-collar jobs or improved social position.

By the 1920s rapid advances in industrialization, transportation, and communication opened up new avenues of work, leisure, and opportunity. Women were granted the right to vote, labor laws were stiffened, and the tax-supported public high school was literally transformed into a true servant of society. The junior high school was established to more effectively bridge the gap between elementary and high school. Federal aid for vocational education increased and strengthened the curricular offerings in the high school, lending respectability to the world of work. Specialized technical and commercial high schools were established to further emphasize preparation for life skills as the curriculum expanded in scope and purpose to meet the diversified needs of a growing and changing society.

The modern day American comprehensive high school has no equal anywhere in the world. Its curriculum has attempted to meet the educational needs of all students regardless of background or ability. As democracy became a reality in the economic, social, and political life of the country, the high school curriculum responded in kind. Today's high schools prepare students for a variety of vocational, industrial, technical, and academic areas. No longer are physical, emotionally, or mentally handicapped students excluded from the system, and in many parts of the country where English is not the primary language for a significant proportion of the population, instruction is provided in both the native language and English. The high school curriculum has changed in a century and a half from a highly selective college preparatory program to a comprehensive educational endeavor directed towards meeting the diverse needs of all students.

## TEACHER EDUCATION

In principle, high school teachers in the late 1800s were required to have four years of training in a college or in a normal school. In practice this was not the case. As a result of compulsory school legislation, a doubling of the population and an increasing pragamatic stance of the secondary school, during the first quarter of the twentieth century, the problem of finding qualified teachers was reduced to the problem of finding any teacher for the schoolroom.

Such emergency practices caused state boards of education and school systems to require minimum training in professional education and subject matter courses. From 1925 to the present day, certification requirements for teachers have been characterized by the following developments: (1) a gradual but steady decrease in the number of hours spent in professional education courses; (2) a variation in the number of hours in subject matter courses seemingly effected by national emergencies as the world wars, the depression, Sputnik, Vietnam, and inflation; (3) an increase in the amount of time spent in full-time practice teaching in the schools; and (4) the use of competency testing for entrance to and exit from teacher education programs.

At the present time secondary level teacher preparation requires at least the completion of a baccalaureate degree with professional training in education including student teaching or an internship. The degree program is usually composed of a general education component, subject concentration in a teaching field, and professional education courses. Teacher preparation at teacher training institutions is organized in such a manner that graduation and completion of the professional training component qualifies the candidate both for a degree and state certification. The general education component consists of English composition, literature, health, music and art appreciation, natural and physical sciences, social sciences, foreign language, and/or mathematics. The subject concentration usually consists of training in a subject content field from approximately twenty-four to fifty semester hours depending on the major, state, and college requirements. The major subject fields encompass mathematics, English, social sciences, physical education, health education, natural or physical sciences, distributive education, business, home economic, industrial arts, foreign languages, music, and art. Usually the total number of hours needed for graduation varies from 120 to 130 semester hours. Any elective hours are used to strengthen the major or to provide for a minor area of preparation. Specialized training in exceptionalities, learning disabilities, and reading are also available. In each state certification requirements determine the minimum subject concentration required. Regional associations, such as Southern Association of Colleges and Schools, and national accrediting agencies, such as National Association of Colleges of Teacher Education, also establish criteria for teacher training programs.

The professional education component usually requires an entrance screening process to determine the prospective teacher's health, hearing, speech, and knowledge skills, including reading, mathematics, and English and usually requires some type of entrance interview before entering the professional education component. The education course work includes history and philosophy of education, educational psychology, adolescent psychology, high school curriculum, subject matter methods in the academic specialization, practical experiences in the school, and supervised student teaching or internship. The student teaching or internship usually varies from eight weeks to a semester in duration and is under the close supervision of a classroom teacher and university supervisor who are responsible for daily, weekly, and overall evaluations for the student teaching experience. In almost every state certification is granted by a state agency, usually the state department of education.

## PROFESSIONAL RESPONSIBILITIES

Professional responsibilities of the teacher center around three major categories of commitment: (1) the profession, (2) student, and (3) community. As a professional, the teacher is responsible for organizing the learning environment of the classroom, including knowledge, skills, and experiences needed by students to function in this society. The duties include being well prepared in one or more subject fields and familiar with effective classroom strategies and able to motivate students to learn. The teacher manages the day-to-day routine, such as roll taking, making assignments, grading papers, and preparing and giving tests, is responsible for the selection of content, and informs parents when students need help or problems arise.

The typical daily teacher's responsibilities usually start at 7:30 to 8:00 A.M. and run until 3:30 to 4:00 P.M. Depending on the school size and teacher qualifications, the teachers have assigned responsibilities for hall, bus duty, lunchroom, and assemblies and as class sponsor, and most teachers have a homeroom of twenty-five to thirty students. In every high school a schedule for extra compensation or reduced teaching loads is granted for debate team, coaching, department heads, etc. In no instance will a teacher have more than two or three different preparations because of being protected by state statutes. Each teacher is provided a planning period that may occur anytime during the school day. The number of students assigned to a given teacher will vary from twenty-five to thirty-five per class with no more than 150-180 students per teacher each day. Some exceptions for class size are provided in typing and physical education classes. During each six or nine weeks the teacher is expected to grade reports and assignments or to calculate grades and to send home interim reports and report cards. During the year various reports and clerical functions are required to meet local, state, and federal requirements.

Another dimension of teacher's professional responsibilities is working with teacher colleagues in planning and participation in faculty and school district meetings. There is also the need to develop a positive working relationship with the building administrator and district personnel and to maintain his or her professional conduct so as to develop a positive, cooperative response to the various publics served by the school.

Finally, the teacher has a professional responsibility to stay active in professional organizations by joining the key professional organizations at the local, state, and national levels, to maintain professional growth through attendance at conferences and conventions, to complete additional graduate course work, to read in professional books and magazines, to participate in in-service training such as workshops, and to conduct research to improve classroom learning.

The second commitment or responsibilities toward students involves ensuring that all individuals' personalities and rights are respected and accepted and at the same time recognizing the need to provide educational opportunity to develop each student to the maximum of their potential through experiences that enable them to grow in self-discipline. Each teacher must try to develop an effective relationship with individual students so that the students can establish successful interpersonal relationships with peers and adults. Teachers should be able to provide counseling and advisement toward career and personal goals and also protect the rights of individual students; maintain a professional and ethical relationship with the student; guide students in their educational experiences; and motivate students to apply themselves in obtaining an education. Thus, careful attention needs to be paid by all teachers to the individual student's needs (Brophy, 1980).

The third commitment implies being a part of the community in which the teacher resides. The teacher on the one hand acts as a citizen but is also a representative of the educational enterprise and, therefore, is a part of the educational decision-making process. A professional commitment to the community implies working with the community to further cooperative arrangements within the community and to assist the community in the establishment of worthy goals. Teachers need to understand the communities' attitudes, values, and conditions existing in the community. In summary, the commitment involves sharing the responsibility to develop general educational opportunities, recognize the right of the public to participate, and individually, assume political and citizenship responsibilities (Timar, 1980).

## ISSUES

Part of the confusion over issues grows in part out of the perplexities of the American society. There would appear to be six questions that need to be answered:

1. What shall be the purposes, role, and functions of the secondary school?
2. Whom shall we educate?
3. How shall we instruct?
4. What philosophy should we teach?
5. Who shall teach?
6. Where shall we teach?

Perhaps, the most persistent and reoccurring question is "What shall be the purposes, role, and functions of the high school?" From 1892 to the present one viewpoint is that the high school existed to prepare the elite for entry into college through the study of humanities, mathematics, and languages. The current movements to define minimum competencies and the "back to the basics" may encourage the revival of the narrow interpretation of the purposes, role, and functions of the high school. In contrast, for sixty years since the recommendations of the Seven Cardinal Principles, we have been trying to extend the curriculum offerings to provide broader educational opportunities for more youth. This has brought on an overextended curriculum trying to serve all students' needs. Thus, the high school in attempting to avoid the narrow specialized program that is inadequate for the needs of today's society and youth has provided standard subjects in high schools, plus the inclusion of educational opportunities in every area of human concern, except religion. Unfortunately, the consequences of the sweeping language of the Seven Cardinal Principles has been the assumption that schools could reform all of society's ills. As a result the schools have undertaken responsibilities they have neither the resources for or the talents to resolve. It is important that the schools limit themselves to a number of tasks and goals they can reasonably cope with in terms of physical and material resources. Perhaps, it is reasonable to assume that the schools are ideally suited to develop intellectual competence and citizenship skills in our society (Martin, 1980).

In response to the question of whom we shall educate, it is imperative that we provide the general education for all citizens but also recognize that specialized training and preparation begin in the high school and that career education can assist in a smooth transition into the world of work (Beane, 1980). At the same time there is a need to provide a forum in which decision-making and choice-making can occur. The question of whom shall we educate also involves several societal issues. High schools are holding more fourteen- to seventeen-year-old youths, and it is undesirable not to attend high schools today. Our society has provided a prolonged period of adolescence during which youth have very little real involvement in worthwhile tasks. The extent of boredom has been documented (Cawelti, 1974). In addition the role of the home is less influential in helping adolescents move from schooling into work, and many parental responsibilities have been passed on to the school. Further complicating the problem is the fact that students are maturing much earlier than two or three decades ago. In fact the curriculum in many instances underemphasizes what young people can do. There is also a continued need to involve the community in education by broadening the educational opportunities in community settings. Learners of all ages should have experiences that are directly related to the needs and demands of the society and community. As the final part of this question, how does one strike a balance between which is more important the child or the curriculum? In any given class you will find the ability ranges from a slow to gifted learner. Mainstreaming has mandated to some degree that children with learning difficulties be placed in regular classroom settings. The argument is about at what point the learning difficulty is severe enough that the child should be excluded from the regular classroom. Both the child and the curriculum are important, and public education takes all adolescents except those who must be institutionalized. However, we have not found a way to make education meaningful to all learners served. It should be noted that part of the responsibility for learning has always and still rests on the learner wanting to learn. Schools do not have the legal authority to make a student learn if he does not wish to do so or to require his parents or guardian to work with him or to be responsible for his learning.

The question of how we shall teach involves decisions about effective methods, training of teachers, and the financing that is provided by the district and state for education. Perhaps the most important concern revolves around the cost of education. The old motto "you get what you pay for" is highly applicable to education. The more expectations that the community has for educating its youth, the more education will cost. There is a great deal of disportional expenditure of funds among the school districts of the various states. Some communities support their schools financially much better than do others. Test scores when measured in terms of financial expenditures have usually born this out. State statutes have attempted to reduce educational expenditures, to equalize expenditures, to improve teachers' instruction through evaluation, to equalize educational opportunities, and to establish minimal competencies

(Fuhrman, 1980). All state statutes need to be carefully evaluated as to whether there is proper planning and implementation. These two previously mentioned concerns are not usually included in the legislation.

In order to answer the question as to what philosophy we should teach, four propositions need to be examined:

1. Secondary schools are primarily a highly selective institution for the intellectually capable.
2. Public schools should perpetuate the conservative side of our American tradition.
3. Secondary schools should assist youth in their present and future needs in our complex society.
4. Schools exist to provide broad-based educational needs for all of society.

Each of the four propositions has an important meaning in terms of the education provided by the public high school. As stated previously in this chapter there is a need to limit the number of tasks and goals that schools can reasonably cope with in terms of physical and material resources. The mandate to provide a general education for all our citizens is established as a principle but the relationship of general education to specialized training, citizenship development, and career education has been subject to many interpretations. The starting point would be to redefine the curriculum of public schools and to provide a sequential framework for the curriculum. However, the movement must be continuous and not started and stopped after one, two, or three years.

The question of who shall teach involves various state certification requirements, preparation programs in colleges and universities, and the availability of teachers to teach. It is estimated that with higher salaries elsewhere and competition from industry, there may well be a shortage of teachers in the later part of eighties. At the present time certification requirements are under review and statutes have been passed in many states, including legislation to carefully screen candidates before they enter the teaching profession and longer probationary periods for beginning teachers. Careful attention is being directed to the teacher's competence, personality factors, and physical and mental health.

In an era marked by steadily declining test scores, the placement of physical, emotional, and mentally handicapped students in regular classrooms, mountains of paper work demanded by local, state, and national legislation, and the presence of armed guards in the schools, placed there to stem the tide of crime and violence, the misbegotten notion that education, particularly in the high school, can cure the ills of society and the perception of the classroom teacher has changed dramatically. Once admired for professional competence and selfless devotion, many teachers have been excused for laziness, lack of interest, and incompetence. Several popular weekly news magazines estimate approximately 20 percent of the nations teachers have not mastered the basic skills of reading, writing, and arithmetic that they supposedly teach. Teachers counterclaim that they are prevented from teaching.

Indecision and lack of control of the system on the part of school officials are cited by teachers who claim that they are reportedly required to implement conflicting administrative policies and procedures associated with mainstreaming, desegregation, and other federally supported programs embraced by the schools. Additional evidence cited by teachers is the increasing rate of violent behavior on the part of students and the schools' inability to maintain discipline and positive student attitudes towards learning. With the attractive incentives and salaries being given by industry, the more competent graduates are being recruited into occupations in industry. Schools are not in a position to compete with private industry.

Responding to the question of where we shall teach requires reviewing size, enrollments, financing, and school buildings. With declining enrollments and high construction costs of new buildings, there is a need to better utilize the present building space. However, many buildings will require extensive renovation to provide broader educational opportunities. The size of the school affects school climate and the ability to communicate between teachers and students. In a high school of 3,000 students it is much more difficult to directly communicate with students than in a high school of 1,000 students. School facilities are predicated on the degree and type of community and parental support given to schools. The ownership of the schools belongs to the community, parents, and patrons of the school district. In the final analysis it is the responsibility of the community to ensure that the best educational opportunities are available to our youth. High schools need to ensure and guarantee that the appropriate learning environment is provided. Parents are responsible for their child's behavior so that learning can occur, and students should have self-discipline to behave so learning can occur in the classroom. If these responsibilities are carefully articulated and implemented, there will be a dynamic high school with an excellent educational opportunity for all youth; if not, there will not be a desirable educational experience for the youth. The future of public education and, more importantly, secondary education is in large part up to the American people. Each citizen, irregardless of his occupational status, has a responsibility to provide and maintain the best educational opportunity for all youth.

## PROFESSIONAL ORGANIZATIONS

National Association of Secondary School Principals
1904 Association Drive
Reston, Virginia 22091

National Education Association
1201 16th Street, N.W.
Washington, D.C. 20036

National Association for Supervision
and Curriculum Development
225 North Washington Street
Alexandria, Virginia 22314

National Council of Teachers of English
1111 Kenyon Road
Urbana, Illinois 61801

National Council for the Social Studies
3615 Wisconsin Avenue, N.W.
Washington, D.C. 20016

National Science Teachers Association
1742 Connecticut Avenue, N.W.
Washington, D.C. 20009

Modern Language Association
62 Fifth Avenue
New York, New York 10011

National Council of Teachers of Mathematics
1906 Association Drive
Reston, Virginia 22091

American Vocational Association
2020 North 14th Street
Arlington, Virginia 22201

American Federation of Teachers, AFL-CIO
11 Dupont Circle, N.W.
Washington, D.C. 20036

## REFERENCES

Beane, J.A.: The general education we need. *Educational Leadership, 37(4):*307-308, January 1980.

Brophy, J.E.: Teacher behavior and student learning. *Educational Leadership, 37(1):*33-38, October 1979.

Cawelti, G.: *Vitalizing the High School.* Washington, D.C., Association for Supervision and Curriculum Development, 1975.

Comments on School Governance. *Educational Leadership, 38(2):*102-110, November 1980.

Faunce, R.C., and Munshaw, C.L.: *Teaching and Learning in Secondary Schools.* Belmont, California, Wadsworth Publishing Company, 1967.

Fuhrman, S., and Rosenthal, A.: School finance reform in 1980s. *Educational Leadership,* 38(2):122-124, November 1980.

French, W.M.: American Secondary Education, 2nd ed. New York, The Odyssey Press, 1967.

Holton, S.M.: *Understanding the American Public High School.* Boston, Allyn and Bacon, Inc., 1969.

Martin, J.H.: Reconsidering the goals of high school education. *Educational Leadership, 37(4):*278-285, January 1980.

McKean, R.C.: *Principles and Methods in Secondary Education,* 2nd ed. Columbus, Ohio, Charles E. Merrill Publishing Company, 1971.

Raubinger, R.M., Rowe, H.G., Piper, D.L., and West, C.K.: *The Development of Secondary Education.* New York, Macmillan Company, 1969.

Risk, T.M.: *Principles and Practices of Teaching in Secondary Schools,* 4th ed. New York, American Book Company, 1968.

Timar, T.B., and Guthrie, J.W.: Public values and public school policy in the 1980's. *Educational Leadership, 38(2):*110-117, November 1980.

# Chapter 6

# THE ADMINISTRATIVE ASPECT
# OF PUBLIC SCHOOLS

Gyuri Nemeth

*G YURI NEMETH was born in Budapest, Hungary, and attended school in Ankara, Turkey. In 1956 he emigrated to the United States with his mother and brother. He graduated from high school in Framingham, Massachusetts, in 1959. He served in the U.S. Army 7th Special Forces from 1959 until 1962. He received both his bachelor of arts degree in social sciences and his masters of education degree in education administration from the University of Delaware.*

*Nemeth taught U.S. History at Framingham South High School in Massachusetts. He also served as assistant dean in the College of Education at Georgia State University, where his doctorate in education administration was conferred. He served as assistant dean and director of student teaching and assistant professor at the University of South Carolina.*

*Nemeth is presently serving as an administrator for DeKalb County Schools in Tucker, Georgia.*

---

## ADMINISTRATIVE POSITIONS

The public schools is a fixture in all communities in the United States. Our children spend the bulk of their years within its walls. We tend to live by the school calendar — planning vacations and other family events around it. Often we take the school system for granted until a tax vote or referendum appears on our election ballot. Then, briefly, we are aware of the financial network that must support the cost of educating our local young citizens.

Even the smallest school districts have seen a marked increase in their need for administrative skills over the past decades. Public education in the United States is now an 81 billion-dollar industry aimed at serving the needs of 43 million children annually. At the local level, administrative skills keep the individual schools operating and serving the needs of the community. Districts oversee, manipulate, and regulate groups of schools. State boards of education orchestrate the bulk of requirements, financial allocations, and other adjudications necessary to ensure a growing, efficient organization within the state. The federal government has become increasingly active in the public education sphere. Within these large categories are thousands of individual jobs that make up the network of public school administrators functioning at all levels to keep the system viable, flexible, and prepared to satisfy the demands of an ever more competitive American population.

The history of education within the United States precedes the birth of the nation. From the time there were children to educate, provision was made for that responsibility.

Our forefathers relied upon homes and churches a great deal to teach the young and there was little uniformity in curriculum. Individual schools were managed by the school master and funded by the community. The city of Cincinatti, Ohio, was the first to establish the role of principal-teacher in 1838, although in 1812 New York had appointed a state superintendent (Campbell, Cunningham, McPhee, & Nystrand, 1970). Even though, as recently as 1900, the average person was formally educated only five years, (Fuller & Pearson, 1969) administrative roles had been enlarged and duties divided as systems had to deal with more students, more money, and more complex educational requirements. Emile Durkheim predicted in the late 1800s that the division of labor would be the rule rather than the exception in our daily lives. His prediction has been realized in many fields, including education, as more and more specialists emerge and, for each specialty, more administrative duties.

Those who aspire to a career in education administration must realize that the field has become extremely varied. The prerequisite for all levels of administration is to gain familiarity with and credibility in the system by working in it. Within the public schools most administrative jobs at the local level are filled from the ranks of school district employees who have worked their way up through the system, particularly within specific curriculum areas. The areas of exception to this rule are those concerned with the actual business side of the school district, although many districts do tap faculty for these positions.

As the education industry has grown, so have educational requirements increased. A bachelor's degree is required for almost all public school administrative positions. At the same time, state certification requirements must be met for the majority of administrative positions. Even upon completing those requirements, many school systems require continuing education in order to advance within the system. As a rule, the general post-bachelor degree requirements may be achieved by taking courses in curriculum, school law, supervision, principalship, interpersonal and group relations, statistics and/or research methods, negotiations, school business management, and finance. Since a graduate degree is becoming a necessity in many school systems, these courses should not be embarked upon haphazardly but in conjunction with a graduate degree or specialist program. Even those individuals involved in the business area of school management, i.e. accounting and data processing, will be more marketable with the addition of education courses to their own degree requirements.

In order to catalog the administrative positions available in the public school sector, one must remember that these duties range in responsibility from assigning specific students to curriculum areas to suit their needs to managing funds at a federal level for schools systems throughout the nation. Needless to say, an individual would have difficulty stepping from a terminal degree program to a top level federal position. However, there is room for a variety of personal interests in administrative positions. The following list categories a few of the positions within the public school system:

1. *Assistant Principal/Principal* — These are two of the most highly visible of all school system administrative jobs. Since they are directly involved with students and with policymaking decisions affecting students, they are the direct line from parents to the hierarchy within a school system. The total job of running a school in agreement with district guidelines falls to the principal. The duties of the principal and assistant principal include faculty supervision, overseeing the physical plant, student discipline, curriculum control, and a myriad other responsibilities. The principal is answerable to the office of the superintendent of schools and is the line between his school and the central administration of the district. The majority of school systems within the United States are now requiring a

graduate level degree in order to attain a principalship. In addition, the individual must satisfy certification requirements and generally must work his way up through the ranks.

2. *Assistant or Associate Superintendent/Superintendent* — These are highly visible positions dealing with both the public and political forces in order to ensure good public relations and adequate financial support for the system. The superintendent is the chief administrative officer for the school district. All policymaking decisions are formalized through the office of the superintendent and his assistants may specialize in a particular area of advisement. Duties at this level are usually clustered and delegated, such as associate superintendent for instruction and assistant superintendent for business. Professional seniority and experience as well as a terminal degree are the most frequent requirements for these positions, although there are still individuals hired at this level who do not have terminal degrees. State certification requirements must be met. The superintendent is generally either appointed by the school board or elected by the citizens of the district.

3. *Director/Supervisor/Coordinator* — Although these titles may vary, they define the role of those in central school district administration who supervise specific areas system-wide. The positions are specialized and may deal with curriculum areas, such as director of special education and supervisor of physical education. They also deal with the running of the support services needed in the system, such as coordinator of food services, and director of transportation. The educational requirements of those individuals acting within the curriculum areas of the system would be similar to those of a principal. The requirements for those in charge of the business aspect of the system may vary widely from district to district.

4. *Legal Officer* — This position is held by someone with a knowledge of legal matters who can evaluate district situations from a legal standpoint and who is to keep abreast of legal precedent that could effect the district. This office reports directly either to the superintendent or to the school board. In some districts an attorney may hold this position; in others an individual who has educational background in school law may be employed. This is a relatively new position and some districts do

not set this responsibility aside from others. However, with rising legal decisions impacting on school system capabilities, it is a necessary field.

5. *Coordinator of Library, Audio-Visual, and Educational Materials Services* — The coordinator is responsible for the inventory of audiovisual equipment and educational materials necessary to supplement and complement district programs. In some instances library supervision is relegated to a separate position depending upon the size of the district. Library supervision entails the staffing and inventory of various school libraries within the system. Although a degree in library science is sometimes necessary, educational requirements generally coincide with those of other directorships.

6. *Attendance Officer* — This office keeps attendance records for state funding and makes predictions necessary for building, staffing, and allocation projects for the district. Education requirements are similar to those for directors, supervisors, and coordinators.

7. *Director of Food Services* — This position entails the staffing of school cafeterias and buying and preparing food in compliance with state and federal mandates. A degree in nutrition or dietetics is often desirable for this position.

8. *Director of Finance and Business Administration* — In some systems the responsibilities entailed in this position are divided. They include pay disbursement, bookkeeping, accounting, auditing, disposal of surplus property, and school plant management. The preparation of the school budget and its proper disposal are usually monitored by this office to ensure legal compliance. The educational requirements for this position include experience within the educational system with some background in business administration.

9. *Personnel Officer* — The head of the personnel office has the primary responsibility for hiring and dismissal recommendations prior to school board action. In addition, duties include recruitment of personnel, hiring, maintenance of fringe benefits, processing retirement, and providing data for certification and salary. In other words, this office is involved with the personnel of the school system from their introduction into the system until the time they leave it. The requirements for this position include a background in other jobs within a school

system and similar educational background to other directorships.

10. *Public Relations Officer* — This individual is considered to be a
spokesperson for the school system on daily matters. This unit is
one of the more recent developments in education as a response
to heavy demand for information by the media. Many public
relations personnel have come up through the ranks although
individuals who have held media-oriented positions are also
marketable for this position.

11. *Assessment Unit* — This unit is usually headed by a director and
its duties are to compile statistical data on students and to conduct research to evaluate the effectiveness of the programs of the
school system. An educational background in statistics and
research is worthwhile for this position.

12. *Support Services Officer* — The large public investment in school
systems necessitates security systems and programs to protect
facilities, grounds, students, and faculty. A background in
police or security work is advantageous for this position.

The administrative officers of a school system are all always
answerable to the highest authority of the system: the local school
board. The board is made up of an arbitrary number (usually based
upon population) of elected individuals who have, collectively, total
power to affirm or deny requests and recommendations concerning
all actions within the system.

Another major source of employment for educators in each state
is the state department of education. Most of the aforementioned
central administration positions within school systems have their
counterparts in the state department of education. For example
there are departments to oversee transportation, data processing,
auditing, food services, textbooks, and secretarial services. There
are three other major functions for the state department of education: the supervision of school districts to ensure compliance with
state statutes, certification of personnel who hold positions having
student contact, and the representation of the state education system
at the federal level. The state superintendent of education is considered to be the spokesperson for education in the state.

Most state department of education positions are not bound by
certification requirements necessary for school system jobs. A
background in education at some level is necessary for all those posi-

tions except business service positions. In order to gain information regarding a specific state department of education, it is best to call the public relations office.

The third category of educational employment opportunities are the professional organizations at the state and local level. In reviewing these associations, an organizational pattern emerges. The elected president of the association is a member of the profession, but an executive secretary and a professional staff are charged with the daily administration of the organization. Professional organizations involved in collective bargaining, such as the National Education Association and the American Federation of Teachers also possess a large staff to administer their ongoing responsibilities. Requirements for positions at this level vary greatly.

## TRENDS IN EDUCATION ADMINISTRATION

For those individuals whose aspirations lean toward positions as educational administrators, a review of new trends and conflicts with which the administrator must deal on a daily basis is worthwhile. Socioeconomic factors are forcing the schools into more controversial roles than ever before, and the administrator must be cognizant of the way in which he can perform his tasks in order to achieve school system goals. Several conflicting areas are as follows:

1. *Political vs. Nonpolitical Action* — Even though the greatest portion of the budget of the local political unit (city, township, and county) is spent on education, the percentage of dollars spent has been decreasing in view of the political actions of other agencies. In order to call the financial needs of the system to the attention of those committttees and agencies responsible for allocations, the school system must forge political alliances. This is a role that the public sometimes finds unacceptable for a service agency, but one that realistically must be recognized and clearly defined within the system.

2. *Curriculum Conflicts* — There are many titles around in which battles have been waged throughout the country in the curriculum wars. Is vocational education more beneficial than general education? Do students gain a better basis for their future from a basic three Rs approach than they do from a varied curriculum in which they can choose from frill courses?

Should students be encouraged to gain general knowledge or to specialize at an early age? Generally individual districts have set guidelines around which they have based their curricula in response to these questions. For the prospective educational administrator, it is wise to formulate an individual philosophy regarding his approach to curriculum and find out how closely a district coincides with that philosophy before filing an application.

3. *Financial Support* — Property taxes constitute a very large portion of the funds allocated to the school system. In 1978, California passed Proposition 13 to reduce ad valorem taxes in that state. In 1980, Massachusetts passed Proposition 2½, which limited property taxes to 2½ percent of the assessed value of the property. At the same time there are ever-increasing demands upon schools to respond to the needs for more and better programs in science, mathematics, and drug education, and thus the need for more specialized faculty personnel is increased. The double dilemma of less revenue to produce more programs is the most trying conflict to face the schools in years to come.

4. *Discrimination* — As society is forced to change, there will continue to be conflict in civil rights areas. Since the schools are bound by legal precedent, they must be the forerunners of court-ordered change. Systems have had to effect changes to alter student and faculty racial balance. Sexual discrimination is an issue in hiring and discipline. Religious discrimination must be considered in curriculum areas. These are but a few of the ways in which schools must be aware of discrimination areas.

5. *Private vs. Public Education* — In 1981 Doctor James Coleman publicized a series of studies that fueled the controversy over the roles of public, private, and parochial schools by stating that better results were attained by students attending private than public schools. The validity of his studies are yet to be tested. However, the possibility that such studies could affect the tax base that supports the public school system is not totally remote. Probably further studies favoring public education will also be forthcoming, although conflict does appear to be emerging in this area.

6. *The Role of the Federal Government* — The cutback of impact funds (funds paid for students whose parents work in tax-exempt locales), reduction of funds for the Elementary and Secondary Schools Act, and the mandate of Public Law 94-142, which directs the school systems to provide an appropriate education for all handicapped children, have resulted in a tremendous financial burden to schools at the local level. The burden of providing funds to support federal court-mandated programs falls to the local community. In order that the schools comply legally, there must be funds available for these programs. However, in many cases the best efforts made locally are not sufficient and often funds must be borrowed from other program or budget areas to satisfy legal requirements. The fact that the federal government is playing an increasing role in mandating new and costly changes in education but is playing a decreasing role in funding is a source of aggravation for school administrators.

The public school administrator is caught between many cross pressures today. However, he is in a position that both reflects and effects societal change and serves his community. There are varied positions in administration that will satisfy the daily occupational needs of many individuals. The public education network is a constantly changing and growing industry that has not been bound by geography, and administration positions within that unit are challenging and fulfilling life's work.

For further information regarding specific career opportunities or other queries about public education in the United States, the following organizations will be helpful:

AASA — American Association of School Administrators
1801 North Moore Street
Arlington, Virginia 22209

AASPA — American Association
of School Personnel Administrators
6483 Tanglewood Lane
Seven Hills, Ohio 44131

AATF — American Association of Teachers of French
57 East Armory
Champaign, Illinois 61820

AATG — American Association of Teachers of German
339 Walnut Street
Philadelphia, Pennsylvania 19106

AATSP — American Association of Teachers
of Spanish and Portugese
Holy Cross College
Worcester, Massachusetts 01610

AEA — Adult Education Association of the United States
810 18th Street N.W.
Washington, D.C. 20006

AIAA — American Industrial Arts Association
1201 16th Street N.W.
Washington, D.C. 20036

ASBDA — American School Band Directors Association
9 Davis Avenue
Dover, New Jersey 07801

ASCD — Association for Supervision
and Curriculum Development
1701 K Street N.W.
Suite 1100
Washington, D.C. 20006

ASFSA — American School Food Services Association
4101 East Iliff Avenue
Denver, Colorado 80222

CBE — Council for Basic Education
725 15th Street N.W.
Washington, D.C. 20005

CEC — Council for Exceptional Children
1920 Association Street
Reston, Virginia 22091

CEEB — College Entrance Examination Board
88 Seventh Avenue
New York, New York 10019

CEFB — Council of Educational Facility Planners
29 West Woodruff Avenue
Columbus, Ohio 43210

HEEA — Home Economics Education Association
1201 16th Street N.W.
Washington, D.C. 20036

IRA — International Reading Association
P.O. Box 8139
800 Barksdale Drive
Newark, Delaware 19711

MENC — Music Educators National Conference
1902 Association Drive
Reston, Virginia 22091

NAASFEP — National Association of Administrators
of State and Federal Education Programs
P.O. Box 1371
Ann Arbor, Michigan 48106

NAEA — National Art Education Association
1916 Association Drive
Reston, Virginia 22091

NABT — National Association of Biology Teachers
11250 Roger Bacon Drive
Reston, Virginia 22090

NAESP — National Association of Elementary
School Principals
1801 North Moore Street
Arlington, Virginia 22209

NAGT — National Association of Geology Teachers
Pennsylvania Bureau of Topographic
and Geological Survey
Harrisburg, Pennsylvania 17120

NAPPA — National Association of
Pupil Personnel Administrators
1950 Mallway
Columbus, Ohio 43221

NASAA — National Association of Student Activity Advisors
NASC — National Association of Student Councils
1904 Association Drive
Reston, Virginia 22091

NASPE — National Association for
Sports and Physical Education
1201 16th Street N.W.
Suite 627
Washington, D.C. 20036

NASBE — National Association of State Boards of Education
444 North Capitol Street N.W.
Suite 526
Washington, D.C. 20001

NASSP — National Association of Secondary School Principals
1904 Association Drive
Reston, Virginia 22091

NCATE — National Council for Accreditation
of Teacher Education
1750 Pennsylvania Avenue N.W.
Room 411
Washington, D.C. 20006

NCSS — National Council for Social Studies
2030 M Street N.W.
Washington, D.C. 20036

NCSSAD — National Council of Secondary
School Athletic Directors
1201 16th Street N.W.
Washington, D.C. 20036

NCTE — National Council of Teachers of English
1111 Kenyon Road
Urbana, Illinois 61801

NCTM — National Council of Teachers of Mathematics
1906 Association Drive
Reston, Virginia 22091

NEA — National Education Association
1201 16th Street N.W.
Washington, D.C. 20036

NSBA — National School Boards Association
1055 Thomas Jefferson Street
Washington, D.C. 20007

NSPRA — National School Public Relations Association
1801 North Moore Street
Arlington, Virginia 22209

NSPA — National Scholastic Press Association
720 Washington Street
University of Minnesota
Minneapolis, Minnesota 55414

NSSE — National Study of School Evaluation
2201 Wilson Boulevard
Arlington, Virginia 22201

NSTA — National Science Teachers Association
1055 Thomas Jefferson Street
Washington, D.C. 20007

NVATA — National Vocational Agricultural
Teachers Association
Box 4498
Lincoln, Nebraska 68504

AFT — American Federation of Teachers
11 Dupont Circle
Washington, D.C. 20036

CCSSO — Council of Chief State School Officers
1201 16th Street N.W.
Washington, D.C. 20036

National Parent Teachers Association
700 North Rush Street
Chicago, Illinois 60611

## REFERENCES

Campbell, R.F., Cunningham, L.L., McPhee, R.F., and Nystrand, R.O.: *The Organization and Control of American Schools*, 2nd ed. Columbus, Ohio, Charles E. Merrill Publishing Co., 1970.

Fuller, E., and Pearson, J.B. (Ed.): *Education in the States: Nationwide Development Since 1900*. Washington, D.C., National Education Association of the United States, 1969.

# Chapter 7

# THE SCHOOL GUIDANCE COUNSELOR

GARY M. MILLER

*G ARY MILLER completed his doctorate in counselor education in 1969 at Case Western Reserve University. He taught at Eastern Michigan University for six years and has been on the faculty at the University of South Carolina since 1975. He has authored and coauthored articles in The Personnel and Guidance Journal, The School Counselor, Elementary School Guidance and Counseling, and other professional publications. Miller has conducted counseling workshops and interpersonal skills training for various populations, including teachers, nurses, and military personnel. In addition to his professional efforts, he enjoys jogging, coaching a youth basketball team, and spending time with his family.*

## INTRODUCTION

This chapter will provide an overview of the development of the guidance movement in American society and the public school setting. A section on the preparation of counselors and the skills needed by them for working with students, school personnel, and parents is presented. Information regarding the responsibilities of the counselor in elementary, middle, and senior high schools will be presented. The final two sections of the chapter focus on current issues facing school counselors as well as information regarding the principle professional organizations to which school counselors belong.

## HISTORICAL OVERVIEW

The evolution of the guidance movement in the United States has had numerous influences. Brewer (1942) noted four principle factors that were interrelated. The division of labor, which required individuals to become specialized in their work efforts, was the first. With some of the specializations emerged the second factor, the growth of technology, which required individuals to master new equipment to complete their work. To understand and be able to work with more sophisticated machinery, people needed specialized preparation, hence vocational education, the third influence emerged. Our democratic evolution as a nation represented the fourth factor. The United States in the early 1900s was relatively free of a class system. With widespread public education, youths were being educated to learn how to live and function in a democracy. This democratic spirit encouraged them to make their own decisions and to develop a greater sense of self-determination. With these factors interrelating the need for assisting people with various issues they would be facing became apparent.

Throughout the twentieth century there have been a number of other factors and events that played a part in development of school guidance programs. Humanitarian efforts supported by philanthropists have attempted to help people better their lives. From these efforts, social reform movements have emerged and throughout our history have attempted to offer services to those in need.

The awareness and understanding of mental disorders affecting people and the establishment of the National Committee on Mental Health in 1909 did much to improve the conditions for people suffering from mental disorders. More humane treatment, focusing on psychological approaches rather than incarcerating people in institutions, was incorporated in treatment plans. Mental health workers were influential in schools as they encouraged educators to understand the identity and insecurity issues faced by students.

The assessment movement represented a new way of examining people and their abilities. In the late 1890s the concept of mental tests was first mentioned by James McKeen Cattell. The first intelligence test was developed in France in 1906 by Binet and Simon. Ten years later in 1916 L.M. Terman revised the Binet-Simon scales for use with American children. The principle thrust in large-group intelligence assessment came with the development of the Army Alpha Test during World War I. From the development of these instruments, individuals were able to systematically gather information about those they were assisting. The testing movement has flourished and the areas of assessment have expanded to examine not only intellectual abilities, but also to encompass special abilities, interests, aptitudes, and attitudes as well as to diagnose difficulties that may need specialized attention.

As early as 1929 the federal government had an influence on guidance efforts. The George Reed Act of 1929 promoted funding for vocational guidance. In 1938 the United States Office of Education created the Occupational and Guidance Services Bureau, but it was not until 1958 that some of the greatest government support emerged. From 1950 through 1955 numerous studies were conducted addressing the dilemma that although many high school graduates had the aptitude and interest for college, many of them did not continue their education. Some students never tried to enter college, and many who did, failed to graduate (Miller, 1961). The National Defense Education Act of 1958 was signed into law by President Eisenhower. One section of the act focused on improving secondary school guidance programs. In the summer of 1959 a total of 2,210 counselors participated in special institutes that were hosted by fifty colleges and universities throughout the United States. The following summer, 2,746 counselors attended eighty-three special summer institutes. Between 1959 and 1961 a total of thirty institutes were conducted during the regular calendar year of the host institutions (Miller, 1961). Although, not funded to the extent of the 1958 act, in 1968 the Education Professions Development Act provided funds for the training and employment of counselors (Shertzer & Stone, 1976).

There has been an evolution of approaches to counseling students in the public schools. The early influences of Frank Parsons, focusing on vocational development, gradually merged with the assessment efforts previously described, resulting in guidance programs that emphasized assessment and vocational planning. In the early 1940s Carl Rogers and his associates began researching the counseling process and from their efforts Rogers developed an approach known as client-centered counseling. The principle emphasis of his theory was that the client had the power to change within one's self and that the counselor's responsibility was to help the person energize the potentialities one has to resolve issues being faced. This approach was seen as highly controversial, for Rogers was placing the counselor and client on equal terms. Prior to this, the counselor was often seen as the expert whose advice would guide people to resolving their problems. Many school counselors were educated by individuals espousing the client-centered approach to counseling.

Other approaches to counseling focusing on behavioral changes for individuals have also emerged and been incorporated into school counseling programs (Aubrey, 1977). Many of these counseling orientations are used on a one-to-one basis or in small group settings.

Shertzer and Stone (1976) have indicated some guidelines counselors use when counseling students. These focus on the development of an understanding and respect between the parties involved in the counseling. The term *rapport* is often used by counselors in discussing the understanding and respect factors. The counselor provides structure in the discussion by clarifying the parts each person will play, the type of help the counselor can provide, as well as the amount of time the counselor has available to the student. Using various interactions, the counselor is able to engage the student in conversation and help the student discuss issues of concern. During this process the counselor listens for the feelings and attitudes discussed by the student. If some information is presented that the counselor is unable to help the client resolve, then the counselor needs to refer the student to the appropriate professional who can provide the needed help. The final phase of the interview is when a smooth termination occurs. During this closing of the interview the counselor may summarize the nature of the discussion and invite the student to return for another session, if the student wishes.

The counselor does not demand that the student change one's feelings, attitudes, and behaviors. The counselor does work at helping the student examine the issues, the choices, and the consequences of the choices one is considering. In this process the counselor respects the integrity of the student and strives to promote the welfare of the individual.

In the early 1970s the development of efforts toward career education emerged to influence school guidance programs. The definition for career education developed by the United States Office of Education states, "Career education is the totality of experiences in which one learns about and prepares to engage in work as part of his or her way of living" (Hoyt, 1974).

Numerous approaches to develop career education efforts have emerged. In the public school setting programs have been designed to include kindergarten through twelfth grade. A principle effort has focused on incorporating information about careers throughout all curricular offerings in the school system. The counselor's role in this effort can vary as schools attempt to provide career information, decision-making, and vocational guidance in all levels of the school's programs. Information regarding career education will be presented in Chapter 11.

School guidance programs exist with a basic set of principles. The programs are designed to help all students in the school. Consequently, counselors are involved in activities with students to help them develop their unique capabilities as individuals. Counselors view students from a developmental perspective. This means that they consider each person's ongoing growth and try to assist students by capitalizing on the strengths within each pupil. Obviously every student is not alike; so the counselor works at understanding the individual differences of students as they participate in different school activities. The guidance program is a systemwide effort wherein a team approach is stressed. Each school's guidance program team includes the counselors, administrators, teachers, parents, and specialists, all of whom influence the student. Each of the previously mentioned groups work together with the goal being the development of students who are capable of living their lives and making decisions for themselves. This effort represents the implementation of our democratic ideals in the lives of individuals.

School counselors function as professionals and have some specific philosophical guidelines that they use. Moser and Moser (1963) view these guidelines as follows:

1. Every person is a dynamic organism with an individual uniqueness of personality and possibilities for growth and adaption.
2. An individual's personality is the composite of two variables: his inherited traits, both physical and mental, and his environment, both present and past.
3. An individual is a growing organism, is in a state of constant change, and his growth can be guided into patterns and channels beneficial both to him and society.
4. Every individual may benefit by having at his disposal assistance in making choices, in promoting his adjustment, and in charting his course for a successful life.
5. It is, and should be the responsibility of the school to develop the guidance services necessary for each student to achieve optimum development.
6. Society may be improved by the optimum development and ad-

justment of its individual members (p. 9).

As can be seen in these six statements, the guidance efforts in schools have a direct relationship to the development of the person and to society as well. The historical and philosophical issues presented provide an overview of guidance in the public school setting. The professional preparation of counselors will be presented next.

## PROFESSIONAL PREPARATION

The Association for Counselor Education and Supervision developed a set of standards for preparing individuals to be counselors (1979). These specific standards are directly related to the personnel selected for counselor preparation as well as the specific kinds of responsibilities that counselors must assume. Geister (1974) described entry-level skills that all counselors should have.

In selecting individuals to enter counselor education programs, faculty members try to ascertain the applicant's potential effectiveness in close personal relationships. Because counseling involves such relationships, it is critical that the counselor is able to become close to another person one is trying to help. Counselor educators are also concerned about an applicant's potential to develop facilitative relationships with people who are at various developmental levels. In addition, the counselor applicant needs to be a person who is open to self-examination and has a commitment to one's own self-growth. The idea of commitment is also stressed as counselor educators seek applicants who are committed to counseling as a career and do not see the position of counselor as a "stepping stone" to some other career they are seeking.

The program of study a counselor trainee enters will have specific requirements. The person will take some academic course work focusing on human growth and development along with courses accenting the social and cultural foundations of society. Courses having an emphasis on the helping relationship of counseling will be required. These provide a background about philosophical issues in counseling, counseling skills, theories, and opportunities to practice various counseling approaches. One is also prepared in consultation skills as well as being taught about different group approaches and how to use them in counseling efforts. The individual learns about life-style and career development, as these may influence potential clients. Appraisal methods using assessment instruments are taught to students, with an emphasis on the counseling use of these instruments. Also the counselor trainee learns about research and evaluation strategies that will assist one in understanding research as well as being able to conduct research and evaluation studies. As in all professions, the individual does have an orientation experience that informs one of the professional responsibilities, the professional role, and organizations and the ethical code governing the counselor as a professional.

The student is also expected to have some educational experiences in the environment in which one hopes to work. Such experiences help in clarifying the role and standards for the counselor in that specific environment. One also learns about the historical, philosophical, and ethical foundation about counseling in a specific environment.

Supervised experiences represent another component in the counselor's formal preparation. These experiences include laboratory activities, wherein one practices specific counseling approaches with other counselor trainees. During this time, observations are made using audio and video as well as direct observations. Through such practice and review of one's skills, the counselor trainee begins to better understand the counseling process and to develop skills appropriate for helping another person.

A second supervised experience is the counseling practicum. This experience may be done at the institution preparing the counselor or at a cooperating setting in the community. It is recommended that the person devote sixty hours of effort over a nine-month time period when enrolled in a practicum. The counselor trainee will be observed and monitored while conducting counseling activities with real clients. Again, one's efforts are critiqued and evaluated by the teaching staff and by the cooperating counselor at the host setting.

The counseling internship represents the final supervised experience for the counselor trainee. In this experience the student is placed in the setting where he or she eventually hopes to be employed. This on-the-job internship consists of 300 hours of experience over a nine-month time period.

At the completion of one's formal education, the counselor is prepared to assist students, school personnel, and parents in a number of specific services. The counseling service is seen by many as the core ingredient in any school's guidance and counseling program. This service is provided to students on an individual basis or in small groups. Its principle focus is to assist the student in developing a sense of self-understanding and an understanding of others and the world in which one lives. As noted earlier, the counseling process is designed to promote self-exploration and learning. In the learning phase of counseling the person gains knowledge and skills necessary for better functioning in one's environment. The skills may range from being able to honestly accept some specific aspect of one's life to learning to listen and communicate more effectively with others. Through being able to identify and deal with issues interfering with one's life, the individual can gain confidence and skills that may generalize to events one may encounter in the future.

The counselor's role in the counseling process is to establish an environment in which the student will be at ease in discussing concerns being faced. In such a situation the student can trust the counselor and see this adult as one who cares and is interested in offering assistance to the student. The counselor can listen to the student and help the student by pointing out discrepancies that may exist in the student's life, eventually assisting the student in facing the issues openly and honestly. In addition, the counselor can help the student learn new ways of facing life along with examining options and their consequences.

In a group counseling situation, the counseling and group members participate in trying to offer assistance to others in a group setting. Counseling groups usually consist of four to eight people in an elementary and middle school setting and from eight to twelve people in a high school setting. The primary focus in group counseling is usually on helping people cope with current life issues and develop ways to better face issues in the future. In some counseling groups students learn specific skills, such as ways to listen to others and ways to clearly state one's viewpoint without being fearful of ridicule or resentment, and the students can learn strategies for confronting issues about themselves and others. An advantage to group counseling is that one is not alone in the group, and members work at helping each other; this has a multiplier effect as compared to individual counseling, involving a single student and counselor. In individual and group counseling the confidentiality of what has been discussed must be maintained. Otherwise the trust and confidence a student may have will be damaged.

The school counselor is also educated in the use of various appraisal instruments. Through one's preparation, the counselor has a knowledge about test construction, test usage, and test interpretation. The counselor is able to select the assessment instruments appropriate to the students with whom one works. After the selection and administration of the tests are completed, it is the counselor's responsibility to interpret the results to the student and others interested in the welfare of the student. The interpretation process can be conducted on an individual basis or in a small group situation.

The counselor helps students, teachers, and parents fully understand the rationale for the school's testing program. The teachers can be helped or the counselor can demonstrate and teach them to use observational techniques with their students. In addition they can assist teachers in developing classroom tests appropriate to the students' and the teachers' subject areas.

In many states, the school's testing program combines tests required by the department of education of the state as well as those tests a specific school deems as necessary for their students. The counselor is the principle person educated in test usage and consequently has responsibility for conducting the program within the school.

Related to the appraisal function is the evaluation function of the school counselor. By developing evaluation strategies the counselor can collect data and information that can assist the school and community in understanding how well the school's guidance and counseling program is functioning. Such evaluation can promote good public relations for the guidance and counseling efforts in the school.

Counselors are responsible for maintaining information services. These services focus on the educational and occupational needs of the students at all levels of education. The educational information can consist of local school programs and policies as well as information about the educational offerings of other schools one may eventually attend. The occupational aspect of the information service provides current resources and data regarding various occupations. This information can help students as they explore and develop tentative choices about the careers they wish to pursue. When working with students as they explore educational and occupational areas, the counselor must emphasize the idea of tentative choice, for one does not want to encourage a student to make a choice too early and consequently to eliminate other suitable options. The information service is one that requires constant reviewing and revising, for it is critical that students be provided with the most current information available.

The placement responsibilities of the counselor rely on some of the information services previously discussed. Through placement the counselor assists students in making choices about the options available to them. Such choices focus on academic offerings within the school, academic offerings outside of school, as well as academic programs one may want to consider upon completion of high school. The placement function also relates to occupations for students. Counselors can develop, along with the help of teachers, local agencies, and employers, a job placement program. Some jobs may be within the school, giving students an understanding about jobs and their responsibilities. Other placements may be in part-time jobs after school or in positions during vacations or at the completion of one's education program. The counselor, through this service, is able to stay in contact with many other people who can be of assistance to students. Again, current information is critical for placement services to be realistic and functional.

Follow-up activities are also stressed as being part of the counselor's function. By developing and conducting systematic follow-ups of one's students, the counselor can gain information as to the kinds of education and occupations graduates have entered. Such information can be valuable in planning and refining further efforts in the guidance and counseling program. It also may help in developing a resource file of people who would meet with students and discuss educational and occupational opportunities.

Counselors prepared to function in elementary and middle or junior high schools spend a great deal of time consulting with people who interact directly with students. Their consulting activities include teachers, administrators, and parents. Through planned consultation, strategies are developed to promote better functioning for those people working with students. The consultant function, as noted earlier, encompasses many activities and helps the counselor reach many individuals.

Coordination of the multiple services within a school's guidance and counseling program is also the responsibility of the counselor. In formal classroom preparation and through practicum and internship experiences the counselor learns how to organize, administer, and coordinate the services previously noted. It is a professional responsibility that the counselor undertakes to ensure that students will have a solid, well-organized program in their schools.

With all of the preparation required for one to become a counselor there are numerous professional responsibilities at various educational levels one must assume. The next section examines some of these.

## PROFESSIONAL RESPONSIBILITIES

The guidance counselor in schools is responsible for a multiplicity of services to students. These have a developmental orientation as noted by the American School Counselor Association Governing Board (1979):

> Developmental guidance is that component of all guidance efforts which fosters planned intervention within educational and other human development services programs at all points in the human life cycle to vigorously stimulate and actively facilitate the total development of individuals in all areas — personal, social, emotional, career, moral-ethical, cognitive, aesthetic — and to promote the integration of the several components into an individual lifestyle (p. 270).

As can be seen, guidance efforts are of a diverse nature, and school counselors at all levels try to incorporate these developmental aspects into their professional efforts.

In elementary schools counselors assist students in developing their self-identities and realizing their likes and dislikes as well as focusing on their interests, skills, and concerns. Children are also aided in clarifying their roles in their family, school, neighborhood, and community. Elementary guidance counselors spend much time and effort helping students develop positive self-concepts and through such efforts enable children to discuss their feelings in a straightforward fashion without the fear of not being accepted. Combined with the issue of self-concept and self-acceptance, children in the elementary school, with the help of the counselor, recognize and accept the limitations they have and are assisted in working toward improving upon their limitations. The counselor also helps the students move beyond self-oriented concerns and through various programs helps students accept others and work toward solving conflicts that may arise in relationships. In focusing on solving conflicts students can learn decision-making strategies, which can be applied to many parts of their lives, resulting in the development of positive attitudes toward learning and working with others. As they work with students, elementary school counselors promote consideration of future plans and roles the students may someday assume. Realistic knowledge and an understanding of how people, their work, and services are interrelated are provided by the elementary school counselor to the students.

The elementary school counselor also has much direct contact with the adults who interact with children in the school setting as well as parents and other adults in the community. As one relates with these adults, the elementary counselor must, according to the American School Counselor Association Governing Board (1978), assist these adults:

> To understand and accept the child's self-concept and work toward determining with them positive changes; then to provide guidance and support as each child endeavors to make those changes.
> To relate to the child as a worthwhile human being so that the child can use acceptable and appropriate relationship behavior.
> To provide teaching, experiences, and opportunities for learning decision-making skills and grant the child the dignity to live with and learn from mistakes without criticism and ridicule, or without "taking over" the decision-making.
> To seek help for themselves when necessary in order to provide the most effective learning environment for the child (p. 201-202).

Such interfacing with other significant adults can do much to promote a positive environment for the development of all children.

In the middle schools and junior high schools, the counselor has some different responsibilities than at the elementary school level (American School Counselor Governing Board, 1978*b*). Children in their preadolescent years are sometimes referred to as transcents, meaning they are between childhood and their young adult years. Consequently, these children have physical, social, and emotional needs that are quite varied. You will recall some of these as presented in Chapter 2.

The specific counseling responsibilities for the middle school counselor focus on assisting the students in developing self-understanding and self-identity. Counseling and related guidance activities are conducted on an individual basis or in group settings. The middle school counselor also assists students through orientation programs to the school they are entering along with helping them in being placed in appropriate educational programs in the school. In addition the counselors offer programs emphasizing career development, including promoting the self-direction and decision-making skills of the students.

Consultation activities with school personnel and parents are conducted by the middle school counselor. In these sessions, test scores, student behavior, curricular plans, and referral sources both within the school and through outside agencies are discussed. Instructional seminars are often given by middle school counselors having an emphasis on topics such as human growth and development, learning styles, parenting skills, and interpersonal skills for teachers and parents.

The middle school counselor is also a public relations person. In this sense, the counselor is in contact with community personnel to present and clarify the counseling program. An emphasis on preventing possible problems for youths is the focus of many of the public relations activities of the counselor. Some typical approaches include newspaper stories or columns, radio and television coverage, and the circulation of handbooks describing the middle school's guidance and counseling programs. These actitivies are important for keeping the public informed regarding one's efforts.

The counselor employed in the secondary school works with students, staff, parents, and community personnel (American School Counselor Governing Board, 1974). As one works with students, one shows respect for the person as an individual having specific rights and responsibilities. Through counseling activities students are helped in the areas of their educational, career, and personal development. By assisting the student in honest self-evaluation leading to self-understanding and the ability to make appropriate decisions, the counselor can enhance the development of positive habits and attitudes in the students. The counselor works with high school students at helping them plan for their career development as well as helping the students explore leisure time activities that lead to personal satisfaction.

As the counselor assists the student in the transition to high school and helps the student examine one's progress as well as one's strengths and weaknesses, there may arise the need for gaining assistance from a local community agency. If such a need does develop, the counselor is responsible for referring the student to the appropriate organization for assistance. Some typical referral sources would include Job Service, the Mental Health Center, Planned Parenthood and other similar agencies.

The secondary school counselor must conduct research. Such efforts can help the counselor examine various factors affecting students, both in and out of school. Data gathered from such efforts can be helpful in developing recommendations for ways to improve various situations for students. Research efforts will also provide feedback to the counselor regarding the nature of the services provided by one's guidance and counseling program as viewed by one's consumers, the students, and the public.

The counselor has access to various kinds of data about each student. Such information can help teachers understand the individuality of each student they teach. Previous educational information and current assessment data can be useful as teachers and counselors strive toward developing curricular offerings appropriate to the abilities and needs of students. The counselor can assist the staff in developing research projects designed to improve the educational programs and services in the school. Through such efforts the school personnel can identify students having special needs and develop strategies for these individuals.

Meeting with parents is another function for the secondary school counselor. Discussions with the parents, student, and the counselor can be very helpful both as the student enters high school and eventually prepares to leave. In such conferences one can discuss the growth and development of the student with the parents. Accurate information about the student's progress, abilities, aptitudes, educational plans, and career goals can also be discussed. During these conferences the counselor may need to clarify the purpose of the school's guidance effort and to provide information regarding school policies and procedures as well as information about various curricular offerings and other opportunities the student may have.

As can be seen in this section, the counselors employed in various levels of education do have similar and yet unique responsibilities to the people they serve. While serving the public, counselors are influenced by numerous societal and educational factors. Some of the current issues and trends are examined next.

## ISSUES AND TRENDS

In several recent publications, some of the current issues and trends facing school counselors have been discussed (Goldman, Carroll, Forsyth, Muro, & Graff, 1978; Shertzer & Stone, 1976; Pietrofesa, Bernstein, Minor & Stanford, 1980). Goldman et al. (1978) questioned the state of school counseling and noted that school counselors are now better prepared than in the past and that many of them seem to have more time to conduct counseling with students. It was cited that counselors need to communicate better with their various publics to help people become better informed as to the role and function of the professional school counselor.

The question of identity was discussed by Goldman et al. (1978). The highly flexible nature of counselors was viewed as having both positive and negative consequences for counselors. On the positive side the flexibility has allowed counselors to respond quickly to changing needs; some would say counselors are almost overresponsive. From the negative viewpoint the flexibility may actually inhibit counselors from developing a solid identity as they are so involved in responding to various situations that they are unable to solidly clarify their professional identity. Pietrofesa et al. (1980) mentioned the efforts counselors have made in responding to societal needs dealing with various issues facing people. For example Congress in 1975 passed PL 94-142, the Education for All Handicapped Children Act, which became effective on October 1, 1977. A free, appropriate public education for all handicapped children between the ages of three and twenty-one is required by this permanent legislation. Although the act does not stipulate how counselors are to work with handicapped children, counselors are involved in many ways as schools strive to meet the educational needs of handicapped children.

According to Pietrofesa et al. (1980) school counselors have also assumed some responsibilities for assisting students with substance abuse problems. Although the school counselors may not be fully trained to counsel these students regarding substance abuse, they are responsible for arranging appropriate referrals to local agencies as well as assisting the students in dealing with school-related issues. From these two examples one can see how counselors, in their efforts to serve various populations, may have difficulty in fully clarifying their identity.

Another issue discussed by Goldman et al. (1978) focused around the base of power for school counselors. Although many groups have voiced opinions regarding the counselors' functions, it is believed that counselors need to have a power base within schools that will help them clearly define their purposes and the nature of the programs they are to provide. Counselors cannot expect others to define their roles for them, but need to be proactive in stipulating what others can expect from them and their programs.

Goldman et al. (1978) also emphasized the need for counselors to function from a developmental perspective. Since the purpose of schooling is to help children develop, it is only logical that counselors can play a major role in the development process. They can assist students in numerous areas ranging from classroom interactions through career development. Counselors, as noted earlier, can work with numerous people who interface with students in the school and assist these people in developing positive ways of working with the students.

Included in this developmental perspective, counselors are using peer counseling efforts (Pietrofesa et al., 1980) to assist students. Peers present less threat to each other than do adults and can be very helpful in assisting each other in dealing with issues facing them. Peers can be models for others and, through assuming responsible duties, they gain confidence in themselves.

A final set of issues facing counselors revolves around their preparation, professional updating, and licensure. Every state requires counselors to meet specific certification requirements (Pietrofesa & Vriend, 1971). These requirements are minimal ones that allow a person to function as a counselor in a public school setting. Due to proliferation of counselor training programs throughout the United States, the quality of preparation for counselors has varied. Recent efforts by the American Personnel and Guidance Association and Association for Counselor Education and Supervision (Stripling, 1978) for accrediting counselor education programs will help in improving the quality of preparation for counselors.

In many states counselors are not required to participate in continuing education efforts. They are often required to renew their certification, yet this is often accomplished by taking additional course work that may or may not be directly related to counseling. In an effort to promote counselor renewal, the American Personnel and Guidance Association conducts yearly workshops throughout the United States focusing on special topics of interest to counselors. In addition, at the yearly convention of the American Personnel and Guidance Association, preconvention workshops are conducted for counselors. Many state guidance association groups are engaging in similar efforts using workshops for promoting counselor renewal.

The licensing of counselors has become a critical issue for the profession. Bluhm and Hardy (1980) documented the licensure movement from 1974 to mid-1980. The American Personnel and Guidance Association and two of its divisions, the Association for Counselor Education and Supervision and the American School Counselor Association, have been very active in promoting counselor licensure in some states. The principle reasons for promoting the licensure of counselors revolve around developing a legal standing for the profession, protecting the rights of people to be served by counselor, and defining the rights and functions of counselors. There have been a number of discussions about licensure, and thus far the states of Virginia, Arkansas, and Alabama have licensing laws for counselors. A total of thirty-two states have active counselor licensure committees, and their efforts toward licensure will be evolving. Although at the present time licensure of counselors in public school settings is not a pressing issue, it may be someday.

These are just a few current issues facing counselors. Other issues will arise in the future and hopefully the professionals will be ready to address them. The professional organizations that offer much support and direction to the counseling profession are presented in the concluding section of this chapter.

## PROFESSIONAL ASSOCIATIONS

School counselors affiliate with the American Personnel and Guidance Association, which has a total of thirteen national divisions focusing on various interest areas to counselors. The various divisions include the American College Personnel Association, Association for Counselor Education and Supervision, National Vocational Guidance Association, Association for Humanistic Education and Development, American School Counselor Association, American Rehabilitation Counseling Association, Association for Measurement and Evaluation in Guidance, National Employment Counselors Association, Association for Non-White Concerns in Personnel and Guidance, Association for Religious Value Issues in Counseling, Association for Specialists in Group Work, Public Offender Counselor Association, and American Mental Health Counselors Association. Each of these can be contacted at the main address of the American Personnel and Guidance Association:

Two Skyline Place, Suite 400
5203 Leesburg Pike
Falls Church, Virginia 22041

As mentioned earlier, these professional groups are very active in promoting counseling and striving to meet the needs of counselors. Through their publications and meetings at the state, regional, and national levels, they have served the profession well and in turn have served society in a professional, concerned fashion.

## REFERENCES

American School Counselor Association Governing Board: The role of the secondary School counselor. *The School Counselor, 21:*380-386, 1974

American School Counselor Association Governing Board: The unique role of the elementary school counselor. *Elementary School Guidance and Counseling, 12:*200-202*a*, 1978.

American School Counselor Association Governing Board: The unique role of the middle/junior high school counselor. *Elementary School Guidance and Counseling, 12:*203-205*b*, 1978.

American School Counselor Association Governing Board: ASCA position statements. *The School Counselor, 26:*270-275, 1979.

Association for Counselor Education and Supervision: *Standards for Preparation in Counselor Education.* Falls Church, Virginia, American Personnel and Guidance Association, 1979.

Aubrey, R.F.: Historical development of guidance and counseling and implications for the future, *The Personnel and Guidance Journal, 55:*288-295, 1977

Bluhm, H.P., and Hardy, N.: Licensure for counselors: An examination of the issues and a status report. *Counseling and Human Development, 12*(9):1-11, 1980.

Brewer, J.M.: *History of vocational guidance.* New York, Harper and Brothers, 1942.

Geister, J.: Counselor educators position statement on entry level counselor skills.

*Michigan Personnel and Guidance Association Journal, 6:* 20-23, 1974.

Goldman, L., Carroll, M.R., Forsyth, L.B., Muro, J., & Graff, F.A.: How are we doing in school guidance? The Moody Colloquium. *The School Counselor, 25:*307-325, 1978.

Hoyt, K.D.: *An introduction to career education.* Policy paper, Washington, D.C., United States Office of Education, 1974.

Miller, F.W.: *Guidance principles and services.* Columbus, Ohio, Charles E. Merrill, Inc., 1961.

Moser, L. E., & Moser, R. S.: *Counseling and guidance: An exploration.* New Jersey, Prentice-Hall, Inc., 1963.

Pietrofesa, J. J., Bernstein, B., Minor, J., and Stanford, S.: *Guidance: An introduction.* Chicago, Rand McNally College Publishing Company, 1980.

Pietrofesa, J. J., and Vriend, J.: *The school counselor as a professional.* Itasca, Illinois, F. E. Peacock Publishers, Inc., 1971.

Shertzer, B., and Stone, S.C.: *Fundamentals of guidance,* 3rd ed. Boston, Houghton Mifflin Company, 1976.

Stripling, R. O: Standards and accreditation in counselor education: A proposal. *The Personnel and Guidance Journal, 56:*608-611, 1978.

Chapter 8

# THE SCHOOL PSYCHOLOGIST

Susan G. Forman and Ann W. Engin

*S USAN G. FORMAN is an associate professor in the school psychology training program, department of psychology, University of South Carolina. Her professional experience also includes positions as Psychoeducational center director, Richland School District I, Columbia, South Carolina: Coordinator of Pupil Personnel Services, Chapel Hill/Carrboro City Schools, Chapel Hill, North Carolina; and school psychologist, D. C. Public Schools, Washington, D. C. Her doctorate was completed at the University of North Carolina at Chapel Hill and her master's and bachelor's degrees were completed at the University of Rhode Island. She is currently Southeastern Regional Director of the National Association of School Psychologists and is a member of the executive board of the South Carolina Association of School Psychologists. She has written numerous publications and papers and has conducted workshops related to behavioral and cognitive-behavioral interventions in schools. Some of her recent publications include the following:*

> *Stress management training: Evaluation of effects on school psychological services. Journal of School Psychology, 1981, 19, 233-241.*
> *Self-statements of aggressive and non-aggressive children. Child Behavior Therapy, 1980, 2, 49-57.*
> *A comparison of cognitive training and response cost procedures in modifying aggressive behavior in elementary school children. Behavior Therapy, 11:594-600, 1980.*

*Ann W. Engin is professor and director in the school psychology training program at the University of South Carolina. Previously she was coordinator of the school psychology program at The Ohio State University, a practicing school psychologist for three years, and a secondary English teacher. She earned a doctorate at the University of Michigan in the combined program of education and psychology, a master of education degree from the University of Toledo, and a bachelor's degree from Western Reserve University.*

*She has been active in professional organizations; past leadership positions include secretary and president of the National Association of School Psychologists (NASP), president of the Ohio Inter-University Council of School Psychology Trainers, and a member of the Division 16 executive board. She was a recipient of two NASP leadership awards. An invited participant in the Spring Hill symposium on the "Future of Psychology in the Schools," Engin was a member of the NASP/APA Steering Committee for the follow-up Conference on the "Future of School Psychology" to be held in 1981.*

*Engin has published widely in professional journals and is on the editorial board of all three school psychology journals: Journal of School Psychology, Psychology in the Schools, and School Psychology Review. Her research interests include the assessment of reading attitudes, simulation in the training of school psychologists, and multifactored assessment theory and practice. With Jane Miller she developed PSYCHISM: a multi-media simulation package for school psychologists. Several recent publications include the following:*

> *Wallbrown, F. H., Levine, M. A., and Engin, A. W.: Sex differences in reading attitude. Reading Improvement, 1981, 18, 226-234.*

> *Wallbrown, F. J., and Engin, A. W.: Reading attitude research: Current status and future directions. In B.A. Hutson (Ed.): Advances in Reading/Language Research, Vol. 111, JAI Press, 1981, 18, 226-234.*

---

## HISTORICAL OVERVIEW

The history of school psychology as a profession is generally conceded to be rooted in both psychology and education. At about the turn of the nineteenth century American educational philosophy was becoming increasingly democratic, emphasizing universal education for youth and recognition of individual differences. Parallel to these developments was the institution of special education classes and the development of assessment technology to quantify the observed individual differences in a more reliable and valid way. Thus, school psychologists initially entered the schools to identify those children who needed special education services (at first mentally retarded pupils) and could best be described as clinical psychologists who were plying their trade in the schools. Arnold L. Gesell is generally credited as being the first official school psychologist in the United States. Hired by the State of Connecticut in 1915, Gesell examined and recommended placement for mentally retarded children. The first acknowledged use of the title school psychologist appeared in the literature eight years later (Hutt, 1923). The early history of school psychology strongly reflects a psychoanalytic philosophy coupled with psychometry and little of the current flavor of social psychology and organizational development coupled with behavioral technology.

Several national conferences have played an important role in the development of school psychology as a profession. The Thayer Conference (held at Hotel Thayer in West Point, New York, in 1954) was the first and undoubtedly the most influential. The report of the conference (Cutts, 1955) is still widely read today and played a seminal role in the evolution of school psychology from a hybrid of clinical psychology to its own unique role. The Thayer Conference resulted in many new training programs, new conceptions and practices, and a recognition of the specialty's place in the psychology and education arena. George Peabody College for Teachers sponsored a conference on school psychology internships in 1963 with support from the National Institute for Mental Health (NIMH). The Bethesda Conference in 1964 discussed many possible role models for school psychology.

A recent conference was held at the Spring Hill Conference Center in Wayzata, Minnesota, in June of 1980. Seventy leaders in school psychology were invited to attend the symposium entitled "The Future of Psychology in the Schools" and to participate in the reconceptualization of the field of school psychology. Sponsored by the School Psychology In-service Training Network housed at the University of Minnesota, the National Association of School Psychologists, and Division 16 of the American Psychological Association, the conference attempted to identify the implications of change for the profession and to begin the difficult but necessary task of developing a blueprint for practice and training in school psychology. The report of the symposium attests to the complexities of charting the blueprint and may be found in *School Psychology Review, 10(2)*, 1981. A follow-up conference sponsored by NASP and Division 16 of APA was held in November 1981 and it generated a specific action agenda for school psychology for the near and distant future.

## PROFESSIONAL PREPARATION

### Training Program Standards

The National Association of School Psychologists (NASP) and the American Psychological Association (APA) have both developed standards for training programs in school psychology. NASP standards have been adopted by the National Council for Accreditation of Teacher Education (NCATE) for approval of sixth year and doctoral level training programs. APA currently approves programs at the doctoral level only. A joint APA-NASP task force is currently collaborating on a joint accreditation process and procedure. Sanctioned by both organizations, this endeavor may change the dual, separate approach to program accreditation that currently exists.

### NASP Standards

NASP contends that acceptable professional training for school psychologists can be provided at the sixth-year level (NASP, 1978a). The requirements for sixth-year programs include a minimum of three years of full time academic study beyond the bachelor's degree, including at least sixty graduate semester hours and a one-year (1,000 hours) supervised internship. Requirements for doctoral programs include a minimum of four years of graduate study including at least 90 graduate semester hours and a one-year (1,000 hours) supervised internship.

A number of basic content areas are specified for inclusion in the training program. Courses in the area of psychological foundations must include focus on human learning, child and adolescent development (both normal and abnormal), and human exceptionality and cultural diversity. Training in the area of educational foundations should include courses in organization and operation of the schools, instructional and remedial techniques, and special education. Psycho-educational evaluation is addressed in courses dealing with psycho-educational assessment, research design, and statistics. The area of intervention is included through training in consultation, behavior modification, counseling, and organization and administration of pupil services. In addition professional issues and standards and ethics in school psychology must be addressed.

Field placements are an integral part of school psychology training programs. Field placements provide opportunities to refine skills and to clarify knowledge gained in the university training program. As defined by NASP, field experiences commonly include practicum and internship or externship (NASP, 1978*b*). Practicum experiences may be offered through on-campus agencies, for example a psychology clinic, or community agencies, such as public schools and mental health centers. Course instruction is usually provided concurrently with the practicum. The experience is usually limited to one academic semester and focus is on a particular aspect of the school psychologist's role. The internship experience is generally offered in the public schools or by an agency that serves school-age children. It is usually full-time and is one year in length in order to approximate the role and function of certified school psychologists. The externship is an alternate form of the internship that is completed on a part-time basis, usually over two years. The internship provides experiences relevant to each of the following areas:

a. Knowledge of public school organization and operation
b. Familiarization with the role and function of the school psychologist
c. Effective utilization of community resources
d. Development of communication and consultative skills and the ability to work as part of a team
e. Development of skills in diagnosis and behavioral analysis
f. Development of skills in remediation and intervention
g. Development of skills in research and evaluation
h. Development of awareness of ethical considerations and legal aspects in school psychology
i. Development of professional growth through continued inservice training, observation, and study

## APA Standards

APA standards for doctoral training programs in school psychology also address course content and field experiences (APA, 1979). Areas of instruction specified include: scientific and professional ethics and standards, research design and methodology, statistics, psychological measurement, and history and systems of psychology. In addition, students must demonstrate competence in four substantive content areas: (1) Biological bases of behavior, for example physiological psychology, comparative psychology, neuropsychology, sensation, psychopharmacology. (2) Cognitive-affective bases of behavior, for example learning, memory, perception, cognition, thinking, motivation, emotion. (3) Social bases of behavior, for example social psychology, cultural, ethnic, and group processes; sex roles; organizational and systems theory. (4) Individual behavior, for example personality theory, human development, individual differences, abnormal psychology. Training in the social and philosophical bases of education, curriculum theory and practice, etiology of learning and behavior disorders, exceptional children and special education, and organization theory and administrative practice is also included.

In addition, APA specifies that field training should be offered through practicum and internship experiences. The practicum should provide for student experiences with client problems and learning of relevant psychological skills. The internship is required as a means of training the advanced student to meet the range of problems the professional school psychologist may confront and involves 1,200 hours in schools or a combination of schools and community agencies.

## State Certification Requirements

Providers of school psychological services are credentialed for practice in the public schools by state departments of education in all fifty states and the District of Columbia (Brown, Horn, & Lindstrom, 1980). A number of terms are used to identify those providing services, including psychometrist, educational evaluator, psychological evaluator, psychological technician, educational diagnostician, associate school psychologist, and school psychologist. A majority of states certify school psychologists at a number of levels depending on training and/or experience.

Many states have course area-based certification requirements, which indicate specified areas in which the applicant must be trained. The four areas most commonly identified are psychological foundations, educational foundations, consultation and intervention, and tests and measurements. Most states specify a master's degree or sixth-year program along with supervised field experience as the minimum entry level requirement.

## PROFESSIONAL RESPONSIBILITIES

School psychologists have a variety of responsibilities and engage in a wide range of activities. Their objective is to facilitate the emotional, social, and academic development of students. Their role involves assessing needs, planning and carrying out intervention programs, and evaluating the effectiveness of these programs. These activities are done with individual students, with groups, and at the organizational level.

### Working With Individuals

Individual students are usually referred to the school psychologist by their teachers because of learning and/or adjustment problems. However, other professionals working in the school, the parents, or the student him/herself can initiate the referral. Informed consent is always obtained from the parents. They must be informed of the reasons for the referral and provided with information concerning the types of assessment procedures to be used and the kinds of decisions anticipated as a result of the assessment.

#### *Assessment*

Assessment is the process of collecting data to be used to make decisions about the educational programs of students (Salvia & Ysseldyke, 1978). After a student is referred for services, assessment begins. When assessing needs of individual students, school psychologists consider a number of areas of functioning, sometimes called multifactored assessment. Academic achievement, emotional-social adjustment, adaptive behavior, sensory-motor development, language development, intellectual functioning, and environmental/cultural influences are areas that are considered.

In assessing achievement, the school psychologist attempts to measure the student's past learning in academic skill areas (reading, arithmetic, spelling, etc.). Social/emotional assessment involves determining the nature of and degree of personal adjustment or behavioral problems. Measures of adaptive behavior focus on social competence outside of school in relation to age and cultural expectations. Sensory-motor tests attempt to determine whether deficits exist in basic processes such as visual, motor, or auditory functioning. Language assessment involves determining the child's level of skill in understanding the spoken word and in verbal expression. Intelligence measures provide information about the student's cognitive development. Intelligence tests have been used to predict success in school and would be more aptly named if they were called academic aptitude tests rather than intelligence tests. They do *not* predict occupational success or success in nonacademic skills, and they do *not* provide a measure of innate capacity or potential.

When assessing these areas, school psychologists use a variety of procedures, considering information from a number of sources. They review student records, interview parents, the student, and school staff regarding the referral problem, observe the student in a number of settings, and administer individual tests. Frequently, school psychologists assess student needs as part of a multidisciplinary team. These teams include a number of different professionals in evaluating student functioning, including regular classroom teachers, special education teachers, guidance counselors, speech and language specialists, school social workers, and school nurses. Results of the individual student assessment are communicated to involved school staff, parents, and when appropriate, to the student.

### Intervention

Information from the individual student assessment is used to develop intervention plans aimed at improving the student's school functioning. Intervention may involve changes in the student's regular classroom curriculum, provision of additional remedial services, or placement in a part-time or full-time program for handicapped students. The school psychologist helps with the development of an Individualized Education Plan (IEP) for each student placed in a program for the handicapped. This includes specification of long-and short-term goals and the methods that will be used to meet these goals.

School psychologists use a variety of techniques in formulating intervention plans aimed at improving academic, social, and/or affective skills. They can recommend and implement academic remedial activities based on specialized teaching techniques or curriculum materials. Many intervention plans are based on behavior modification techniques (Blackham & Silberman, 1975; O'Leary & O'Leary, 1977). Behavior modification is the application of learning theory and experimental psychology to the problem of altering maladaptive behavior. Four major types of behavior modification procedures are used by school psychologists. Operant conditioning involves modifying behavior by altering the consequences of behavior. Social modeling involves providing real or symbolic models who demonstrate a behavior that a student is attempting to acquire. Counterconditioning procedures are used to alleviate anxiety problems by helping the student substitute more adaptive responses, such as relaxation, in problem situations. Cognitive behavior modification focuses on helping students change thoughts as a means of developing more appropriate and constructive behavior.

In addition to behavior modification, school psychologists use other approaches to facilitate social and emotional adjustment. Reality therapy approaches focus on helping the student learn to satisfy his needs while behaving responsibly. Individual/developmental approaches attempt to modify the way students deal with social relationships and responsibilities with an emphasis on examining the purposes of behavior and alternatives in a given situation. Play therapy techniques are used with young children (under ten). Play provides the young child, who has not mastered language, with a way of expressing internal thoughts and feelings.

*Indirect Services.* The school psychologist may provide indirect or direct services to the student as part of the intervention plan. Indirect services focus on helping individuals who have major responsibility for the education and development of the student to interact with him or her constructively. Indirect services may also involve helping other professionals formulate a treatment program for the student. Thus, the school psychologist functions as a consultant to others who deal with the student (Bergan, 1977). Indirect services include consultation with the child's teachers regarding classroom management practices and specialized curricula or teaching techniques that will help meet the student's needs. Parent consultation is also provided concerning ways of improving academic, social, and emotional development (Abidin, 1976). The school psychologist may also serve as a liaison with other community agencies that may be able to provide services for the student, such as local mental health centers or social service agencies.

*Direct Services.* Direct services consist of intervention programs that are carried out by the school psychologist. Direct services may be provided in the form of individual counseling or remedial activities. Individual counseling may be aimed at improving interpersonal and communications skills, improving emotional adjustment, or providing support during crisis situations. Other remedial activities may be aimed at improving academic skills.

### Evaluation

Follow-up services are provided for all referred students. This involves obtaining information concerning whether or not intervention programs have been successful and may include parent, teacher, and student interviews, classroom observations, and/or additional testing. This information is used to determine whether intervention programs should be continued or modified.

## Working With Groups

When working with groups of students, classroom observational data, test results, and input from school staff and parents are used to determine needs and develop intervention programs. The school psychologist may be involved with preventive and/or remedial activities.

### Prevention

Preventive activities focus on strengthening the emotional and social development and building psychological health in all students (Clarizio, 1979). Indirect preventive intervention may include parent education programs that focus on basic behavior management techniques, communication skills, and methods of facilitating school success. Direct preventive intervention may include affective education sessions with whole classrooms aimed at helping students develop personal coping and social skills.

## Remediation

When intervening indirectly with groups of students who have identified problems, the school psychologist may consult with the classroom teacher regarding behavior management programs aimed at improving academic achievement and behavior of an entire class or small group of children with similar needs. Consultation may also be provided for small groups of teachers who have students with similar kinds of academic or behavioral problems or for small groups of parents with children who have similar problems. Direct intervention may take the form of group counseling sessions aimed at improving emotional and social adjustment. Evaluation of these group intervention programs is an integral part of the school psychologist's responsibilities and may be accomplished through analysis of information obtained from questionnaires, interviews, observations, and/or tests.

## Organizational School Psychology

Some school psychologists also work at the organizational level (Gutkin & Tieger, 1979). This involves assessing the mental health and special education needs of an entire school or school system. This may be done through surveys, through group needs assessment sessions at the school or district-wide level, by examining school or district-wide group test results, and/or examining trends in individual student referral problems. Once a school or district-wide need has been established, school psychologists can help other school personnel meet that need in a number of ways. They can assist in planning new programs that can be carried out by reallocating currently existing resources. For example a school psychologist might assist in developing a screening program in order to improve the effectiveness and efficiency of identification of students for programs for the handicapped. They can provide in-service training for other school staff in areas related to the amelioration of learning or behavioral problems and facilitation of social/emotional development. A school psychologist might provide in-service training to school staff in behavior modification techniques, communications skills, or self-management procedures in order to improve teachers' interactions with students. They can also assist in obtaining state and federal grants that provide funds for development of new programs. For example a school psychologist might assist other administrators in obtaining funds to implement an intervention program aimed at decreasing disruptive or aggressive behavior. School psychologists then assist in evaluating these programs in order to help school administrators make decisions about feasibility and effectiveness.

## PROFESSIONAL ORGANIZATIONS

There are two major national professional organizations for school psychologists, the American Psychological Association (APA) and the National Association of School Psychologists (NASP). Both national professional organizations are of importance to school psychologists, but each has a different overall mission.

The APA was founded in 1892 and represents all of psychology with a membership of approximately 40,000. Full members must possess a doctoral degree. Associate membership is available to psychologists without the doctoral degree. APA publishes the *American Psychologist* monthly with articles on current issues in psychology and theoretical and practical treatises in the broad aspects of psychology. Within APA there are forty divisions representing various subareas, such as experimental psychology, clinical psychology, counseling psychology, etc., and special interests, such as psychotherapy, population psychology, and psychology of women. Division 16, the school psychology division, has approximately 2,000 members.

The National Association of School Psychologists was formed in 1969 exclusively as a professional organization for school psychologists. In contrast to APA, which derives its identity and strength from its large numbers of psychologists and diversity of their interests and commitments, NASP devotes itself exclusively to the interests, standards, and overall conditions of practice of school psychology. It was established to provide a national communication and problem-solving forum for practitioners and is characterized by its ability and willingness to respond rapidly to identified concerns of problems from the field. NASP currently has approximately 7,500 members, the majority of whom possess master's degrees.

APA and NASP are best viewed as complementary organizations. Membership in APA keeps one abreast of developments in generic, scientific, and academic psychology, whereas NASP affiliation enables one to be at the forefront of applied practitioner interests.

The addresses of the two national organizations follow:

American Psychological Association
1200 Seventeenth Street, N.W.
Washington, D. C. 20036

National Association of School Psychologists
1629 K. Street, Suite 520
Washington, D. C. 20006

It should also be noted that thirty-eight states currently have school psychology organizations at the state level and many regional organizations, both formal and informal, exist.

## PROFESSIONAL JOURNALS

There are three journals devoted exclusively to the theory and practice of school psychology. The *Journal of School Psychology* is the oldest journal in the field, having been established in 1962. *Psychology in the Schools* was subsequently published in 1964, and the *School Psychology Digest,* a publication of the National Association of School Psychologists, first appeared in 1972. The latter publication was recently renamed the *School Psychology Review.*

Following are the current editors and addresses for the three journals:

Thomas Oakland, Editor
*Journal of School Psychology*
College of Education
Department of Educational Psychology
The University of Texas
Austin, Texas 78712

Gerald B. Fuller, Editor
*Psychology in the Schools*
Department of Psychology
Central Michigan University
Mt. Pleasant, Michigan 48859

George W. Hynd, Editor
*School Psychology Review*
Department of Educational Psychology
325 Aderhold Hall
University of Georgia
Athens, Georgia 30602

## ISSUES AND TRENDS

The major issues and trends in the profession of school psychology can be best viewed as emanating from three distinct but complementary pressures and influences: (1) the complex and dynamic changes in the economic, social, moral, and psychological fabric of American society, (2) the tension between the static and the changing role of the educational enterprise within American society, and (3) the normal growing pains of a fledging profession as it simultaneously attempts to define and refine its uniqueness and affinity in training and practice with other professions.

### The Changed American Society

The changes in American society in the twentieth century, particularly since the 1940s, have been dramatic and unparalleled in previous history. Just a few examples will suffice to demonstrate the magnitude of the changes. The nuclear family (typically viewed as a working father and stay-at-home mother with two normal children) is no longer the dominant pattern in society. Only one out of every seventeen families is as depicted above (Edelman, 1981). More mothers work than do not work and the trend is predicted to continue (U. S. Department of Commerce, 1980). Women with preschoolers living with husbands had an employment rate of over 43 percent in 1979, and single mothers with preschoolers in the same year had a rate of nearly 60 percent (Hoffman, 1980). Growing divorce and separation rates result in one out of every five children under eighteen living in a single-parent family (Bronfenbrenner, 1980). The American divorce rate doubled between 1965 and 1978 and is reported as the highest in the world (Hetherington, 1979). Stable neighborhoods are decreasing as approximately 18 percent of all families change homes every year (Bureau of Census, 1977).

Family interaction has been further diminished by an omnipresent technological marvel: television. Consider that the average preschooler views 27.5 hours of television a week, and the average high school graduate has spent 18,000 hours watching television in comparison to 13,000 hours in school (Van Dyck, Robbins, Gordon, & Hannibal, 1979). In addition, moral standards have changed over the last several decades, and juvenile and adult crime rates in rural as well as urban areas have generally been increasing. All in all, both the modes and standards of American life have been altered significantly.

## Changing Expectations of the Schools

The school in society has changed just as dramatically. Although the purpose of the schools is still viewed primarily as the teaching of the three Rs, the schools have been called upon increasingly to assume other responsibilities that previously resided in the home or church. For example school curricula now include sex education, vocational education, moral education, drug education, affective education, driver education, consumer education, ad infinitum. Not all educators and certainly not all parents agree with nor like the expanded roles expected and/or assumed by the schools. Thus, we see alternative schools appearing in districts for parental choice ranging from "back-to-basics" to "free" school settings.

Local schools that in principle have autonomy for educational practices and procedures now receive more and more mandates from federal government and judicial sources. Busing for integration, mandates of due process hearings before suspension or expulsion of pupils, requirements that curriculum offering and sports programs be free of sex bias, and regulations regarding the access to school records by parents and children are but a few examples of the profound influence on the schools by these external forces.

It should also be noted that parents have declining faith in the schools and seriously question their effectiveness as standardized test scores continue to decline. On the other hand teachers are leaving the field in large number, experience burnout to an unprecedented degree, and blame parents for permissively raising children without the structure, discipline, and high expectations that prepare children to meet the academic and social demands of the schools. The evolving nature of the schools subject to legal, legislative, and social changes will continue to affect the practice of all educational personnel.

## Continuing Definition of School Psychology Practice

As a relatively young profession, school psychology has devoted considerable time, effort, and countless pages of polemic in its journals to the responsibilities, skills, and personal characteristics of psychologists who function in the schools to facilitate the optimal educational opportunities and emotional and social development of America's children and youth. The role and function of literature over the years has clearly outlined a generalist in psychology and education who can bring to bear a variety of skills and problem-solving strategies for all children in the school setting. It is perhaps ironic that as this consensus clearly transformed the perceptions of individual school psychologists and school districts that employed them, a major piece of federal legislation, Public Law 94-142 (The Education for all Handicapped Act discussed in detail in Dean McIntosh's chapter), has served to require more time of most school psychologists in the traditional assessment role. Thus, school psychologists are currently torn by desires to assure the free and appropriate education to all handicapped children to meet both the letter and intent of the law and by their responsibilities to all children within the school system. It is clear that school psychologists must work with other educational professionals to develop more effective and efficient procedures to assess the needs of and plan effective interventions for handicapped individuals so that there will be time to devote to the needs of the other nonhandicapped children as well.

Another major professional problem is also related to P. L. 94-142. The law specifies that ". . .testing and evaluation materials and procedures utilized for the purposes of evaluation and placement of handicapped children will be selected and administered so as not to be racially or culturally discriminatory." The theory base and technology to assure such nondiscriminatory assessment is currently lacking. Thus, school psychologists as well as other educational personnel are required by law to perform "best practice" when such has not been adequately defined nor consensually validated. Equally talented, humanitarian school psychologists differ on the ways and means to meet the intent of the law ranging from the elimination of all standardized, norm-referenced assessment to maintaining the status quo in assessment practices and instruments.

Two recent court cases serve to illustrate the dilemma for school psychologists. Judge Peckham, in the highly publicized *P. v. Riles* case in California, ruled that disproportionate placement of minority group children in special education classes was due in large part to invalid IQ tests. He therefore, enjoined the use of IQ tests for assessment and placement of black children in EMR classes in the State of California. Judge John Grady, a federal judge in Illinois, ruled in *PASE v. Joseph P. Hannon* that IQ tests could be used in the assessment and placement of black children in the Chicago public schools. Both cases have been appealed and it is likely that the United States Supreme Court may eventually rule in the matter and thus judicially mandate best practice. Overall the increasingly influential role of the legislative and judicial branches of government into educational and school psychology practice is a noteworthy trend.

Another issue relevant to professions in general is the rapid creation of new knowledge and technology, which necessitates the continuous professional development of individuals. At both the individual and organized group levels school psychologists must use existing, continuing education channels and develop new, innovative ways to keep abreast of the latest developments in psychology and education. Self-renewal must become as automatic as paying the electric bill each month in order to maintain one's status as a professional and to mitigate the effects of burnout, which is beginning to affect the profession in greater frequency and intensity.

Oftentimes overlooked as an issue is the pressing need for those within the educational system to perform the research and development function, which can inform practice and enable us to make our important decisions about children's lives on the basis of data rather than personal preference or speculation. It is shocking to realize that many educational practices continue because of faith validity (strongly felt beliefs that something works) rather than because of actual evidence that the practice is worthwhile, or alternatively, better than an equally appealing practice to someone else. More than ever before citizens and educators must unite to determine not the best curriculum for all children at all ages but what curricula and educational practices are best for which kinds of children at what periods in their cognitive and affective development.

In essence, the issues and trends in school psychology overlap to a large degree with those in society and the schools, as they are all intimately interconnected. What is becoming more and more clear is that school psychologists like every citizen must become more informed about and involved in a meaningful way with the political process so that the society can rationally plan for and bring about needed national and state policies for children (Bevan, 1980; Edelman, 1981). We must be proactive rather than reactive.

One analogy will serve to point out the economic and life quality aspects of this approach. As a country we have been warned by energy and economic experts for at least at decade that the depletion of oil reserves in the major oil producing countries was both imminent and inevitable. Yet to date we still hear otherwise intelligent people claiming that the fossil fuel shortages and escalating prices are fake and due to profiteering of Arabs as well as American businessman, and as yet America has no comprehensive energy policy and research program to help us prepare for the present and the future. Thus, inflation and escalating balance of trade deficits continue to sap our national and individual economy and to create a general despair about the future.

The schools of the United States are neither so good as the apologists would have us believe nor so poor as the critics depict, but the schools are in dire need of concerted action to plan for the conceptual and related economic resources for the future. Let's not continue to bemoan the state of education in the scheme of national and state priorities but rather seize the moment to create the society and the schools within it that more effectively assess and meet the needs of our children and youth. The fact that our children are our most precious commodity has been often said but too little acted upon. May all society's members and educational personnel join together to nurture this most precious national resource in new and creative ways.

## REFERENCES

Abidin, R. R.: *Parenting Skills.* New York, Human Sciences Press, 1976.
American Psychological Association. *Criteria for the Accreditation of Doctoral Train-*

*ing Programs and Internships in Professional Psychology.* Washington, D. C., 1979.

Bergan, J. R.: *Behavioral Consultation.* Columbus, Ohio, Charles E. Merrill, 1977.

Bevan, W.: On coming of age among the professions. *School Psychology Review, 10* (2), in press.

Blackham, G. J., and Silberman, A.: *The Modification of Child and Adolescent Behavior.* Belmont, California, Wadsworth, 1975.

Bronfenbrenner, U.: Ecology of childhood. *School Psychology Review, 9:*294-297, 1980.

Brown, D. T., Horn, A. J., and Lindstrom, J. P.: *The Handbook of Certification/ Licensure Requirements for School Psychologists.* Washington, D. C., National Association of School Psychologists, 1980.

Clarizio, H. F.: School psychologists and the mental health needs of students. In G. D. Phye, and Reschly, D. J. (Eds): *School Psychology Perspectives and Issues.* New York, Academic Press, 1979.

Cutts, N. E. (Ed.): *School Psychologists at Mid-century.* Washington, D. C., APA, 1955.

Edelman, M. W.: Who is for children? *American Psychologist, 36:*109-116, 1981.

Gutkin, L. B., and Tieger, A. G.: Funding patterns for exceptional children: Current approaches and suggested alternatives. *Professional Psychology, 10:*670-680, 1979.

Hetherington, M.: Divorce: A child's perspective. *American Psychologist, 34:*851-858, 1979.

Hoffman, L. W.: The effects of maternal employment on the academic attitudes and performance of school-aged children *School Psychology Review, 9:*319-335, 1980.

Hutt, R.: The school psychologist. *Psychological Clinic, 15:*48-51, 1923.

O'Leary, K. D., and O'Leary, S. G.: *Classroom Management.* New York, Pergamon Press, 1977.

National Association of School Psychologists: *Standards for Training Programs in School Psychology.* Washington, D. C., 1978a.

National Association of School Psychologists: *Standards for Field Placement Programs in School Psychology.* Washington, D. C., 1978b.

Salvia, J., and Ysseldyke, J. E.: *Assessment in Special and Remedial Education.* Boston, Houghton-Mifflin, 1978.

U. S. Department of Commerce, Bureau of the Census: *Population Profile of the United States: 1979, Population Characteristics.* Current Population Reports, Series P-20 No. 350, May 1980.

Van Dyck, N. B., Robbins, M. P., Gordon, A., and Hannibal, M. E.: *Profiles of Children in the United States. NCCT Forum, 2:*15-23, 1979.

# Chapter 9

# THE ROLE OF THE SPECIAL EDUCATOR

DEAN K. MCINTOSH

*D EAN K. MCINTOSH is associate professor and chairman of the Department of Special Education, College of Education, University of South Carolina. He received his bachelor's degree in social science education from Colorado State University. His master's degree was obtained from the University of California at Los Angeles in guidance and counseling and his doctorate was from UCLA in special education. He has been a public school teacher at the junior high level in southern California and a faculty member in the College of Education at the University of Hawaii and West Virginia College of Graduate Studies.*

## INTRODUCTION

Probably no other area of education has had such rapid growth, general overall interest, and federal government involvement within the past ten years as has the field of special education. Administrators of special education programs are consistently recruiting highly trained personnel in almost every area of special education. There is a dire need to fill many vacant positions in schools in urban, suburban, and rural areas in literally every state of the nation. And, there seems to be little lessening of the need for teachers in this field.

Numerous authors have attempted to define the term *exceptional children.* Some include the total range of handicapping conditions through gifted, while others limit the definition to only the physically handicapped. There are those who claim only the gifted should be labelled as exceptional. Kirk and Gallagher (1979) have proposed an all-encompassing definition that meets the generally accepted criteria of most experts in the field today. They define the exceptional child as follows:

. . . the child who deviates from the average or normal child (1) in mental

154

characteristics, (2) in sensory abilities, (3) in neuromotor or physical abilities, (4) in social behavior, (5) in communication abilities, or (6) in multiple handicaps. Such deviations must be of such an extent that the child requires a modification of school practices, or special education services, to develop to maximum capacity (p.3).

Even this definition leaves many gray areas, such as how much deviation is required before a child can or should be labelled as exceptional and what is a normal education. Basically these and other questions must be answered based on each particular individual.

Education for the exceptional student can best be described as specialized instruction including, but not limited to, methods, materials, and management that helps meet the individual and unique needs of any child thus classified. The degree and content of the specialized instruction again depends on the specific individual, his/her label, and severity of the problem.

Most special educators tend to group exceptional children into one or more of the following nine categories:

1. Mental Retardation
2. Behavior Disorders (Emotional Disturbance)
3. Learning Disabilities
4. Hearing Handicapped
5. Visually Handicapped
6. Physically Handicapped
7. Speech and Language Handicapped
8. Severe and Multiply Handicapped
9. Gifted and Talented

It can readily be seen how a child could easily be classified and placed into two or more of the above categories. An example would be a mentally retarded student with both limited vision and hearing who also has some related behavioral disorders.

An additional category some authors have included in this list is that of socially disadvantaged. However, there remains a great amount of controversy as to whether this is indeed a separate and viable category of exceptionality.

## HISTORY

Historically, special education can be traced back to the period 3000 B.C. (Hewitt and Forness, 1974), in which early man accepted, rejected, or often gave preferential treatment to those who were physically and/or behaviorally different from their fellow man. Generally this period was dominated by the survival of the fittest, coupled with a large amount of superstition. As man moved into the eighteenth and nineteenth century, the trend slowly, but surely, was toward both more humane treatment and scientific acceptance of the person who deviated from the norm. By the nineteenth century both physicians and educators were involved in assisting the exceptional individual. For example Dorothea Dix actively worked to make life better for the mentally ill; Louis Braille developed the braille code so that the blind could read; Itard studied and wrote about Victor, the "Wild Boy of Aveyron"; Seguin established a school for the feeble-minded in Paris and later migrated to the United States to set up the first residential school for the retarded; and Montessori adopted Seguin's methods and materials for the mentally retarded and later for the normal child. Others equally active, such as Samuel Howe, showed how the deaf-blind could be taught to read and communicate. Anne Sullivan, a visually handicapped individual, graduated from Perkins in 1886, the same year Helen Keller was born, and later became her teacher and mentor. Alexander Graham Bell invented the telephone that opened up a totally new world to the deaf and hard-of-hearing in the form of hearing aides. Indeed, the nineteenth century was a very active period in terms of interest in, and assistance to, the exceptional individual. In the latter half of that century, the interest resulted in public school classes throughout the United States for retarded, deaf, blind, and orthopedically handicapped persons.

The twentieth century brought an emphasis on intelligence testing and intelligence quotient (IQ) scores. Beginning in France, Binet made an effort to identify the mentally retarded through formal standardized testing. Terman refined this early effort with the result being the Stanford-Binet Intelligence Scale. He instituted a movement toward intelligence evaluation for the classification of many groups of exceptional individuals that remains active to date. In addition, Terman began his lifelong study of the gifted that culminated in a major longitidinal study, which is scheduled to run far into the twenty-first century.

Mental illness was studied and treated by Freud. Pavlov began his study of conditioned reflex, which was to later become the foundation of behavior modification. Strauss intensively studied brain-injured children while Lehtinen became actively involved in their overall education, including restructuring their physical environment for better learning conditions.

By the 1950s federal legislation for the handicapped was instituted in the form of training and research grants administered through the United States Office of Education. From 1957 through 1975 there have been at least thirteen distinct federally legislated laws dealing with the exceptional individual, including specific legislation for retarded and deaf, and additional laws pertaining to professional personnel preparation, research, demonstration, regional resource centers, and funds for state schools.

The major piece of legislation enacted has been Public Law 94-142, *The Education for all Handicapped Children Act,* passed by Congress in 1975, to take effect in 1977. Many have labelled it as the Bill of Rights for the Handicapped (Goodman, 1976), and most feel it is one of the most significant pieces of educational legislation to come from Congress in the twentieth century. In essence it provides a free and appropriate education for all handicapped children ages three through twenty-one.

This act ensures needed special education services will be available for all handicapped of appropriate age levels, but explicitly excludes the gifted. In order to guarantee such services the federal government requires each state to submit a state plan to the commissioner of education, with a number of assurances regarding these services. In turn, each local district must submit a plan to the state for the same general assurances. In essence, each school district and each state within the United States, if they are to receive federal funds to assist the handicapped, must put in writing their commitment to the education of those individuals and in turn must be willing to have the federal government do periodic audits of their plans to be sure that they are in compliance. This is the first time that such stringent regulations have been applied to funds for the handicapped.

Among the more profound of the legal rights guaranteed to the handicapped under Public Law 94-142 is the assurance that all handicapped children will have developed for them, with parent or guardian input and participation, an Individualized Education Plan (IEP). The IEP, in reality, is the mechanism by which the handicapped student is guaranteed a free and appropriate education in a least restrictive environment through a tailor-made program. The IEP must be written by an interdisciplinary team that includes, but is not limited to, (1) a representative from the local educational agency (district) who is qualified to provide special education services or to supervise such persons, other than the student's teacher, (2) the student's teacher; (3) parents and/or guardian, (4) the student, if appropriate, and (5) any other individual who may be present at the request of either parent or agency. In the initial IEP, a member of the original diagnostic team or someone knowledgeable about evaluation is also required to be in attendance. The IEP includes the following:

1. A statement, or statements, of the youth's current level of performance based on an individualized assessment
2. A statement of both annual goals and short-term objectives
3. A statement regarding the specific educational services to be provided
4. A detailed description of the amount of time the youth will be able to participate in the regular programs
5. The projected dates that services are to be initiated and the anticipated duration of all such services
6. Objective criteria that are capable of being evaluated with proper procedures, and also determine, on an annual basis, at least, whether the instructional objectives were achieved (Kameen and McIntosh, 1979).

It can be seen how the above requirements profoundly affect both the training and classroom responsibilities of both regular and special educators and how many additional persons become directly involved in the services to the handicapped. The parents, or guardians, also assume a much more important role in their children's education than ever before because of their direct involvement in planning their child's educational future. Although, as previously mentioned the gifted are explicitly excluded from Public Law 94-142, a number of states have, by their own volition, already developed IEP models for the gifted, even if they are not required to do so by law.

For the first time there is accountability for what is taught to the student, on the part of the school and teacher. Since both long- and short-term goals are listed, along with specific services to be provided, there is a built-in evaluation factor, both in terms of teacher success and in terms of student learning and success of learning. Such accountability, while feared by some teachers and administrators, is generally accepted as a very positive move on the part of most. They also see the parent's direct involvement in the writing of the IEP as an accountability factor placed on the parent that previously has not been present in the school system. With parent, student, and teacher all involved in the total education of the student, only a better and more acceptable education program will result, with all parties feeling both a responsibility and commitment to such a plan. In fact, in a number of states, parents of normal children are beginning to question if such an IEP should not be written for all students, handicapped and nonhandicapped.

## PREPARATION OF SPECIAL EDUCATION PERSONNEL

Professional personnel working in the field of special education vary from teachers's aides with high school degrees through persons who hold doctorates in a variety of specialized administrative functions. They vary in services they provide to exceptional individuals, ranging from severely retarded through gifted; from multiply handicapped (physically and/or mentally) through normal; and with varying levels of sensory and/or emotional impairments. In order to meet all these abilities and disabilities, many different types and levels of trained professional personnel are required and an extremely diverse amount of ancillary assistance will be needed. All of these persons in one form or another need specialized training and/or education.

### Special Education Teachers

By far the majority of the positions available in special education are in classroom teaching. While certification requirements vary from state to state and from specialty to specialty, literally every state in the nation requires the classroom teacher to have a minimum of a bachelor's degree in special education and/or regular education. If a degree is required in regular education (elementary or secondary), then normally additional hours will be needed in a specialty area. The special education teacher will most often be employed in a self-contained or resource room setting. If the present trend continues, the area most in demand will be teachers in resource rooms.

A typical resource teacher normally works with mild to moderately handicapped students classified as educable mentally retarded, emotionally disturbed (behaviorally disordered), or learning disabled. The gifted are also often served through a resource room model. In most instances the students will be scheduled into the room throughout the day, usually in fifty minute blocks, and will be seen for a minimum of two fifty-minute periods per day; however, the amount of time can vary based on the student's academic weaknesses and/or needs. Normally emphasis is placed on remediation of basic school subjects, but with the gifted the underlying emphasis is on enrichment rather than remediation.

As a resource teacher basic skills will be needed in curriculum development and adaptation, classroom management, and diagnostic testing and interpretation. The teacher will also need to implement an Individualized Education Program for each child assigned to the class. Working with regular class teachers, as well as ancillary personnel and parents, will demand a high priority.

The skills of a self-contained teacher will be quite similar to those of a resource room teacher. The major difference is the teacher will be working with one exceptionality and the degree of handicapping conditions usually ranges from moderate to severe. Therefore, there may be less overall contact with the regular class teacher than in a resource setting.

A number of other types of educational arrangements can be provided to meet the unique educational needs of exceptional children. For example itinerant teachers are employed in many rural and sparsely populated areas to work with low incidence populations, such as blind/partially sighted, deaf/hearing impaired, and the gifted. The number of students served and the distances travelled vary from situation to situation. In general the teacher spends a part of each day in one school and then moves to the next. Schools can be visited one or more times each week. For students, who for a variety of reasons cannot attend school at all, most districts offer homebound or hospital instruction. In such cases the teacher literally travels from home to home and hospital to hospital providing instruction for a limited number of hours per day or week.

Some teachers of the handicapped may also be housed in residential hospital or institutional settings. The role assumed here is very similar to the public school. The population served has more severe types of problems than in public schools and close cooperation with professionals, such as physicians, psychologists, and psychiatrists, in a total therapy program will be required.

All the above discussed positions demand so many skills that most colleges and universities are moving to a bachelor's degree plus additional units. Some now require thirty hours beyond the bachelor's degree in order to be a special education teacher. Others require more or less, depending upon state certification requirements and level of training. Many special educators agree that a teacher in a resource room actually needs more skills than a self-contained teacher due to the variety of the handicapped being taught each day, the necessity for meshing together the resource room and the regular curriculum, and the importance of ongoing dialogues with regular teachers, parents, administrators, and ancillary personnel. However, few state departments of education differentiate, to date, between the two when awarding certificates. Many experts within the field also oppose a newly graduated teacher at the bachelor's level being immediately placed in a resource room. They prefer self-contained or regular classroom experience prior to assuming a resource room role.

## TEACHER ROLES OUTSIDE THE CLASSROOM

### Consultants

In addition to classroom assignments there are positions available in school districts as a consultant. Normally these are filled by teachers who have had successful classroom experiences in the exceptionality for which they have been assigned consultant responsibilities.

Consultants normally work out of a central office and provide direct services to the classroom teacher. Curriculum and classroom management are typically top priority items. According to Public Law 94-142, since all handicapped children are required to have individual educational programs written for them, and many school districts utilize this format for gifted students, the consultants then become the so-called resident experts in this area. Testing, evaluation, and parent conferencing are major skills required of any consultant under the terms of this law.

Each state department of education has a branch that is specifically responsible for the overall education of exceptional children. Persons employed in such offices assume a consultant role similar to that at the district level but on a statewide basis. Much of the work responsibility is closely tied to Public Law 94-142. As a result a significant amount of their time is spent in contact with district directors and consultants rather than class room teachers. As with district consultants they normally will have had successful classroom teaching experiences with exceptional children, coupled with school or district-level administrative background.

## Aides

There continues to be a need for aides in many special education classes. Employment opportunities vary directly with the state and district funds allocated for such positions. Generally teachers of the more difficult-to-teach students, especially in self-contained rooms, receive the services of an aide. For example most teachers of emotionally handicapped, visually impaired, hearing handicapped, and trainable, severely, and profoundly retarded have such assistance, and many residential and hospital settings make extensive use of them. Teachers of the mildly handicapped rarely have aides.

Aides are not normally required to hold a bachelor's degree. However, many do because of the nationwide overproduction of elementary teachers. They serve in this capacity while awaiting a classroom teaching position. Aides normally are the teacher's "right arm" and provide much direct instruction under the supervision of the classroom teacher. Rarely in this day and age are they relegated to the ditto machine or errand running.

A number of colleges and universities throughout the nation provide two-year programs for the specific training of paraprofessionals in the field of special education. For the person interested in such a position this is by far most expeditious path to pursue.

## Administration

As in every profession a limited number of persons serve in administrative capacities. Each school district normally has an over-all director of special education. Each district has its own unique administrative arrangements and chains of command, thus title and responsibility may vary. Generally, the director is responsible for the overall administration of the program, including budget, personnel utilization, curriculum, and proctoring of and adherence to state and federal regulations and related activities. Being involved in the IEP placement meeting also is a major responsibility. Because of the administrative type of responsibilities given to this person, the district normally looks for someone who is not only a successful teacher but also has proven administrative ability and has taken additional specialized course work in special education, administration, and curriculum and instruction. Many states have specific credentials which must be obtained before a person can assume such a role. More and more frequently, the director holds a doctorate (Ed.D. or Ph.D.) in special education administration.

## ANCILLARY PERSONNEL

A number of ancillary positions are always available in every school district. These positions are assigned to persons outside the field of special education, but who provide specialized and limited types of services to the exceptional individual. Some of these will be discussed briefly.

### Psychological Services

Literally every school district employs school psychologists whose major responsibility may be the identification of exceptional children through testing and observation. They obtain individual IQ test scores on children referred for evaluation and also do additional testing as required by the district and/or state guidelines. They serve as members of the IEP placement team. In addition, they are often asked to participate as the experts in behavior and classroom management, mental health, programming, and test interpretation. These persons normally hold a minimum of a master's degree in school psychology.

## School Guidance Counselors

Guidance counselors serve a very important role in working with exceptional children, including the gifted. These students, by their very nature, often need additional assistance in understanding both self and others. Lack of acceptable interpersonal skills may be one of their major disabilities in the school and community. The guidance counselors, because of specialized training, are normally able to provide valuable assistance in this area, both on an individual basis and in small groups. They can also be very helpful in gaining the acceptance of exceptional children by their normal peers within the school and community.

Counselors normally have a bachelor's degree in elementary or secondary education. They then take specialized course work at the post-bachelor's, master's, and/or doctoral level before assuming positions in the schools. Traditionally the majority have been employed at the secondary level, but as more emphasis is placed on the elementary exceptional child, they are found with more regularity in the elementary settings.

## Speech and Hearing Specialists

By their very nature, many exceptional children need services from these specialists. Some need them on a long-term basis while others may need very limited and short-term assistance. Hearing handicapped, low functioning retarded, and cerebral palsied are examples of those groups typically requiring assistance. In many states these persons have become *communication disorders specialists* and have broadened their training and experience to work in language acquisition and development, another area needed by numerous exceptional children in each school. They work both with individuals and small groups and in and out of the classroom. Most are master's degree level trained.

## Social Workers

Often the social worker is called upon to assist in providing services to the handicapped. Because parents are an integral part of the

IEP and due process, the social worker may be needed to coordinate activities among the home, school, and other services available to the parents and child outside the educational setting. Social workers may also be used to assist parents in the IEP process itself. Generally social workers hold master's degrees and may be employed by the school district or public and private agencies. A general knowledge of the handicapping conditions is a necessity for a social worker in today's society.

## Summary

By no means have all the personnel associated with the education of exceptional children been discussed. The above section is representative of types of services generally needed and points out the necessity for most persons in the school and support system to have more than just a passing knowledge of the exceptional child, both inside the school setting and outside in the community, especially with the present trend of placing children in the regular classes and with normal peers as much as possible each school day.

## TRENDS AND ISSUES

Probably more than any other area of education today, the field of special education is in a transition state. This has been brought about by legislation, parent interest groups, teacher training institutuions, research, and a general overall awareness on the part of the general public that the exceptional individual can, and should be, a worthwhile member of society. Money spent in the educational process is money well spent, for it makes the individual become a more active and involved member of society in an adult world. A number of trends and issues will be discussed. Because of space limitations, only some of the more significant have been chosen.

### Least Restrictive Environment (Mainstreaming)

Public Law 94-142 requires that each handicapped individual be educated in the least restrictive environment. To the educator this means in the most normal class setting as possible. In essence the least restrictive educational environment of all would be the regular classroom with no additional educational services whatsoever, whereas the most restrictive might be considered to be the home-bound instruction in which the student has no contact with any classroom or with any other student. In the current literature this is often referred to as *mainstreaming.* It basically means the placement of the student in the most normal classroom as possible, based upon the student's own unique strengths and weaknesses and upon the placement as agreed to by the parent or guardian and the IEP placement committee meetings.

Of course, many levels of services are provided between the two extremes of total integration, or total isolation. One example would be the *special education consultant* to the regular teacher. In the mainstream model the students remain in the regular class for the total day with all special services being provided through the class teacher or through the consultant who comes to the regular class and works with the exceptional children in their own class. In a *resource room* the student receives special education services for a specific amount of time each day in a separate classroom, while still another model is the *self-contained special education class* in which the students remain in a regular school but the majority of the day is within a special class. Finally there is the *self-contained day school* in which the students remain in public education but in a separate school with specially trained personnel. In addition nonpublic, specialized day and residential facilities can be included. These most often are private specialty schools for the learning disabled, retarded, or emotionally disturbed. Most states have traditionally provided for the severely mentally retarded, the seriously emotionally disturbed, and the deaf and blind in the form of state residential schools. However, with the advent of Public Law 94-142 there has been a trend back to the public schools within the student's own community because of the emphasis being placed on the placement of any handicapped student in the least restrictive environment. For many of these it has been determined that a state residential school is indeed far too restrictive and an alternative needs to be provided.

To the regular educator this movement has profound implications as the vast majority of the identified special education students in the public schools are presently served in resource room settings. As a result a significant portion of each day is spent with the regular educator and in the regular classroom. Normally the exceptional student found in a resource room setting is the mildly handicapped mentally retarded, learning disabled, or emotionally disturbed type, and gifted and visually and hearing handicapped are also more and more being served under such a model. This means the regular educator must gain at least basic knowledge in special education in order to provide the necessary educational remediation for the handicapped and gifted children. The teacher must work with the special educator in both the development and implementation of the IEP. Most colleges and universities are meeting these newly required skills through a variety of techniques such as (1) a minimum amount of required coursework in the special education department as part of the undergraduate total program; (2) a cognate in special education with a specific number of required courses being taken with that department; (3) a double major at the undergraduate level in elementary or secondary education and special education; or (4) a total undergraduate major in special education in which the student is prepared to teach a variety of handicapped students within a number of different educational settings upon the completion of the degree.

## Deinstitutionalization

This topic has become a national issue with a trend that has, and continues to be, a very potent force within the educational system. Because of the many court decisions and federal laws passed within the past fifteen years, many people previously placed in institutions have begun to be returned to the community. Some have been placed in regional centers, others in halfway houses, and others back to their homes. Those of school age have been made the responsibility of the public schools in the area in which they presently live. This has been especially noticeable with the retarded, emotionally disturbed, hearing handicapped, and visually handicapped. Many of the larger state institutions housing these populations have come under severe criticism for a variety of reasons. As a result of both this and the mandate from Public Law 94-142, there has been a steady movement away from the institution back to the local community through a variety of support systems, all of which emphasize community-based education. Students previously housed in these settings are now becoming the educational responsibility of the local schools. In turn an additional burden is placed on districts to provide the most appropriate education in the least restrictive environment. The end result is, for the most part, a very constructive move toward a more normalized life for those previously institutionalized. But, again this move has a tremendous effect on the colleges and universities in training of teachers and upon the responsibilities of both regular and special education teachers in the public schools. This is only one more example of the expanding role of the schools in providing for the overall education of the handicapped.

## Normalization

This is a very closely aligned topic with deinstitutionalization, and for many it is a philosophy rather than a technique. The overriding theme is that exceptional individuals have all the rights and privileges of the normal, thus they should be integrated within the educational, physical, and social mainstream of society to the greatest extent possible. Group homes for the handicapped in a typical residential setting is an attempt at normalization. The home members live in a large family arrangement, use public transportation and facilities, and are employed within the community whenever possible. Such a trend has obvious implications for the schools and community-based service providers. Once again, schools will be called upon to provide additional educational services to yet another handicapped population.

## Additional Current Issues and Trends

Although space permits only a brief listing of other issues and trends in the field today, they should at least be discussed briefly. Much more information is available on each topic in traditional texts in the field of special education.

*Rights of the Handicapped.* This topic has been, and continues to be, a priority area. In the past too many persons labelled as handicapped literally lost all of their privileges as a citizen of the United States. With current and ongoing legislation and parent interest group involvement, the rights of this group will continue to be protected, and the rights of all free persons will inherently be theirs.

*Prevention of Handicapping Conditions.* This is a number one priority in the United States today. Advances in medicine, psychology, and related fields are helping to drastically reduce the prevalence of some types of handicaps. As science and medicine continues to make advances, the effects will be greatly felt in the field of special education.

*Early Intervention Programs.* Programs of this type are receiving a great amount of attention from a number of different sources. The federal government each year funds research, demonstration, and teaching in this area. The basic intent of any such program is to reach the handicapped child very early and to institute a number of major interventions so that by the time the child reaches school, some or all of the handicapping conditions will be alleviated sufficiently so as to not interfere with the normal school learning process. Preschool classes for the handicapped are now available in most states, and colleges and universities are in the process of training personnel to work with the very young handicapped.

*Recreation for the Handicapped.* Many persons in the field are deeply involved in recreation for the handicapped. Realizing the physical and mental limitations of many of the handicapped, professionals in physical education and related areas have begun to develop programs specifically designed to assist this group of individuals to enjoy life as much as possible, while maintaining good physical and mental health through a long-term recreational program.

## Summary

While only a few of the current issues and trends have been touched upon, they are exemplary of the tremendous growth of research and expansion of knowledge that is literally exploding in the field of special education. All these topics discussed and their related results indeed increase roles and responsibilities of not only special educators but all professionals who work with the handicapped and gifted in any way in the public and private sector of education or in related services.

## PROFESSIONAL ORGANIZATIONS

There are numerous organizations that serve not only the professionals in all areas of this field, but also parents and the exceptional individuals themselves. While some are exclusively professional organizations, most welcome inquiries and elicit membership from any interested persons. Some of the most prominent are listed below. Current addresses are listed, however it is advisable to check before sending any correspondence to determine if the address is still current.

Alexander Graham Bell Association for the Deaf, Inc.
3417 Volta Place, N.W.
Washington, D.C. 20007

American Association on Mental Deficiency
5101 Wisconsin Avenue, N.W.
Washington, D.C. 20016

American Printing House for the Blind
1839 Frankfort Avenue
Louisville, Kentucky 40206

American Psychological Association
1200 17th Street, N.W.
Washington, D.C. 20036

American Speech and Hearing Association
10801 Rockville Pike
Rockville, Maryland 20852

Association for Children with Learning Disabilities
2200 Brownsville Road
Pittsburgh, Pennsylvania 16201

Association for the Severely Handicapped
Garden View Suite
1600 West Armory Way
Seattle, Washington 98119

Closer Look
National Information Center for the Handicapped
1201 16th Street, N.W.
Washington, D.C. 20026

Convention of American Instructors of the Deaf
5034 Wisconsin Avenue
Washington, D.C. 20016

Council for Exceptional Children
1920 Association Drive
Reston, Virginia 22091

National Association for
the Education of Young Children
1834 Connecticut Avenue, N.W.
Washington, D.C. 20009

National Association for the Gifted
8080 Spring Valley Drive
Cincinnati, Ohio 45236

National Association for Retarded Citizens
2709 Avenue E, East
P.O. Box 6109
Arlington, Texas 76011

National Foundation March of Dimes
1275 Marmaroneck Avenue
White Plains, New York 10605

National Council for the Gifted
700 Prospect Avenue
West Orange, New Jersey 07052

National Perinatal Association
Suite 420
1015 15th Street, N.W.
Washington, D.C. 20005

President's Committee on Mental Retardation
Regional Office Building #3
Seventh and D Streets, S.W.
Room 2614
Washington, D.C. 20201

United Cerebral Palsy Association, Inc.
66 East 34th Street
New York, New York 10016

Orton Society
8415 Bellona Lane
Baltimore, Maryland 21204

## REFERENCES

Goodman, L. V.: A bill of rights for the handicapped. *American Education, 12:*6-8, 1976.

Hewitt, F., and Forness, S. R.: *Education of Exceptional Learners.* Boston, Allyn and Bacon, 1974.

Kameen, M. C., and McIntosh, D.K.: The counselor and the individual educational program. *The Personnel and Guidance Journal, 58:*238-244, 1979.

Kirk, S. A., and Gallagher, J. J.: *Educating Exceptional Children.* Boston, Houghton Mifflin, 1979.

*Chapter 10*

# ROLES AND RESPONSIBILITIES
# OF THE
# READING SPECIALIST

RICHARD E. KEMPER

*R ICHARD KEMPER received his doctorate in education in reading and language arts from the University of Pittsburgh in 1970 and has been with the University of South Carolina for eleven years. Prior to his return to full-time teaching in the fall of 1980, Kemper had administrative positions with the College of Education, including assistant dean for Graduate Regional Studies, director of South Carolina Desegregation Center, and director of the Model Schools Project and Special Training Institutes. He has been actively involved in writing grants for the College of Education and school districts throughout South Carolina and the Southeast. He has also done extensive consultant work in reading and educational management for school districts, colleges and universities, publishing companies, and state education agencies in South Carolina and nationally. Kemper is currently associate professor of education in the Reading Department at the University of South Carolina, where he is involved in teaching, grant writing, and services to public schools.*

---

The role of the reading specialist is relatively new in American public education. Smith (1963) reports that it was during the period 1935 to 1950 that school districts began to appoint special personnel to supervise reading, and "the term reading consultant made its initial appearance in educational literature" (p. 31). A review of educational literature reveals that throughout the 1940s few references are made to school personnel who would resemble today's reading specialist. Gates (1947) mentions the specialist in reading, but no explanation of the role and responsibilities of such personnel is given. During the 1950s the role of the reading specialist became a more frequent topic in educational books and journals. During this period Durrell (1956) writes that many school districts had created reading consultant positions to provide more effective reading instruction. He includes one school district's description of the duties, qualifications, experiences, and professional training required of a reading consultant. This description suggests that the reading consultant was expected to work with the school administration, teachers, supervisors, and community to plan, implement, and evaluate the total school reading program. Beginning with the 1960s and moving into the present, the concept of the reading specialist has become more and more firmly established in public education. Increasing numbers of school districts, both large and small, employ specialists in reading, and in contrast to the period of the 1940s and before, current educational literature contains numerous articles, chapters, and books dealing with the topic of reading specialists.

## PROFESSIONAL ROLES AND RESPONSIBILITIES

To a great extent the roles and responsibilities of special personnel in reading are situation specific and are categorized with a variety of titles, including reading consultant, reading supervisor, reading coordinator, remedial or developmental reading teacher, special teacher of reading, reading teacher, and reading specialist. The particular title, role, and responsibilities assigned to special reading personnel tend to vary from work setting to work setting and from author to author. For instance Otto, McMenemy, and Smith (1973) refer to the remedial specialist as "one who is highly trained in the techniques of diagnosis and remediation and who is called in to deal with learning problems as they arise" (p. 407). Robinson (1972), with a somewhat different point of view, describes the reading consultant as one who works with school staff to improve the reading program. Botel (1972) suggests that the reading specialist should have primary responsibility for working with teachers in the area of professional development. Referring to the variety of titles associated with special reading personnel, Kinder (1969) points out that "whether a reading title guarantees anything about the person holding it is largely a matter of geography — a matter of the state or local school district in which the person works" (p. 381).

A number of attempts have been made to clarify the relationship between the titles of special reading personnel and associated roles and responsibilities. These efforts have met with varying degrees of success in terms of producing consistency between titles and job roles and responsibilities. They do, however, provide a comprehensive picture of the variety of expectations and possibilities associated with positions for special reading personnel.

One of the major efforts at describing the roles and responsibilities of special personnel in reading was carried out by the International Reading Association (1968), which developed the following definitions of roles and list of related responsibilities of reading specialists:

I. Definition of Roles

Reading personnel can be divided into two categories:

Those who work directly with children either as reading teachers or reading clinicians; and those who work directly with teachers as consultants or supervisors with prime responsibility for staff and program.

A. Special Teacher of Reading

A Special Teacher of Reading has major responsibility for remedial and corrective and/or developmental reading instruction.

B. Reading Clinician

A Reading Clinician provides diagnosis, remediation, or the planning of remediation for the more complex and severe reading disability cases.

C. Reading Consultant

A Reading Consultant works directly with teachers, administrators, and other professionals within a school to develop and implement the reading program under the direction of a supervisor with special training in reading.

D. Reading Supervisor (Coordinator or Director)

A Reading Supervisor provides leadership in all phases of the reading program in a school system.

II. Responsibilities of Each Reading Specialist

A. Special Teacher of Reading

Should identify students needing diagnosis and/or remediation.

Should plan a program of remediation from data gathered through diagnosis.

Should implement such a program of remediation.

Should evaluate student progress in remediation.

Should interpret student needs and progress in remediation to the classroom teacher and the parents.

Should plan and implement a developmental or advanced program as necessary.

B. Reading Clinician

Should demonstrate all the skills expected of the Special Teacher of Reading and, by virtue of additional training and experience, diagnose and treat the more complex and severe reading disability cases.

Should demonstrate proficiency in providing internship training for prospective clinicians and/or Special Teachers of Reading.

C. Reading Consultant

Should survey and evaluate the ongoing program and make suggestions for needed changes.

Should translate the district philosophy of reading with the help of the principal of each school into a working program consistent with the needs of the students, the teachers, and the community.

Should work with classroom teachers and others in improving the developmental and corrective aspects of the reading program.

D. Reading Supervisor

Should develop a systemwide reading philosophy and curriculum, and interpret this to the school administration, staff, and public.

Should exercise leadership with all personnel in carrying out good reading practices.

Should evaluate reading personnel and personnel needs in all phases of a schoolwide reading program.

Should make recommendations to the administration regarding the reading budget.

The International Reading Association's document uses the term reading specialist in a generic sense and proposes broad responsibilities or tasks for each specialist category. In a somewhat different vein, Botel (1972) proposes that the primary role of a reading specialist should be one of helping teachers in the area of professional development. He presents the following list of specific responsibilities for such a position:

1. Coordinating of the reading and language arts professional development program.
2. Responding to teacher requests for assistance.
3. Helping teachers in all subject areas to determine the instructional levels of their pupils and the reading levels of the of the textbooks used in their classes.
4. Helping to adjust materials and methods in the light of pupil differences.
5. Helping teachers develop competency in teaching directed reading lessons in all subjects.
6. Helping teachers find alternative instructional strategies for teaching subject matter when textbooks are too difficult for some or all of their pupils, and demonstrating effective classroom techniques.
7. Setting up procedures for identifying and diagnosing pupils who need special remedial help.
8. Coordinating the evaluation and selection of reading and language arts textbooks, tests, and other media.
9. Organizing a reading materials resource center.
10. Supervising the work of special reading teachers.
11. Helping parents understand their role in influencing their children's language and reading development.
12. Initiating and supervising pilot, experimental, and innovative instructional strategies.
13. Orienting new teachers in the program.
14. Keeping the staff informed regarding research findings and new theories and helping teachers implement them.

Robinson (1965) contends that the title reading consultant is more appropriate than reading specialist to describe reading personnel who are assigned primarily to work with teachers. He proposes the following seven roles for the reading consultant: resource person, advisor, in-service leader, investigator, diagnostician, instructor, and evaluator. While reading consultants, as described by Robinson, work occasionally with children, their primary responsibilities are in the areas of helping teachers; designing, conducting, and interpreting reading related research within the school system; communicating with parents, teachers, and administrators about reading programs within the school or school system; and, planning and assisting with the implementation of the total school in-service program.

Another view of the roles and responsibilities of reading specialists is presented by Smith, Otto, and Hansen (1978) who propose that "reading specialists generally function either as teachers of students with special needs or as consultants to administrators and classroom teachers" (p. 221). They place reading specialists in several specific roles, including reading coordinator, central office reading consultant/teacher, and elementary school reading teacher. For each role they list specific tasks or responsibilities:

A. Reading Coordinator

Designs and directs new developments in the instructional reading program, K-12.

Provides in-service education for central office reading consultants, teachers, and administrators.

Interprets the reading program to the board of education and community groups.

Assists in developing systemwide testing procedures relevant to the reading program.

Advises and cooperates with nearby universities in teacher education and research relative to reading.

Aids in the recruitment, interviewing, and selection of reading program personnel.

Designs and directs reading research.

Attends and participates in meetings relevant to the school system's reading programs.

Disseminates information regarding reading program development throughout the school system at the local, state, and national levels.

Visits classrooms with the approval of school principals to assist in evaluating teachers and improving their capabilities in the area of reading instruction.

Assists the director of curriculum development in the preparation of course outlines and teaching guides.

Assists in the evaluation and selection of textbooks and other resource materials.

Works with the central office reading consultants to coordinate the reading curriculum from kindergarten to grade

12.

B. Central Office Reading Consultant

Aids school staffs in developing objectives for reading instruction in the schools assigned.

Organizes and conducts in-service education programs for classroom teachers and for reading teachers assigned to individual schools.

Aids the reading coordinator in research relative to the reading programs being conducted in the schools assigned.

Investigates materials for the academic level assigned and recommends their purchase to teachers and principals.

Aids the reading teacher and the principal in developing and evaluating special instructional programs.

Aids the reading teachers in a continual evaluation of each school's reading program.

Studies the latest writings and research on reading instruction at the academic level assigned and communicates this information to teachers and administrators.

Works with reading teachers for initiating projects that will benefit from a temporary team approach.

Diagnoses and prescribes instruction for seriously disabled readers.

Communicates frequently with central office reading consultants assigned to other schools and other academic levels.

Works with the reading coordinator and other central office reading consultants to coordinate the reading curriculum from kindergarten to grade 12.

Supervises reading teachers in their work with teachers and students.

Introduces innovative reading programs and materials to the schools assigned.

Serves on textbook and other committees that affect reading in the schools assigned.

Gives classroom demonstrations for teachers.

Conducts in-service meetings and classes for reading teachers, classroom teachers, administrators, and parent groups.

C. Secondary School Building Consultant/Teacher

Develops and maintains, with the help of central office reading consultant, a systematic development reading program residing in the content areas by helping content area teachers incorporate the teaching of reading into their curriculums.

Develops and teaches special classes, seminars, and workshops, and supervises individualized study projects for students with special reading needs, which may be remedial, corrective, or accelerated.

Advises the principal and central office reading consultants regarding desired reading program development.

Implements, with the help of central office reading consultants and guidance counselors, a testing program and communicates information regarding students' reading abilities to their content area teachers.

Administers diagnostic reading tests to specially referred students and on the basis of the test results recommends special materials, assignments, and achievement expectance to their teachers.

Teams with reading teachers in other schools and with central office reading consultants to conduct short-term projects or in-service work in another school.

D. Elementary School Remedial Reading Teacher

Organizes a systematic plan of referral and instruction for disabled readers likely to profit from individual or near-individual teaching.

Diagnoses and gives remedial instruction to students with reading disabilities.

Acts as a resource person for the principal and teachers in reading to the employment of materials, methods, etc., for reading instruction.

Diagnoses and prescribes corrective programs for mildly disabled students likely to profit from corrective help by their classroom teacher.

Confers with central office reading consultants regarding systemwide reading program development in the elementary school.

Pikulski and Ross (1979) approach a description of the reading specialist by summarizing, from educational literature, the skills and attitudes that they feel would be expected of a successful reading specialist. They categorize these skills and attitudes into three areas:

1. Knowledge — information generally of a technical-professional nature that the specialist should have available to dispense or apply as needed.
2. Interpersonal — personal social qualities and attitudes that should allow the specialist to interact more effectively with students, teachers, administrators, and people in general.
3. Administrator — skills that should allow the specialist to contribute actively to the organization, guidance, and direction of the reading program.

In a discussion of reading specialists, Bader (1974) writes that "the roles of the reading specialist are so many and varied that he literally has a job that cannot be done" (p. 37). While this may be something of an overstatement, it is obvious from the previous descriptions that reading specialist positions are complex and require a comprehensive set of technical and personal knowledge and skills. It is impossible to predict the exact responsibilities that will be assigned to a given reading specialist. As was mentioned above, that will depend upon the state or school district in which the specialist is employed. It is possible, however, to predict generic performance areas that will be expected of a reading specialist, regardless of titles. The roles and responsibilities presented previously suggest a number of such areas. For instance a reading specialist can expect to perform as a teacher. Whether this teaching is directed toward students, administrators, parents, or teachers, the reading specialist will need to be an accomplished teacher. Second, reading specialists must have planning skills. As with teaching, planning may be in relation to different groups, but the reading specialist will need to do planning. Third, the reading specialist must be able to demonstrate an in-depth knowledge of reading. This may be in the form of demonstrations of teaching techniques, explanations of reading programs or reading research, identification of instructional material to meet special reading needs, documented support for or rejection of specific programs or approaches to reading instruction, or any number of actions that clearly demonstrate the reading specialist's comprehensive knowledge and understanding of the total field of reading. Fourth, the reading specialist will evaluate. Student performance, instructional materials, program effectiveness, testing programs, and instructional techniques are a few of the areas in which any reading specialist will be expected to demonstrate competency in evaluation. Finally, the reading specialist must communicate effectively with students, teachers, supervisors, administrators, school board members, and the general community. Without effective communication skills, the reading specialist cannot succeed.

How the reading specialist develops the skills required for success on the job depends on previous work experiences and education. Generally, however, much of the reading specialist's professional competence will depend on the quality and nature of his or her professional training.

## PROFESSIONAL PREPARATION

Just as the roles and responsibilities of reading specialists are specific to different situations, so too are the professional preparation requirements. Such requirements vary from state to state and are usually linked to a particular college or university and/or the certification requirements of a state department of education. In 1969 Kinder reported that twenty-three of fifty states required reading certifications as follows:

Reading Specialist (9)
Special Teacher of Reading (8)
Reading Supervisor/Coordinator/Director (7)
Reading Consultant(4)
Remedial Reading Teacher or Clinician (8)

However, as Otto, McMenemy, and Smith (1973) point out, it is difficult to make generalizations about certification requirements for reading specialists, since "specific specialty areas and types of preparation vary widely from state to state" (p. 408). A study by the International Reading Association (1979) reveals that there is little in common from state to state, school to school, and job to job regarding required professional preparation of special reading personnel.

While there is diversity in the required qualifications for reading specialists, educational literature does contain some suggestions for the professional preparation and experiences of special reading personnel. The International Reading Association (1968), in conjunction with its description of the roles and responsibilities of reading specialists, has recommended the following minimal qualifications for the different categories of reading specialists:

I. General (Applicable to all Reading Specialists)

Demonstrate proficiency in evaluating and implementing research.

Demonstrate a willingness to make a meaningful contribution to professional organizations related to reading.

Demonstrate a willingness to assume leadership in improving the reading program.

II. Special Teacher of Reading

Complete a minimum of three years of successful classroom teaching in which the teaching of reading is an important responsibility of the position. Complete a planned program for the Master's Degree from an accredited institution, to include:

A. A minimum of twelve semester hours in graduate level reading courses with at least one course in each of the following:

1. Foundations or survey of reading

A basic course whose content is related exclusively to reading instruction or the psychology of reading.

2. Diagnosis and correction of reading disabilities

The content of this course or courses include the following: causes of reading disabilities; observation and interview procedures; diagnostic instruments; standard and informal tests; report writing; materials and methods of instruction.

3. Clinicial or laboratory practicum in reading

A clinical or laboratory experience which might be an integral part of a course or courses in the diagnosis and correction of reading disabilities. Students diagnose and treat reading disability cases under supervision.

B. Complete at undergraduate or graduate level, study in each of the following areas:

1. Measurement and/or evaluation.

2. Child and/or adolescent psychology.

3. Psychology, including such aspects as personality cognition, and learning behaviors.

4. Literature for children and/or adolescents.

C. Fulfill remaining portions of the program from related

areas of study.

III. Reading Clinician

Meet the qualifications as stipulated for the Special Teacher of Reading and, in addition, complete a sixth year of graduate work to include:

A. An advanced course or courses in the diagnosis and remediation of reading and learning problems.

B. A course or courses in individual testing.

C. An advanced clinical laboratory practicum in the diagnosis and remediation of reading difficulties.

D. Field experiences under the direction of a qualified Reading Clinician.

IV. Reading Consultant

Meet the qualifications as stipulated for the Special Teacher of Reading. Complete, in addition to the above, a sixth year of graduate work to include:

A. An advanced course in the remediation and diagnosis of reading and learning problems.

B. An advanced course in the developmental aspects of a reading program.

C. A course or courses in curriculum development and supervision.

D. A course and/or experience in public relations.

E. Field experiences under a qualified Reading Consultant or Supervisor in a school setting.

V. Reading Supervisor

Meet the qualifications as stipulated for the Special Teacher of Reading. Complete in addition to the above, a sixth year of graduate work to include:

A. Courses listed in 1, 2, 3, and 4 under Reading Consultant.

B. A course or courses in administrative procedures.

C. Field experiences under a qualified Reading Supervisor.

These recommendations set by the International Reading Association appear to be representative of the certification requirements for special reading personnel in many states. In addition many schools and colleges of education have adopted these suggestions as a part of their programs for the preparation of special reading personnel. They provide, perhaps, the best available set of guidelines for persons interested in preparing to become reading specialists.

The colleges and universities that offer programs for the preparation of reading specialists and the differences in the nature and content of these programs are too numerous and varied to describe here. A publication by the International Reading Association (1973) provides a detailed description of graduate programs for the training of reading specialists. This guide contains the following information for some 200 graduate programs in reading throughout the country:

1. Degrees offered
2. Courses offered
3. Number of students enrolled
4. What students do when they finish the program
5. Background and current activities of faculty members in the program
6. Special resources, centers, clinics, laboratories, and institutes available
7. Name and address of person to contact for further information

The above publication should serve as a helpful guide to anyone interested in identifying a graduate program in reading. It should be remembered, however, that such programs tend to change considerably over time, and direct contact with personnel in a particular program will be necessary to obtain a current description of its content, resources, and degree offerings.

## TRENDS AND ISSUES

Reading specialists' roles, responsibilities, and required preparation are nearly as varied as the school districts that hire them, the state departments of education that certify them, and the colleges and universities that train them. To a certain extent this diversity is good since it represents the attempts of the different agencies involved to respond specifically to a state's or school district's particular identified needs in reading. However, prospective and currently employed reading specialists should be aware of the following factors growing out of this situation that are directly related to their professional growth and employment:

1. Professional programs for training special reading personnel vary not only in content, but also in quality. Bader (1974) suggests that colleges and universities have been training reading specialists to diagnose and remediate youngsters on an individual or small group basis and have done little for specialists who are or will be responsible for organizing and directing a total reading program. Austin (1968) also suggests that many colleges and universities provide incomplete or inadequate training programs for special reading personnel. Before beginning a program at a particular college or university, it is best to investigate the reputation of the program with school district and state department of education personnel as well as recent graduates. Every effort should be made to assess the content and quality of a program in relation to a specific reading specialist position.

2. Differences in the meanings of job titles can pose problems for the prospective reading specialist. Before deciding on a career as a reading specialist, it is best to learn what specific titles mean in the school district where you intend to work. A reading specialist in one school district may spend considerable time in supervisory or administrative tasks and a minimum of time teaching reading. Different distributions of responsibilities may be expected in another district.

3. Certification requirements for special reading personnel are different from state to state, and a reading specialist in one state may be a reading consultant or a reading clinician in another. Persons who are working toward reading certification in a state where they do not intend to be employed should learn about the specific certification requirements of the state where they expect to work.

4. Titles and position descriptions are often misleading and represent only a portion of the responsibilities of any job. Before accepting a position as a reading specialist, it is important to find out what the person who held the position before did on a day-to-day basis. If the position is new, it may be best to learn what teachers and other specialists or supervisors perceive as the primary responsibility of the position.

## PROFESSIONAL ORGANIZATIONS

A number of professional organizations exist for teachers, supervisors, university professors, and other professional personnel who are directly or indirectly involved in the reading professions. The organizations listed below generally hold annual meetings or conferences and publish periodic journals, newsletters, and other material related to reading and reading instruction. Details concerning publications, conferences, and membership costs can be obtained by writing directly to the organization of interest:

International Reading Association
800 Barksdale Road
P.O. Box 8139
Newark, Delaware 19711

College Reading Association
S.W.B.C., 623 South Pike
Bolivar, Missouri 65613

National Reading Conference, Inc.
1230 17th Street N.W.
Washington, D.C. 20036

American Reading Forum
309 Aderhold Hall
The University of Georgia
Athens, Georgia 30602

## REFERENCES

Austin, Mary C.: Professional training of personnel. In Robinson, Helen M. (Ed.): *Innovation and Change in Reading Instruction.* Chicago, University of Chicago Press, 1968, pp. 357-396.

Bader, Lois, A.: The reading coordinator: Key to an effective reading program. In Duffy, Gerald J. (Ed.): *Reading in the Missle School.* Newark, Delaware, International Reading Association, 1974, pp. 34-45.

Botel, Morton: A proposed staff organization for reading-language arts. In Carlson, Thorsten R. (Ed.): *Administrators in Reading.* New York, Harcourt, Brace, Javanovich, Inc., 1972, pp. 41-59.

Durrell, Donald D.: *Improving Reading Instruction.* New York, World Book Co., 1956, p. 336.

188     *A Consumer's Guide to the Public School*

Gates, A.I.: *The Improvement of Reading,* 3rd ed. New York, The MacMillan Co., 1947, pp. 131-132.

International Reading Association: *Graduate Programs and Faculty in Reading.* Newark, Delaware, 1973.

International Reading Association: Roles, responsibilities and qualifications of reading specialists. *Journal of Reading, 12(1):*60-63, October 1968.

International Reading Association: What's in a name: Reading specialist? *Journal of Reading, 20(7):*623-628, April 1979.

Kinder, R.F.: State certification of reading teachers and specialists: Review of the national science. In Figurel, J. Allen (Ed.): *Reading and Realism.* Newark, Delaware, International Reading Association, 1969.

Otto, W., McMenemy, R.A., and Smith, R.J.: *Corrective and Remedial Teaching,* 2nd ed. Boston, Houghton Mifflin Co., 1973.

Pikulski, John J., and Ross, Elliott: Classroom teachers' perceptions of the role of the reading specialist. *Journal of Reading, 23(2):* 126-135, November 1979.

Robinson, H. Alan: *Guiding the Reading Program.* Chicago, Science Research Associates, 1965.

Robinson, H. Alan: New patterns in the secondary school. In Carlson, Thorsten R. (Ed.): *Administrators and Reading.* New York, Harcourt, Brace, Javanovich, Inc., 1972, pp. 242-263.

Smith, Nila B.: Reading: Seventy-five years of progress. In Harris and Sipary (Eds.): *Readings on Reading Instruction.* New York, David McKay Co., 1963.

Smith, R., Otto, W., and Hansen, L.: *The School Reading Program.* Boston, Houghton Mifflin Co., 1978, pp. 214-241.

# Chapter 11

# VOCATIONAL AND CAREER EDUCATION

LEONARD MAIDEN

*L EN MAIDEN is the distributive teacher educator at the University of South Carolina. He has been in vocational education since 1948 as a student, teacher, supervisor, and teacher educator. Maiden has degrees from Virginia Commonwealth University, The University of Virginia, and the University of South Carolina. In addition to his duties in vocational education, he currently serves as director of undergraduate studies in the College of Education at the University of South Carolina.*

## VOCATIONAL EDUCATION

Vocational education has developed in response to philosophical, economic, and sociological trends in our society. Basic to the vocational education philosophy is the belief in the worth of every individual and the right of that individual to pursue a vocation suited to his or her interest and needs. Vocational education leaders and sponsors of the federal vocational education acts espouse the belief that vocational training should be a part of every individual's education. There is also widespread belief that it is inseparable from general education and is of tremendous value as a teaching-learning method for general education.

### Vocational Education Defined

Vocational education as an educational philosophy and program has many definitions, based upon its function and relationship to a given educational system. Some confusion over the nature of vocational education has developed because of the wide variety and inclusive phrasing of these definitions. What is considered vocational education in one school district may be considered technical, occupational, or career education in another school system. For pur-

189

poses of clarification, vocational education in this discussion will be interpreted as any form of education, training, or retraining designed to prepare individuals to enter or continue in paid employment in any recognized occupation. This broad definition expresses the concept established by federal acts directed toward vocational education. Specific programs offered through vocational education include agricultural education, business and office education, distributive education, trade and industrial education, health occupations education, and home economics education. Vocational guidance and career counseling have been included as a part of vocational education as a result of federal legislation, which provides funding for these services. The prime target population for vocational education is high school students. Through prevocational education programs, students are guided in career selection. In vocational education they are trained for the occupation of their choice. Other individuals participating in vocational education programs include the following:

1. Young people and adults in junior colleges and technical schools or similar postsecondary schools
2. School dropouts from sixteen to twenty-five who have temporary low skill jobs and need part-time vocational training while they continue working
3. Persons with academic, physical, or other handicaps that require special modified vocational education programs
4. Adults needing to update their job skills through vocational courses.

### Historical Perspective/Legal Basis

Although vocational training in various forms has played an important part in the preparation of our society's work force since the birth of our nation, it was not until the success of the land grant institutions established under the Morrill Land Grant Act of 1862 that public secondary schools began to explore the possibilities of the development of public vocational education programs within the public school system. One of the most influential groups in the early stages of the promotion of the vocational education concept was the National Society for the Promotion of Industrial Education, which was organized in 1906. The society enlisted the support of leaders in every state and worked with Congress to call attention to the need for industrial education and to secure partial funding for vocational education.

From 1906-1917, the concept of a public vocational education program was analyzed and reviewed by educators and legislators. During the planning stages, the value of public vocational education became evident. However, because of the mobility of labor and the inability of the states to develop vocational education programs, vocational education's only hope was to acquire federal funding, which could establish appropriate standards and uniformity among various vocational programs.

By 1917 public and congressional support for vocational education resulted in the passing of the first vocational education legislation, the Smith-Hughes Act. The Act provided 7 million dollars annually to be allocated for education in vocational agriculture, trades and industry, and home economics education. Under provisions in the Smith-Hughes Act, requirements were established for the submission of state plans, the establishment of state boards for vocational education, qualifications of teachers, and the duration of vocational programs. The nearly fifty years following the passage of the Smith-Hughes Act were marked by a series of federal acts that broadened the purposes of vocational education and expanded support for occupational training programs. The Vocational Education Act of 1963 represented the most comprehensive vocational legislation ever passed by Congress. The act provided a basis for state and local agencies to expand vocational education into broader objectives, such as career exploration and preparation for advanced and highly skilled vocational technical programs in any occupational field that does not require a baccalaureate degree. Funding for vocational education increased from an initial 60 million to 225 million dollars over a five-year period.

The vocational education amendments of 1968 doubled the previous appropriations to be spent for vocational education. The amendments were an attempt to break down the barriers between academic, general, and vocational curricula so that no young person would be denied an opportunity to prepare for work of his choice. The 1968 amendments established a national advisory council on vocational education and similar advisory councils at the state level.

## Vocational Education: Curriculum and Administration

The total curriculum of each vocational program is based upon the specific occupational needs and interests of the students. Training received through a comprehensive vocational program is designed to provide the student with the basic job entry skills needed to get a job in the student's chosen career field. While each individual vocational program will have its own unique curriculum, the following service areas are typical for most diversified vocational programs:

Agriculture Education
Health Occupations Education
Marketing and Distributive Education
Occupational Home Economics
Office Occupations Education
Trade and Industrial Education

The specific courses offered through these programs depend upon the number of students, the availability of suitable equipment and classroom space, and the philosophy of the school. Some vocational programs place more emphasis on theoretical instruction; others place more on practical instruction, which prepares the student for a specific occupation. Examples of specific skill-acquiring courses offered under the major service areas are as follows:

Agriculture Education
    Agricultural production
    Agricultural mechanics
    Ornamental horticulture

Health Occupations Education
    Practical nursing
    General health occupations
    Nursing assistant

Marketing and Distributive Education
    Distributive education
    Fashion merchandising
    Salesmanship

Occupational Home Economics Education
    Child care

Commercial cooking
Housing and home furnishings
Office Occupations Education
  Accounting
  Office procedures
  Shorthand
  Typing
Trade and Industrial Education
  Air conditioning and refrigeration
  Automotive mechanics
  Building construction
  Cosmetology
  Graphics
  Masonry
  Plumbing

## Curriculum Structure

There are a wide range of instructional methods that are used in vocational education programs. While the traditional lecture and mastery of theory approaches are useful and necessary for some aspects of the vocational curriculum, the nature of vocational education programs requires skill mastery as well. For vocational programs to be effective, the student must master both theory and method or skill. This facet of vocational education has led to the development of a performance-based vocational curriculum in many programs. Performance-based vocational education simply means the student is told in advance exactly what task (or skill) is necessary and how well he or she will be expected to perform the task. Instruction is based on job-relevant tasks, and the final test is the performance or mastery of the task.

## Vocational Education Centers

Vocational education centers designed to meet the occupational training needs of a cluster of high schools have been developed in some states. Many educators are opposed to the concept of vocational schools located on sites physically separated from comprehensive secondary schools. In a number of states, a compromise has been struck whereby the vocational center enrollee remains a student at a parent high school and is transported to a center for vocational classes. A major argument for the vocational center is that skill courses may be offered that cannot be justified in an individual high school because of laboratory costs and/or student interest. This practice is especially applicable to the skill development courses in the trades and industry service area where the equipping of an appropriate laboratory is relatively expensive. Vocational education programs at individual vocational centers offer in-depth skill training in a modern setting and in areas where business/industry need skilled workers. Students train for two or three hours per day at the vocational center. The remainder of the school day is spent in academic classes in the feeder high school.

### Cooperative Vocational Programs

Many vocational centers have *cooperative* vocational education programs that train students at the vocational center and then place them in real job situations related to their training. Students in cooperative vocational programs earn credit for on-the-job training in addition to credit earned in the classroom.

### Advisory Councils

Each federally funded vocational education program has an advisory council composed of key leaders from local business/industry. These councils are helpful in keeping the vocational programs responsive to the needs of the business and industry sectors in the community.

### Staff Training

Each vocational program at an accredited vocational education center or public school is required to provide a well-organized in-service education program for professional personnel in addition to regularly scheduled faculty meetings. Staff members should be involved in the planning and evaluation of these activities, which are designed to focus on the problems, needs, purposes, and goals of the vocational education program.

## Outlook for the Future

There are some national future trends that will have a dramatic impact upon vocational education. The major trend influencing vocational education is the continuing technological boom. Rapid changes are expected in the many technical occupations. According to Robert Scanlon, only one in five jobs that will become available through 1985 will require a college degree, while there will be a 50 percent increase in the number of technicians and professional workers, accompanied by a decrease in the demand for laborers. The increasing importance of rapidly changing technologies in energy, communications, transportation, medicine, and computer science is also predicted by many futurists. The bulk of the new jobs of the future will also be service oriented, rather than in manufacturing and production. The need for skilled and middle management personnel will grow tremendously. Education faces the task of providing workers of the future with a means of upgrading their skills and knowledge in order to keep pace with rapid occupational changes. Although the birth rate in the United States is expected to continue declining, women and handicapped individuals are expected to continue entering the work force in increasing numbers and competition for skilled technical jobs will increase.

It is apparent that the advances in and redirection of technology will place increased emphasis on vocational and technical training. Some vocational courses will expand rapidly, others will become obsolete, and mere reliance on a steady core of traditional vocational education courses will not be possible. The importance of career awareness and planning will increase, as will the need for comprehensive programs of guidance and counseling.

The need for alternative forms of education will increase, especially as the median age increases. On-the-job training, work study, and cooperative training programs will play an important part in vocational education in the future as costs for vocational equipment rise and taxpayer pressure reduces the availability of expensive, up-to-date technological equipment.

## CAREER EDUCATION

It has been argued by many that schools must have a change in outlook and reallocation of funds in recognition that all students must be prepared for the world of work. The curriculum must reflect this understanding and eliminate the idea that only less capable students will be oriented toward work. This has been a recurrent theme since the vocational education amendments of 1968. Conference papers following passage of this act stressed a systems approach to education emphasizing development of marketable skills, decision-making abilities, and knowledge of self. Career education took form and assumed a definition as a restructured form of education involving vocational and general education, while focusing primarily on people rather than specific jobs.

### Career Education Defined

The term *career education* was probably coined by Sidney P. Marland, Jr., Commissioner of Education (1971), as he emphasized that the only two routes available after school should be continuing education or employment.

In *An Introduction to Career Education,* Kenneth Hoyt (1975, p. 4), director of the Office of Career Education, defined career as "the totality of work done in his or her lifetime" and education as "the totality of experiences through which one learns about and prepares to engage in work as part of her or his way of living." Career education is a combination of many concepts available at various times in American education.

Career education is not another word for vocational education, and it does not require a complete change in our educational system. It requires change within the present structure of the present system. It extends from very early years of a person's life until the later years enabling people to have more power in making decisions about life roles.

### Career Education Model

In 1972 the United States Office of Education began development of four conceptual models for career education. These are being tested and revised, and are as follows:

1. School-Based Model 1
   Insures that students will leave school with self-knowledge, purpose, skills, and awareness of career options.
2. Employer-Based Model II
   Insures that students will leave school with the same understanding as above, as well as specific skills and knowledge for a career.
3. Home/Community-Based Model III
   A career-oriented approach for adults no longer in school. It employs mass media, referral programs, counseling, and integration of these by the Career Education Extension Service.
4. Rural Residential-Based Model IV
   Has as its objective the provision of rural families with employment capabilities suitable for the area and improvement of family living.

The school-based model has been the most successful.

Career education in schools usually begins with the awareness stage in kindergarten through third grade. The child needs exposure to the concepts and practice in the cultivation of skills. Awareness of self, of different occupational roles, of responsibility for one's own actions, of classifying and decision-making skills, of cooperative social behavior, and of respect for others and their work all take place during this stage.

Grades fourth through sixth are involved with the accomodation stage of career awareness. Included here are development of concepts related to self, development of concepts related to the world of work, assuming more responsibility for planning one's time, application of decision-making and classification skills, development of desirable social relationships, and development of work attitudes and values.

The orientation stage in grades seventh through eighth involves clarification of a self-concept; understanding of the interrelated structure of American economic, occupational, and technological systems; assuming responsibility for career planning; development of one's inquiry and problem-solving skills; development of socially responsible behavior and more mature social relationships; appreciation of work as a valued social institution.

The exploration and preparation stage follows for grades ninth through twelfth. Goals involve crystallization and implementation of a self-concept, executing plans to qualify for career objectives, commitment to implementation of a career plan, application of problem-solving skills, understanding the dynamics of group behavior in a work environment, and acquiring the discipline of work.

Postsecondary goals usually include more precise career selections, more refined job skills, and skills that lead to productive leisure or retirement.

There is very little formal teacher preparation for career education. In-service training constitutes the majority of training. Conferences, workshops, retreats, and seminars are held through local schools and professional associations. Some universities have been successful in infusing career education awareness concepts into teacher education programs. Small steps, such as involving college students in helping plan and carry out local projects and programs, are usually the best way to start.

Implementation of a career education program requires the collaborative efforts of the business-labor-industry community, counseling and guidance personnel, home and family members, educational administrators, school boards, and classroom teachers.

The business-labor-industry community will provide work experience. Their employees will serve as resource personnel and participate in career education policy formulation.

Counselors will assume a major role because they are experts in consultation, coordination of pupil personnel services, and human relations competence. They also have a unique insight into student needs. Home members can help students acquire good work habits and positive attitudes. Educational administrators will emphasize career education as a primary goal and provide leadership, materials, and finances.

The classroom teacher will probably bear the major responsibility for integrating career education into the classroom. Since career education involves not one particular subject area, all teachers will be involved. Familiar techniques are used, including interview, research, discussion, bulletin boards, hands-on activities, field trips, learning centers, shadowing, internship, and simulation. Most of these are activity centered and can extend outside of the classroom. Counselors, parents, librarians, community persons, or retired people may be included in the teaching process in their specialty areas. The teacher plans the learning experience, but others may help carry it out. Teachers need to appreciate the value of these experiences, know of available resources, have planning time, and be certain that these activities enhance other learning activities. The teacher must understand that career education is not an additional subject but an emphasis and attitude to be interwoven into the existing curriculum. There is no set time limit, and no subjects need be dropped in order to include career education. Career education helps meet occupational needs of students while enhancing their knowledge in subject areas. This overlapping is the goal.

## Career Education Outcomes

Specific learner outcomes to be gained from career education were outlined in *An Introduction to Career Education, A Policy Paper of the U.S. Office of Education* by Kenneth B. Hoyt (1975, p. 11). Students leaving school (regardless of age or grade level) should be —

1. Competent in the basic academic skills required for adaptability in our rapidly changing society
2. Equipped with good work habits
3. Capable of choosing a personally meaningful set of work values that foster in them a desire to work
4. Equipped with career decision-making skills, job-hunting skills, and job-getting skills
5. Equipped with vocational personal skills at a level that will allow them to gain entry into and attain a degree of success in the occupational society
6. Equipped with career decisions based on the widest possible set of data concerning themselves and their educational-vocational opportunities
7. Aware of means available to them for continuing and recurrent education once they have left the formal system of schooling
8. Successful in being placed in a paid occupation, in further education, or in a vocation consistent with their current career education
9. Successful in incorporating work values into their total personal value structure in such a way that they are able to choose what, for them, is a desirable life-style

There are basic implications that follow these goals. Initial implementation of career education will not be expensive, but the complete reform of the system will be expensive. Additional funds will be needed for remedial and alternative educational systems. The single educational system that will follow will be less expensive and more beneficial in the long run. Education will no longer be isolated but will join forces with all other segments of society and provide a collaborative effort.

## Career Education Outlook

Evaluation study results have been received that indicate the benefits of career education. The most favorable results seem to apply to career education programs that have been in operation for the longest period of time. Evidence has been found of improved academic skills, improved work values, improved career decision-making skills, improved occupational and interpersonal skills, greater knowledge of educational/vocational opportunities, and an increase in students' sense of control over their lives. Evidence is usually on the positive side, but more studies must be done, and better evaluation techniques must be developed for a more complete picture.

The career education concept is still evolving. The developmental nature of career education means that studies are needed to determine its effectiveness. The particular career education treatment must also be evaluated.

Career education may experience setbacks because of incomplete acceptance by educators or incomplete understanding and implementation of its goals. Educators may only visualize it as being confined within school walls, and this would be a mistake. Professional jealousies or negotiation for funds might interfere. Career education, however, is a response to the life needs of individuals, advocated by individuals and groups from all areas of the population. It has demonstrated its acceptability as a direction for change to educators and the general public. If career education receives widespread application, it may answer the call for educational reform, which has been heard persistently around the United States.

## PROFESSIONAL ASSOCIATIONS

Individuals interested in securing more information regarding vocational and career education can contact the following organizations:

The American Association
of Career Education Coordinators
2952 Halifax Lane
Montgomery, Alabama 36116
Phone: 205-832-5085

American Vocational Association
2020 North 14th Street
Arlington, Virginia 22201

National Association for Career Education
The National Center for
Research in Vocational Education
Ohio State University
1960 Kenny Road
Columbus, Ohio 43210

## REFERENCES

Calhoun, Calfrey C., and Finch, Alton V.: *Vocational and Career Education: Concepts and Operations.* Belmont, Wadsworth Publishing Co., Inc., 1976.

Finn, Peter: Integrating career education into subject area classrooms. *The NAASP Bulletin, 62:*64-70, 1978.

Goldhammer, Keith, and Taylor, Robert E.: *Career Education: Perspective and Promise.* Columbus, Charles E. Merrill Publishing Co., 1972

Hoyt, Kenneth B.: *An Introduction to Career Education.* Policy paper of the U. S. Office of Education. Washington, D. C., U.S. Government Printing Office, 1975.

Marland, Sidney P., Jr.: Marland on career education. *American Education, 7:*25, 1971.

# Chapter 12

# COMMUNITY-BASED, LIFELONG EDUCATION

H. LARRY WINECOFF AND W. JACKSON LYDAY

*H LARRY WINECOFF is a professor of education at the University of South Carolina. Winecoff holds a master's degree in educational administration from the University of North Carolina, a doctorate in international relations education from New York University and has done post-doctoral work in community education through the University of Virginia. Winecoff is currently the associate director of the Center for Community Education Development at USC.*

*W. Jackson Lyday is an associate professor of education at the University of South Carolina. Lyday holds a master's degree and doctorate in curriculum and instruction from the University of North Carolina. He is the director of the Center for Community Education Development at USC and legislative chairperson for the S.C. PTA.*

*Lyday and Winecoff have been actively involved in community-based education for the past ten years and have published numerous articles in the areas of community, adult, continuing, and career education.*

## INTRODUCTION

In our rapidly changing, highly technical and mobile society, there is a tendency, as suggested by Alvin Toffler, Schumacher, and others, for the individual to feel alienated, frustrated, and powerless to control even the immediate environment. Having become accustomed to a relatively high standard of living, inexpensive power and fuel supplies, and a system of disposable goods, communities across the country are having difficulty in the 1980s adjusting to the economic, political, and ecological realities of a postindustrial society, which has challenged traditional systems, values, and life-styles.

The world of the eighties is far different from that envisioned in the dreams of world leaders only a few decades ago. While it is true that individual standards of living have increased at a steady and rapid rate, the quality of life has fluctuated dramatically and is today in what is perhaps one of the sharpest and lowest declines in recent history. We have only to scan the headlines of U.S. papers to grasp the impact of our plight:

— Corruption hits highest political office
— Crime rate doubles
— Vandalism hits new high
— Delinquency up 37 percent
— 100,000 senior citizens starving in the central city
— Hard drugs reach into the elementary school
— Gasoline prices to double again
— Police involved in syndicate pay-offs
— Half of all crimes go unreported
— Top officials involved in surveillance of over 75,000 U.S. citizens
— Neighborhood vigilante groups organize to protect their homes
— Inflation continues record climb
— Unemployment hits new high

Concern over excessive concentration of power, bigness, loss of control, and mistrust has caused governmental, educational, and business leaders at all levels to seek more effective, efficient ways of preparing both young and old to cope with ever-changing problems and of delivering human services to better meet community and individual needs. In this country the question is not so much where do we find the resources to solve the complex problems that face us, but rather, how do we effectively organize the multiresources we have to best solve these problems? Since the industrial revolution, the trend has been toward centralization and consolidation, toward bigness and mass production, and toward a government removed from the people. The anxieties and frustrations of today are gradually forcing the pendulum to begin moving in the opposite direction — away from ever-increasing growth and toward a concern for improving the quality of life for each individual and at an affordable price.

This implies a need to rethink priorities and procedures on the part of government, education, and business/industry and to provide for more local decision-making and input into the analysis and determination of change and growth as well as training programs. Such rethinking and reorganization must provide for more economical, better coordinated, more relevant, and accessible services to the potential client.

It is within this context that the two related concepts of community-based education and lifelong learning are making a resurgence as part of the formal educational system not only in the United States but in virtually all countries of the world.

There are, however, problems in defining, describing, and assessing the degree and impact of both community-based education and lifelong learning since by nature they are being adapted and applied in various forms and through different institutions and agencies in each community.

There is little doubt that both concepts are of major importance in public education today and are receiving considerable attention at every level — local, state, national, and international.

The purpose of this chapter is to examine the background and underlying philosophies of community-based education and lifelong learning; to review the parameters of the public school based movement in light of the social realities of the eighties; to identify major components, issues, and trends of the movements; and to examine implications these movements have on the training of educators and other human service delivery personnel.

Most community-based and lifelong educational programs have grown out of necessity rather than out of a systematic planning process. As local communities have attempted to improve the quality of life for citizens of all ages, community institutions have been brought into the process and charged with an educative, training, and, often, a problem-solving function.

Both community-based education and lifelong learning are elusive terms to which an infinite number of definitions and interpretations have been ascribed. Primitive societies first engaged in a process of lifelong, community-based education for survival long before formal institutions were established. As educational institutions have evolved, matured, and become formalized, the sense of education designed to meet local community needs for all citizens has often been bypassed as a common organizing or philosophical basis. Educational institutions at all levels are, and have long been, criticized for being too far removed from the "real world" community, for remaining aloof from the social problems of the day, and for practicing elitism in client selection and/or treatment. The complex and frustrating social and economic problems of the latter half of this century are forcing established institutions to respond or are generating new, more responsive institutions to more nearly assist in meeting community needs, wants, and interests.

It is safe to say that lifelong, community-based education has been prevalent since man began developing organized social patterns. Since that time, however, it is virtually impossible to trace the threads of the movements into this century. It could be argued that the first Massachusettes School Act established schools in this country that were fully responsive to community needs of both youth and adults. It can be debated that the Land Grant Colleges were the first formally established adult, community-based institutions designed to extend the learning process for large numbers of adults. The multipurpose "little red school house," which served as a community center providing a wide range of academic, social, and welfare needs, might be called the first community school.

In subsistence or primitive societies, education is, of necessity, informal and based on personal and group survival. Such an approach is probably the purest form of lifelong, community-based education. When a community develops a surplus economy, time can then be allocated to the development or improvement of skills and knowledge during leisure hours. Thus, as education evolves from a means of survival toward an end unto itself, it becomes more highly formalized and gradually moves away from primarily responding to the survival needs of a community.

The degree to which educational agencies and institutions respond to community needs is generally related directly to a combination of at least two factors: basic survival and crisis or threats to community security. Periods of high economic well-being generate a greater abundance of leisure time and, hence, the ability of a society to support education on a more abstract, philosophical level, which often is not directly related to immediate survival. An economic decline forces education into a partnership with its community in search of means for recovery. The curriculum is turned more toward occupational, job-related, and economic factors that have practical, immediate application rather than to the liberal and fine arts.

The industrial revolution illustrates this fluctuation of education in relation to the economy. In the early years of the revolution, education was survival-oriented and limited to a few years of formal schooling for the lower class while the academy served the upper class with a liberal arts curriculum. As the surplus of goods grew and fewer man hours were required for production, new forms of educational institutions emerged to replace the academy. The emergence of Benjamin Franklin's juntas, the formation of learned societies, and the Chataugua-type conference centers marked the beginning of an expanded mission for education in the twentieth century. Perhaps the most notable and permanent result of this new thrust was the American high school with its expanded role in occupational training.

The economic-educational relationship is subject, however, to other influences, particularly those of local or national security. For example the United States during the late fifties was involved in the aftermath of a war economy with production still high in response to national and international postwar demands as well as the requirements of the Korean conflict. Education was enjoying a period of perhaps the greatest degree of public support in its history with the children of the baby boom and returning veterans filling the classrooms. The public enjoyed education and made relatively few hard-nosed, practical demands during the fifties as the pendulum swung away from the tight community survival needs of the World War II years.

It was in the midst of this public "love affair" with education that what has been described as one of the world's most meaningful and relevant audiovisual aids appeared in the skies as Russia launched Sputnik. Almost overnight the educational world responded to a national crisis with a practical, applied arts curriculum emphasizing science, math, and foreign languages in an effort to regain a primary position of world power.

In the broadest sense of the term, all education is community-based. The degree to which an educational agency or institution responds to community needs, interests, and concerns is determined not only by the philosophical orientation of the institution but also by the prevailing economic climate and unpredictable crisis situations, particularly those related to local or national security.

## DEFINITION, CHARACTERISTICS, AND COMPONENTS

Lifelong, community-based education is a concept or movement rather than a specific program; it is more nearly a philosophical premise than it is a well-defined operational procedure or organizational pattern.

As we enter the eighties, the definition of terms in the field of education oriented toward community needs has grown increasingly more complex and at times confusing. There has been a rather large number of distinct community-based educational movements in this and other countries during the last decade, and it appears that the list is steadily growing.

The nature of lifelong, community-based education, based as it is *on* each community, makes a universal definition inappropriate and probably undesirable. There are, however, a number of common characteristics that most efforts exhibit:

1.  It is *process oriented.* The process of community involvement in all phases of operation is a critical element. The direct active participation of community members in the decision-making process gives each community its own opportunity as well as challenge to define and delineate its own efforts.

2.  It involves *collaborative decision-making* among all of the partners involved in the process. This will include community members and school personnel in collaboration with other agencies and organizations that serve that community (social services, churches, PTA, cooperative extension, adult education, League of Women Voters, mental health, public health, recreation, and the like).

3.  It requires a *continuous assessment* of individual and community needs, wants, concerns, and interests through comprehensive assessment techniques that directly involve those to be served.

4.  Its *programming* is based *on* the concept of *community*, through which a healthy sense of belonging, self-sufficiency, and purpose can evolve; its programming is based *in* the community so as to be readily accessible to all residents and its programming is *for* the community to meet its own identified needs, interests, concerns, or wants.

5.  It is a process that *actively involves* large segments of the commu-

nity in the total educational process, which includes the regular kindergarten through twelfth grade program as well as afternoon, evening, weekend, adult, continuing, leisure, and life skills and other programs or activities. Active involvement means sharing in the decision-making, developmental, planning, implementation, and evaluation aspects; it is far more than simple participation as a learner, teacher, or resource person.

6. It has as a goal the satisfaction of both *individual* and *community* interests and needs — ultimately an improvement in the quality of life through a true sense of community.

7. It is *lifelong* and *recurring* based on the premise that education is not confined to a set number of years but rather is needed throughout every phase of our lives as we encounter new challenges, new feelings, and new problems.

8. It requires both *speed* and *flexibility* in responding to changing community needs (a rapid, immediate response at the critical time when the need is most pressing, current, or important) and flexibility in *timing* (time of day, day of week), *location* (to be most accessible), *delivery mode* (lectures, discussion meetings, problem-solving groups, films, TV, etc., whatever is most appropriate to the situation), and *type of response* (one-time service, service with follow-up, formal, or informal education programs, counseling, and the like.)

9. It requires the direct involvement, and thus coordination, of all community agencies and organizations involved in the delivery of human services.

There are a number of somewhat distinct programs that exhibit many of these characteristics and that might be considered as lifelong and community-based. Movements such as adult education, citizen education, life skills education, career education, continuing education, leisure education, and recurrent education are just a few of the many programs that fall into this category. However, perhaps the fastest growing concept at the public school level that most nearly meets all of the above characteristics is what is commonly referred to as *community education*.

## THE CONCEPT — COMMUNITY EDUCATION

### An Island Apart

Many schools are like little islands set apart from the mainland of life by a deep moat of convention and tradition. Across this moat there is a drawbridge which is lowered at certain periods during the day in order that the part-time inhabitants may cross over to the island in the morning and back to the mainland at night. Why do these young people go out to the island? They go there in order to learn how to live on the mainland (Carr, 1942, p. 35 as cited in Cook, 1977, p. 1).

The concept of community education has been expressed in a variety of ways. There is no monolithic, carved in stone definition. Rather there exists probably as many definitions as ways in which the concept has been implemented. For the purpose of this writing, however, the following descriptions seem sufficient to introduce the reader to its general nature.

Jack Minzey has stated that "Community Education is a philosophical concept which serves the entire community by providing for all of the educational needs of all of its members. It uses the local school to serve as a catalyst for bringing community resources to bear on community problems in an effort to develop a positive sense of community, improve community living and develop the community process toward the end of self-actualization" (Minzey, 1972, p. 19).

In 1968, the National Community School Education Association surmised that . . . "community education is a comprehensive and dynamic approach to public education. It is a philosophy that pervades all segments of education programming and directs the thrust of each of them towards the needs of the community. . . . It affects all children, youth and adults directly or it helps to create an atmosphere and environment in which all men find security and self-confidence, thus enabling them to grow and mature in a community which sees its schools as an integral part of community life" (NCSEA, 1968, p. 6).

Van Voorhees said community education results in "a process whereby communities become involved in their own problems and needs. It does not do things for people but through people . . . a process that is continuous and changing over the life span of a community's efforts and somewhat different in every community" (Van Voorhees, 1968, p.3).

According to Baas, "community education is a concept based on a process of education for children, youth, and adults. The process refers to the organization of the community into appropriate size units to facilitate interaction, identification of local resources, and involvement of people in the solution of their own problems and the problems of the community. It is an effort to capture a sense of community without eliminating its pluralism" (Baas, 1973, p.2).

Finally, the Community Education Office in the U.S. Department of Education considers community education "as a process of people in the community coming together in a public facility to discuss their needs, interests, and problems. They devise solutions to fit these needs, using locally available resources and skills. It is people working together in a group which is small enough for them to identify with: the community. As a group they accomplish what they cannot do as individuals" (National Community Education Advisory Council, 1980, p.3).

While each expression is somewhat unique, the essence of each is the same: Community education is an avenue for helping people identify and resolve their own needs and problems. The primary agent in facilitating the concept has been the local school.

## Historical Development of Community Education

The development of community education has been an evolutionary process. Many forces — cultural, social, educational, recreational, and others — contributed to the contemporary concept of community education. Thorough histories of community education have been written (Cook, 1977) for the purview of the consumer if he or she chooses to research it, however, the purpose here is to provide a condensed version of that history, to highlight those major historical data that bear on community education as it is perceived today.

Community education began in this country as early as 1642 when the State of Massachusetts mandated compulsory education with the passage of the Act of 1642. The school in this era became a center for community activity. Social events, community meetings, and even religious services were normal occurrences in the school environment.

Revoked colonial charters and Indian wars took their toll on the development of public education, and subsequently private schools and academies came into existence but placed little emphasis on community education. Church and denominational schools stressed separation of church and state, and laws restricted the use of public school property. These conditions stymied the growth of community education. By the middle 1800s, however, some eleven states (Indiana and others) had passed legislation supporting the extended use of school facilities.

The Civil War had a negative impact on education generally and community education was no exception. However, toward the end of the nineteenth century and the early twentieth century a number of very significant forces gave impetus to community education. One was the Chautauga movement, begun in 1874, which clearly supported the idea of education for the total community, not just the young. Another was the establishment of settlement houses in New York City and Hull House in Chicago in which opportunities existed for creating new learning and recreational programs among the underpriviledged. In 1902 the social center movement promoted the integration of school and community with John Dewey as its major spokesman. He believed that schools must become embryonic communities, active with the type occupations that reflect the life of the larger society and permeated with the spirit of art, history, and science (Dewey, 1949, p.27).

Community-based educational programs continued to expand in the early 1900s through agricultural programs financed by federal funds. Enactment of the Smith Lever Act of 1914 provided funds for education through county extension services, such as county agents. The Smith-Hughes Act, passed in 1917, granted money to high schools for the first time to be used for vocational classes. The passage of this act enabled school administrators to offer vocational, agricultural, home economics, and trade courses as part of the curriculum.

In the 1920s three specific community-related thrusts occurred that were to have great impact on community education. In 1929 Elsie Clapp began what has come to be known as the first community school (Ballard) in Louisville, Kentucky. Secondly, the implementation of John Dewey's idea of relating learning to the environment complemented the community education movement. "Learning certainly, but living primarily, and learning through and in relation to this living" (Seay, 1974). This theory influenced educators to plan community-oriented curriculums. A third and perhaps most important factor, the Great Depression, ironically became a plus for community education. To ease the impact of the Depression, the federal government sponsored programs to provide jobs and training for people to help themselves. Projects such as Tennessee Valley Authority not only provided jobs, but developed unique learning experiences for community members (Seay, 1974). Other government funded programs during the Depression years were the Civilian Conservation Corps, Works Progress Administration, Public Works Administration, and Federal Emergency Relief Administration. These programs, too, provided training, jobs, and even recreational activities and put the community education concept into practice, often through the use of local advisory planning boards (Seay, p.72).

Following the 20s a most significant event took place in Flint, Michigan: the development of the first urban community education model. By 1936 about fifteen centers were operating there, and Flint has served, with support from the Charles S. Mott Foundation, as the lighthouse of the movement since that time.

Berridge states in summary that "The period from 1900 through the early 1930s was significant in the later development of community schools and community education. Writers of this period advocated the marriage of education and community. For the first time the importance of the child's environment was discussed in relationship to his total education" (Berridge in Hickey, 1969). Community education growth was interrupted by World War II, but by the 1950s, it was expanding once again. Unemployment, new technology, and interrupted education all gave impetus to communities developing educational programs for all ages.

In the 1960s the federal government passed many acts that promoted the growth of community education. Most of this *Great Society* legislation was concerned with improving education for the economically deprived. In 1962 the Manpower Development and Training Act was passed to train unemployed persons for jobs. In 1963 and 1968 the vocational education acts were passed to update the 1917 laws on vocational education. The Elementary and Secondary Act of 1965 (with amendments in 1968 and 1970) covered the funding of a number of programs that impacted the life of the total community. The Adult Education Act of 1966 placed the Office of Economic Opportunity under the Office of Education with the stipulation that provisions be made for literacy training and adult basic education. The Vocational Rehabilitation Act of 1967 provided training opportunities for persons to secure and maintain employment (Cook, 1977). Obviously there were many other bills passed during this period with as much or even greater impact, but suffice it to say, it was a very important decade for furthering the idea that school and the community were integrally tied to the educational process.

The 1970s ushered in many changes in community education at the national level. One was the endorsement of community education by many national groups, such as the PTA, national board of directors of the Jaycees, and National League of Cities. Also the National Community School Education Association changed its name to the National Community Education Association to "emphasize the total community orientation rather than the much more limited lighted schoolhouse idea earlier associated with the community school concept" (Olsen and Clark, 1977, p.70).

In 1971 the *Community Education Journal* was first published, and significant legislative steps were taken. The Community School Development Act, part of the 1974 amendments to the Elementary and Secondary Education Act, was passed by Congress in 1973 and signed by President Gerald Ford on August 21, 1974. This federal legislation made funds available to (1) assist local public school systems in implementing Community Education, (2) to train Community Education personnel, and (3) to disseminate information on the community education concept and to establish a National Advisory Council. In 1978 this was followed by the Community Schools and Comprehensive Community Education Act (Porter, edited by Kaplan, 1975).

Since 1974 growth in community education has been phenomenal. Currently leadership in the federal government is provided by the Office of Community Education, established in 1975 within the U.S. Office of Education. Also the Community Education Clearinghouse and the National Community Education Association provide leadership and material dissemination on the national level. Other data indicative of the status of community education today include the following:

Nearly ten thousand Community Schools in over 700 school districts are in some stage of community education development

Fifteen to twenty states (eight to ten with funding) have or are considering community education legislation

The "greying" of America is being reflected in increased educational programming for older Americans

Increasing state dollar commitments, for example North Carolina — 3 million dollars and Alaska — about 2.5 million, in community education this year.

Professional organizations also played a major role in the development of community education. There is now a strong network of over forty state associations and a National Community Education Association (NCEA) that has played a major role in the development of community education across the country.

Also there is an international community education association that was founded to promote and foster the growth of community education worldwide. Its membership now represents among others Austrialia, England, Mexico, New Zealand, Portugul, Fiji, and the U.S.A. This association will play an increasingly significant role as countries around the world embrace the concept of community education. Evidence of the international expansion of community education can be seen in the fact that with the support of Partners of the Americas, the Organization of American States, the Mott Foundation, and private contributions, three inter-American community education conferences have been held (1976, 1978, 1980) involving representatives from more than twenty-two U.S. states and sixteen Caribbean, Central, and South American countries. An inter-American center for community education development was established in the Washington, D.C. Partners of the Americas Office in 1979. Subsequently a Brazilian national center for community education development was established in 1980 with two additional centers planned: one in Spanish-speaking South America and one in Central America or the Caribbean.

This section has provided only a brief historical overview of the emerging concept of community education. Because of the wide range of programs, events, and legislation that contributed to the growth of the movement, one might still ask, exactly what is included in the concept of community education?

## Major Components

Authors vary somewhat in their idea of the basic components of community education, but Kaplan, after an extensive review of the literature, suggests that most authorities agree that community education includes the following six basic elements:

Community Organization and Development
Utilizing Community in Kindergarten Through Twelfth Grade Programs
Citizens Involvement and Participation
Interagency Coordination, Cooperation, and Collaboration
Lifelong Learning and Enrichment Programs
Expanded Use of School Facilities Community Schools-Community Centers

## Community Organization and Development

A primary underlying principle of community education is that of helping community residents to identify and solve local problems with available resources. This process involves community organization, development of leadership and problem-solving skills, identification of community needs, as well as coordination of resources. Most authorities agree that the ultimate goal of community education is the improvement and enhancement of individual and community life.

## Utilizing Community in Kindergarten Through Twelfth Grade

This feature of community education directly impacts the kindergarten through twelfth grade program by involving community resources in regular school programs. This might take the form, among other things, of bringing in volunteers from the community, utilizing speakers, having field trips, or perhaps even utilizing materials contributed to the instructional programs. Coordination is traditionally done by a community school coordinator with substantial input from the community school advisory council as well as with individual teachers.

### Citizen Involvement and Participation

This is a very broad feature of community education. It includes community participation through such things as advisory councils, volunteer programs, and afternoon and evening programs and serves to give community persons (parents and nonparents) a sense of ownership in the schools.

### Interagency Coordination, Cooperation, and Collaboration

This component encourages the most effective and efficient use of community resources in meeting community needs. Duplication of services is minimized as the school and other agencies in the community design and deliver programs collaboratively, often at the local school level.

### Lifelong Learning and Enrichment

Schools remain open in the afternoons, evenings, weekends, and summers to serve the learning needs of all ages and groups. Offerings typically include a wide variety of courses, skill training, enrichment academics, recreation, social events, and community development activities.

### Expanded Use of School Facilities

School buildings, gyms, and playgrounds are potentially available twenty-four hours a day, seven days a week, fifty-two weeks a year for community use. In this model, the traditional academic program for the young remains a very important use of the facility but by no means the only one. The facility rather becomes accessible to many human service agencies that cooperatively provide a wide variety of services, activities, and programs.

These components are complementary in many ways and in sum provide a process for individual and community development with the local school serving the primary facilitative role.

## TRENDS AND ISSUES

Today (1981) American public education is experiencing what is perhaps its lowest level of public support in this century. The public schools are not only being vociferously questioned by the press, but they are also being sternly called to task through the courts over issues ranging from teacher dismissal and student discipline procedures to a lack of desegregation, a lack of relevance, and an inability to adequately teach basic academic and life skills. Every indicator points to more legal entanglements in the coming years. The rapid growth of teacher's unions and more aggressive teacher's associations have added to the likelihood of tougher negotiations and massive strikes or walkouts over the coming years.

A number of other factors are directly influencing public education today:

The traditional school-aged population (six to eighteen years) is declining.

The older population (forty-five and older) is increasing (as people live longer) numerically and gaining proportionately in political power (individuals with no public school aged children).

Over half of the adult population regularly engages in some form of continuing education.

Most adults will change jobs at least three times (often requiring major retraining).

Technology is changing more rapidly every year and consequently requiring regular retraining for both worker and consumer.

Single parent families are becoming more prevalent as are families with both parents working (both require extended child care/educational services).

The shortened work week and/or flex-work time has made longer periods of nonwork time available to families and individuals.

Such complex and perplexing problems faced by the public schools have caused an alarming number of citizens to abandon public education, especially in our larger cities. This movement away from public education was summed up by the president of the National Congress of Parents and Teachers when she said in 1975 that "the schools no longer belong to us." Thus, public schools are today facing one of their major challenges. They are being required by law and mandate to expand their range of operations and services while budgets are being frozen or reduced. Simply stated the public schools must be revitalized to assure the citizenry that they are relevant and capable of carrying out their primary mission of education for the world of today and tomorrow.

Colleges and universities are faring little better. They are under attack for graduating students who do not seem to possess basic life and job skills, for remaining aloof from the reality of community, state, national, and international problems, for producing more professional and white-collar workers than there are openings, and for failing to provide communities, business, and government with assistance needed to cope with the complex problems of the eighties. The violent student protests of the late sixties and early seventies have given way to more subtle unrest as students struggle to become employable.

If public schools and institutions of higher education are to regain a position of high public support, they must continue to develop alternative approaches to program improvement that are both lifelong and community-based. The dilemma in which our society and our public schools find themselves paradoxically holds great potential for revitalizing the educational process. What is required are relevant program modifications; bold, creative leadership; and a building of trust among communities and schools. Collaborative relationships, both in spirit and through formal programs, aimed at joint, mutually beneficial efforts to solve pressing social problems and to improve the quality of life of all citizens, seem mandated by public reaction and economic necessity. Such a thrust can be made if training programs in community-based education and human service delivery are redesigned to better reflect the need for cooperative relationships among agency personnel and reflect the growing need for providing lifelong, continuing education for all citizens.

## MANDATE FOR TRAINING

Recent congressional actions exhibit a national concern for lifelong, community-based educational programs as does legislation in many states calling attention to the need for a coordinated national, state, and local effort that can maximize the fragmented efforts of varied human resources and minimize the cost to the individual and the state.

Lifelong, community-based education is not a new concept. Where it is operational it is a total, integrated educational delivery system that encompasses all physical and human elements in the community in a planned, organized, and coordinated program.

There is evidence that the nature of work and the increasing mobility of people in society are creating new demands for intellectual, technical, and interpersonal skills. This demand is intensified by increasing life expectancy, which will require structured and informal creative avocational and leisure pursuits.

The absence of coordinated efforts to meet this wide range of human needs can result in competition and overlapping and fragmented activities at the state and community levels. Such unplanned outcomes of legitimate activities may also create need gaps of a significant nature.

A coordinated program of lifelong, community-based and community-centered education is a rational mechanism to meet the wide range of human needs. However, such coordination must be accomplished in a context that recognizes the unique role of existing institutions, agencies, and groups, and it will require leadership competencies that are not now being developed in most present educational training programs.

Therefore, it is essential that staff development and training programs be redesigned so that individuals can be trained to provide expertise in the planning and coordination of all community-based educational programs. Programmatic and interpersonal skills must be commensurate with the responsibility to coordinate such distinct but related activities conducted by and under the auspices of various groups, such as public schools, social and health agencies, recreation agencies, fraternal and religious groups, civic organizations, trade associations, business and industrial firms, unions, and professional associations.

Few existing training programs have components that prepare personnel to develop and manage community-based programs. Some exceptions to this are community education and continuing education but even here the majority of course work is in areas such as school administration rather than specific management training or collaborative planning and decision-making. This is not at all surprising since lifelong, community-based education programs, at least in the formal sense, are relatively new on a national and international scale.

The time, then, seems opportune for leaders in this broad movement to explore new and different training options that are community-based themselves and that model collaboration so that feelings of territoriality and competition are reduced and delivery of services can be accomplished in a cost-efficient and cost-effective manner to all citizens.

The model explored here is one attempt to answer this need. In this approach full collaboration and coordination is required from three primary "communities": the professional community (associations such as adult and community educators, secondary and elementary principals, school superintendents, teachers, school boards, social, health, and recreation workers, and the like); the geographic community, (state departments and agencies, etc.); and the college or university community. Each of these components has specific functions within the training model.

The professional community has the responsibility of specifying minimum generic and specialized competencies that persons must possess to be qualified to serve in a leadership role in these community-based areas. Through this mechanism, training objectives could be constantly updated and would accurately reflect current training needs.

The geographic community has the responsibility of specifying educative needs that are above and beyond the training requirements set by the professional community. This ensures that unique local needs as well as standards are met through the training model.

The role of the college or university is to engineer or orchestrate an educational delivery system that produces qualified persons according to professional and local community specifications. Central to this higher education role is the design of training programs that foster the development of the necessary skills and competencies as set forth by both professional and local communities. A second function is to monitor participant progress within the program and to assure quality in terms of participants. A third function, and one of key importance, is to assure that minimum standards (such as those set by the various accrediting agencies) are adhered to within the training program. Fourthly, the college or university would assume the responsibility of providing quality assurance and quality control in the training process.

Having suggested a way of organizing for training community-based education leaders, it seems appropriate to explore what the content of such a program might look like. Is there, indeed, sufficient commonality in terms of the training needs of managerial personnel among the various community-based activities to warrant an integrated training program? Community-based education leaders in several states have responded in the affirmative. Generally the following broad competency areas should provide the nucleus of such an integrated program:

Program Development
Program Management, Supervision and Evaluation
Instruction
Human Relations and Communications
Student Development Services
Professionalism

Leaders in community-based areas must be able to develop programs based on community needs. To do this they must be able to assess community needs, which requires skills in selecting appropriate needs assessment strategies, in actually conducting a comprehensive assessment and in making some order from the data once it is collected. Also, using the data, the manager must be able to establish priority needs, to derive program goals and objectives, to design a program plan, including evaluation, and to develop an implementation schedule.

Proper budgeting is another skill that the manager must possess. This requires the ability to select a budget system and components therein consistent with institutional and program requirements. He/she must also be skilled in budget negotiation.

One skill area that seems to be increasingly important in program development is grantsmanship. Outside monies from federal, state, and foundation sources have become essential to many programs. Briefly, some specific skills that are important here are the ability to locate funding sources appropriate to program goals, to write a fundable proposal, and to successfully submit and negotiate a grant request.

Equally important as program development is program management. Of the skills needed for successful program management, staff selection and development is perhaps most critical. This generally includes the ability to assess program needs, match these with qualified staff while assessing staff needs and designing training experiences based on the assessed needs. All of this, of course, would need to be accomplished within given policy and operational parameters of the institutions involved.

Supervision is another vital function of the community-oriented manager. He/she must be able to design and carry out a comprehensive supervisory program for all personnel. Being able to assess and improve individual and group performance toward personal and institutional goals is a key subskill in demonstrating effectiveness in this competency area.

Needless to say, the ability to organize, implement, and evaluate various programs is the nucleus of the program management component. Staffing, facilities management, materials, and equipment use are only a few examples of skills that leaders should have in order to operate a successful program.

Another general area of competency required to manage a community-based program is instruction. Briefly, the manager should be expected to have a working knowledge of such things as basic principles of curriculum construction, various instructional methods, delivery modes, alternative learning activities, and evaluation strategies. Also an understanding of youth and adult learning theory and various approaches to classroom organization will help the manager be more effective.

Little mention has been made so far of the need for the manager to be able to design appropriate developmental experiences for his clients. He must have a knowledge of basic principles of growth and development and the ability to help students make viable choices personally and professionally.

Human relations and communication is another key area in the training program. In this component competence would be developed in such things as interpersonal relations, institution/community relations, and group processes and procedures. This would include the ability to establish, train, and help maintain advisory councils, to develop and maintain a good public information program, and to engineer interagency cooperation. Also in this component the manager would develop basic group process skills and demonstrate the ability to work effectively with persons and groups of differing cultural backgrounds.

Finally, the trainee must be able to plan and carry out a program for his own self-improvement in order to keep relevant and current. This will include the ability to renew his philosophical positions, to update his knowledge of changes and innovations in the field, and generally to develop consistency between his beliefs, values, and attitudes and his professional behavior.

Although the list of competencies being briefly summarized here is certainly not as exhaustive nor detailed as it might be, the idea is that generally these competencies would be applicable to leaders in all community-based, lifelong learning programs. Each participant in the training program would be expected to master each of the competencies according to criteria established by the professional, geographic, and institutional communities. This task of developing these criteria is currently underway in many communities and promises to be one of the more difficult stages in the development of the training program. Also realizing that there are some unique skills and competencies required in perhaps each of the community-oriented activities being considered, ways are being explored so that program participants might specialize in one of the particular areas. This would, of course, require mastery of additional competencies beyond those generic competencies listed previously in this chapter.

Finally, it should be noted that the growth of this phenomenon of community-oriented education has been so rapid that a great need already exists for retraining. Persons in many different positions and community agencies find themselves in roles that call for skills related to assessing and resolving community problems and need additional training that promotes the development of these skills.

Since the growth of community-based, lifelong learning is currently so fragmented and broad-based, a real need exists for persons working in the field to be aware of and able to coordinate training efforts with learning activities other than those in his/her own primary area. It is anticipated that much of the instruction in the training program would be done in the field by adjunct faculty (field professionals) who are on the cutting edge of the movement. Not only does this approach increase relevance in the instructional program, but it also would provide more flexibility in terms of time, place, and content of training sessions, therefore, significantly improving the quality and time of response to expressed training needs.

In this chapter an attempt has been made to give the reader some insight into the need for, indeed the demand for, lifelong, community-based education. A brief history of the evolution of the movement has been provided, and one illustration of the concept, namely community education, has been described along with current issues and trends that will help shape future development. Implications for training were presented and a generic training model was discussed.

It would appear that as the eighties begin, local, state, and national needs and problems will provide more impetus for the development and expansion of lifelong, community-based education facilitated through the public schools.

## PROFESSIONAL ASSOCIATIONS

National Community Education Association
1201 16th Street, N.W.
Suite 305
Washington, D.C. 20036
(202) 466-3530

International Association of Community Educators
14th Level, Nauru House
80 Collins Street
Melbourne 3000, Australia

National Center for Community Education
1017 Avon Street
Flint, Michigan 48503
(313) 238-0463

## REFERENCES

Baas, Alan M.: *Community Schools.* Educational Management Review Series, #24, December 1973.
Boone, E.J., Dolan, R.J., and Shearon, R.W.: *Programming in Cooperative Extension Service — A Conceptual Schema.*
Cook, Nancy Cassity: *The Historical Basis for Community Education: A National and South Carolina Perspective.* Unpublished doctoral dissertation, University of

South Carolina, 1977.

COPE: *Career Education Module for Education 620.* Columbia, South Carolina, University of South Carolina (Mimeographed), 1975.

Dave, R.H.: *Foundations of Lifelong Education.* Bimsford, New York, Pergamon Press, 1976.

Decker, Larry E.: *Foundations of Community Education.* Midland, Michigan, Pendell, 1972.

Dewey, John: *The School and Society.* Chicago, University of Chicago Press, 1949.

Dobbs, Ralph C.: Leisure as a component. *Lifelong Learning: The Adult Years,* November 1977.

Hesburgh, Theodore M., Miller, Paul A., and Wharton, Clifton R., Jr.: *Patterns for Lifelong Learning.* San Francisco, California, Jossey-Bass Publishers, 1973.

Hickey, Howard W., and Van Voorhees, Curtis: *The Role of the School in Community Education.* Midland, Michigan, Pendell, 1969.

Kaplan, Michael H. (Ed.): Public schools: Use them don't waste them. In Porter, Sylvia: *Your Money's Worth.* Charlottesville, Virginia, Mid-Atlantic Center for Community Education, 1975.

Keppel, Frederick P.: Education for adults and other essays. New York, Columbia University Press, 1926. Freeport, New York, Books for Libraries Press, Inc., 1968.

Knowles, Malcolm: *The Adult Learner: A Neglected Species.* Houston, Gulf Publishing Company, 1973.

Learning opportunities for adults. Participation in adult education, 1977. *Organization for Economic Cooperation and Development,* Vol. IV.

Minzey, Jack D., and LeFarte, Clyde: *Community Education: From Program to Process.* Midland, Michigan, Pendell, 1972.

Ohliger, John: *Introduction to Adult Education: Syllabus for Education 672.* Columbus, Ohio, Ohio State University (mimeographed).

Olsen, Edward B., and Clark, Phillip A.: *Life-Centering Education.* Midland, Michigan, Pendell, 1977.

Rosenthal, Edward L.: Lifelong learning: For some of the people. *Lifelong Learning: The Adult Years,* December 1978.

Schumacher, E.F.: *Good Work.* New York, Harper & Row, 1979.

Schumacher, E.F.: *Small is Beautiful.* New York, Harper & Row, 1973.

Seay, Maurice: *Community Education: A Developing Concept.* Midland, Michigan, Pendell, 1974.

Skager, R., and Dave, R.H.: *Curriculum Evaluation for Lifelong Education.* Bimsford, New York, Pergamon Press, 1977.

The National Community Education Advisory Council: *Community Education: The Federal Role.* Hunter, Utah, Bill Woodruff Company, 1980.

Toffler, Alvin: *The Third Wave,* New York, William Morrow & Company, 1980.

Yarrington, Roger: *Lifelong Education Trends in Community Colleges.* American Association for Community and Junior Colleges, 1978.

# Chapter 13

# CITIZEN PARTICIPATION IN EDUCATION

MARY C. JACKSON AND MARY HOUSE KESSLER, PH.D.

*MARY C. JACKSON is currently the director of the School Advisory Council Assistance Project at the College of Education, University of South Carolina. She has worked extensively over the past four years to design and implement training programs for educational personnel and citizens associated with school advisory councils. Her previous experience includes that of a classroom teacher, school psychologist, and coordinator of leadership training with the Project.*
*Mary House Kessler, Ph.D., is a teaching associate in the College of Education at the University of South Carolina. She is the coordinator of publications and materials development for the School Advisory Council Assistance Project. Prior to this position, she was an assistant professor in the College of Education at the University of Hawaii-Manoa.*

## HISTORICAL OVERVIEW

The United States has historically represented itself as a nation committed to citizen participation in governmental decision-making. The themes of citizen participation have varied from simple citizen support to full citizen control. Thomas Jefferson laid theoretical foundations of citizen participation and shaped the entire democratic system as the principal author of the Declaration of Independence. Jefferson believed in the "common man" and fiercely defended the concepts of free schools, popular self-government, equal representation in legislatures, and a general hierarchy of republics working together to preserve the worth of all individuals. Consequently, the Jeffersonian perspective has become virtually synonymous with the American democratic system of governance (Walker, 1978).

The modern precept of citizen participation emerged as a result

The authors thank Mrs. Kathleen Taggart, staff assistant of the School Advisory Council Assistance Project at the College of Education, University of South Carolina, for her patience and diligence in the preparation of this chapter.

of industrialization, urbanization, growth of government and business, and improved technology. The traditional notions and theories addressing citizen participation have been revised to reflect a more realistic view of the ordinary or common man. Jefferson's "ideal" citizen has been characterized as an individual caught up in an urbanized, mass society with a passive view of the participatory function (Walker, 1978). Further, there seems to be no prescriptive solution to how people can best cope with the responsibilities of citizenship given the complex demands of modern society. The role of citizens in government has become a critical theme that contemporary American policymakers have judicially and cautiously debated. The need to expand the opportunities for individuals to influence and participate in administrative decision-making has become an arena for reform that features citizen participation as the main attraction.

The Advisory Commission on Intergovernmental Relations cites three differing but interrelated movements that perpetuated the evolution of citizen participation in modern government: (1) a continuing effort to expand the suffrage, (2) perennial drives beginning in the 1820s to "reform" the political processes by which candidates are nominated, and (3) recurring efforts to expand direct popular control of governments (Walker, 1978). From these movements came written legislation and policy that eventually gave practical meaning to Jefferson's thoughts of popular sovereignty, political equality, minority privilege, and individual rights. Most importantly, these movements expanded the electorate and provided a stage for active political reform.

The growth of government also aided the citizen participation movement in the United States. The call for improved bureaucratic competence and accountability resulted in decentralization and the creation of dozens of commissions to oversee governmental service efforts. The advent of increased citizen participation resulted as a response to failing administrative accountability mechanisms. The merit system, professionalism, and improved personnel classification schemes all failed to produce a more accountable public service. Instead, the combination of expanding government services, civil service coverage, delegation of discretionary authority by legislatures, and the loss of executive powers over agencies heightened the public's demand for new mechanisms of administrative accountability. Government was increasingly viewed as self-perpetuating, self-serving, wasteful, and generally exempt from public scrutiny. Public skepticism replaced public faith in the government's ability to respond effectively and efficiently to society's needs. As a result, two reform efforts were initiated: (1) improved political participation designed to strengthen the executive and legislative branches' control over the public service through the vote and (2) increased direct citizen participation in and control over administrative processes (Walker, 1978).

The first approach strengthened executive management by allowing the popularly elected chief executive to effectively discharge administrative duties. Legislatures responded through "sunset" legislation, legislative vetos, improved committee staffing, tougher and more strenous control of administrative procedures, ethics legislation, "sunshine" laws, and increased oversight activity.

The second approach, citizen participation and control of administration processes, was grounded in the notion that even the most responsive elected officials cannot consistently find the time, motivation, or staff to mount a sustained administrative oversight/accountability effort. There were feelings that the increased authority afforded the chief executives could also be abused without proper accountability controls (Walker, 1978). In other words, the cure could be deadly without certain prescriptive precautions!

The two interpretations merge in practice in that legislatures and chief executives must establish through law or policy the directives that set forth citizen participation opportunities and responsibilities. Basically, these directives take two forms. The first form is that of general procedural acts to facilitate citizen access to information and review of administrative accountability in the planning and implementation of programs. The second form is that of specific enabling legislation or statutes that require agencies or jurisdictions to establish citizen participation programs (Rosenbaum, 1976).

Federal initiatives in the form of legislation have greatly expanded and aided citizen participation efforts. The Federal Administrative Procedures Act of 1946 followed by subsequent amendments, supplemented by state and local enactments, the Freedom of Information Act (1966) and the National Environmental Policy Act (1969) all represent major legislative steps to formally mandate citizen participation involvement in administrative decision-making (Rosenbaum, 1976).

## Conclusion

The evolution of citizen participation in American government is a pluralistic collection of both liberal and conservative perspectives. The increased emphasis on practical applications of Jeffersonian ideals coupled with historic circumstances that launched the drive for democratic innovations, such as expanding the electorate, democratizing the nominating process, and progressive reforms, all worked to broaden the franchise of direct popular control of governments. In these efforts, citizen participation was given legitimate meaning and became a primary mechanism for administrative accountability.

Democratic innovations, such as citizen participation, are subject to ambiguities as well as inconsistencies. Barriers to effective citizen participation remain a constant reminder of the realities associated with change and the pervasive propensity of formal complex organizations to ultimately resist change. Yet, efforts persist to promote the viable aspects of political equality, democratic reform, and Jefferson's belief in keeping government close to the people. Citizen participation efforts have become firmly entrenched as one process in answering public policy and leadership questions as well as promoting change in both the government and people.

## CITIZEN PARTICIPATION: THE EDUCATIONAL PERSPECTIVE

Citizen participation in the modern American education system takes many forms and represents a diverse array of purposes and political trends. The upsurge of participatory efforts in schools was an outgrowth of social movements in the 1960s and 1970s, consumerism, and the reality of the Watergate investigation. Parents, perhaps better than other special interest groups, learned about the benefits of community development through social reform, the ability of citizens to challenge big government and big business, and the validity of ordinary people questioning administrative decisions and policies. Most importantly, parents, students, and other consumers of public education began a movement to make bureaucratic and professional institutions more responsive (Davies, 1976a).

Ironically, many of the issues that sparked an increase in citizen activism also fueled the fires of public apathy. Many people have

Table 13-I

## CITIZEN PARTICIPATION INITIATIVES IN EDUCATION

| | |
|---|---|
| 1. CITIZEN PARTICIPATION ACTIVITIES DESIGNED TO RESOLVE IMMEDIATE PROBLEMS<br><br>Example: Temporary advisory committees, special task forces, blue ribbon committees. Such "one issue" committees are usually appointed and disband once the issue is resolved. | 2. CITIZEN PARTICIPATION ACTIVITIES DESIGNED TO INVOLVE PARENTS MORE DIRECTLY IN THEIR CHILDREN'S EDUCATION<br><br>Example: School volunteer programs, parenting programs designed to help parents learn ways to be more effective parents, and special parent-child programs are examples of such programs initiated at the federal, state, and local levels. The degree of actual parent/citizen participation varies with the project or program. |
| 3. CITIZEN PARTICIPATION ACTIVITIES DESIGNED TO USE COMMUNITY RESOURCES TO ENRICH LEARNING OPPORTUNITIES<br><br>Example: Community Education is the primary process that focuses on the use of the community as a major resource for learning; other examples include special topic study programs for students, internships, student tutoring, and counseling programs. | 4. CITIZEN PARTICIPATION ACTIVITIES IN PLANNING, POLICY DEVELOPMENT, AND DECISION MAKING<br><br>Example: School advisory councils and committees, Title I councils, community advisory committees. These councils are often part of a three-tier plan that involves the school, attendance areas, and the district in that each level is represented by a council or committee. |

become totally preoccupied with their own private lives while others are simply struggling to make a living. It is helpful to differentiate, citizen participation in schools according to function. The Institute for Responsive Education views activities and programs according to four major initiatives (Davies, 1976a) (*see* Table 13-I)..

All approaches to citizen involvement in education have two-sided objectives: (1) the parent/child point of view that advocates a more responsive educational system in respect to student, parent, and community needs and (2) the school district/professional educator point of view that advocates a more responsive and supportive citizenry for educational goals and budgets.

There are many approaches initiated and implemented by both educators and citizens to improve public education. Yet, when school systems attempt to define the purposes of citizen participation there is a need to become specific, to refine the roles and responsibilities, and to clearly state the rules that govern each approach. The following approaches represent general models for citizen participation in education. These are the most common approaches that currently exist in many school districts in the nation.

## Parent Teacher Groups & Associations

Groups such as the National Parent-Teacher Association or other parent-teacher organizations are somewhat formal organizations that work toward promoting and supporting public education and getting the best possible education for children and youth. Membership in these groups is on a voluntary basis and, in some such organizations, participation by nonparents is encouraged. They work toward their goal of improving public education by undertaking specific projects and, as a group, taking a public stand on certain education issues. Parent-teacher groups are typically organized and managed outside of the formal education organization. This type of citizen participation effort exists in nearly every school district in the United States and often has existed longer than any other citizen participation group.

## Volunteer Programs

School volunteer programs enable various school services to be offered when necessary funding is not available. The actual services provided by the school volunteer program depend on the needs of the individual school and on the skills and interest of the volunteers themselves. Volunteers can provide help in the classroom, counseling department, school library, school grounds, athletic department, health room, etc. Volunteers give their time and skills to the improvement of education within a specific school. Many volunteer programs are highly organized and do have a school staff member that organizes, directs, and helps implement the program. There are national associations for school volunteers that also offer technical assistance and expertise to local volunteer program organizations. The most successful volunteer programs are often those that are highly structured and employ at least one staff member who assumes responsibility for the program (either district or area wide) and provides training for school volunteers in respect to their roles, responsibilities, and functions.

## Community Education

Community Education is a concept that requires and promotes the development and cooperation of all community resources to work toward the solution of problems. It encourages the maximum use of local school facilities and community resources. School facilities are an integral part of the total resources of a community and the Community Education concept advocates expanded use of public school facilities to meet community needs (Frank, 1977).

Community Education provides an opportunity for people to work together to achieve community and self-improvements. As citizens become involved in the decision-making process, a climate of mutual respect, acceptance, and understanding of differences develops and results in improved community relations. Through cooperation and communication the schools become community schools, which are operated in partnership with civic, business and lay leaders, as well as community, state, and federal agencies and organizations. Community schools offer lifelong learning and enrichment opportunities in education, recreation, social, cultural, health, and other community services. Programs are coordinated and developed for citizens of all ages, ethnic backgrounds, and socioeconomic groups.

Community school programs are often planned based on the vice of a community school advisory council. These councils typically have representatives from all factors of the community. They are broad-based, and the main goal of such councils is to establish a mechanism by which citizens will begin to analyze their community's needs and to assist in determining future directions. The Community Education concept suggests that programs are by-products of rational decision-making (Nance, 1975).

## Advisory Councils

Citizen advisory councils in the public school system emerged from the educational reforms of the 1960s and from federal legislation that mandated advisory councils as one criteria for federal aid to education. Councils are now widespread throughout the United States, specifically in providing advice to the superintendents, boards of education, principals, and teachers at the building level (Jones, 1978). Such states as California, Florida, and South Carolina have legislatively mandated school advisory councils on a district and/or building level. Elsewhere, advisory councils exist according to board policy or school policy.

The functions of advisory councils include inquiry, information, needs identification, program development, and evaluation (Clark, 1982). The councils assist the schools in planning and organizing. Councils may recommend policies, promote cooperation from community resources to meet education needs, or provide technical assistance. While the council does advise decision-makers, the final responsibility for most educational decisions remains with the educational administrators and school boards.

## GENERAL PURPOSES OF CITIZEN PARTICIPATION PROGRAMS

The models that schools and districts choose to help implement citizen participation efforts are diverse. The rationale behind each model is usually tied to one or more of eight general purposes of citizen participation.

1. To give information to citizens (a one-way communications effort usually directed from the school or district level)

2. To get information from citizens (a one-way communications effort usually directed by the schools or districts but often includes a related school/parent organization, such as a PTA or volunteer program)
3. To improve public decisions, programs, projects, and services
4. To enhance acceptance of public decisions or school board decisions in respect to programs, projects, and services
5. To supplement public education/agency work through volunteerism
6. To alter political power patterns and the allocation of public resources
7. To protect individual and minority group rights and interests
8. To delay or avoid the making of difficult public education decisions

These eight general purposes are neither mutually exclusive nor separately achieved in practice. For example, local PTAs give information to parents and educators and get information from and about them. The key to any of the approaches involves enhancing the interaction between the formal educational system and its constituents. The focus should be on improved two-way communication that will ultimately lead to improved decision-making, improved programs, and greater support for public schools.

The following checklist is a modified version of a similar checklist originally developed by Robert A. Aleshire (1970). It provides a more detailed view of the eight purposes of citizen participation. This detailed chart focuses on public education systems and citizen participation efforts regarding those systems.

### Citizen Participation Checklist

1. Give information to citizens/parents about the schools.
   A. Disseminate information.
   B. Inform and educate the public and community.
   C. Answer citizen questions.
   D. Notify citizens of actions taken by local school board, county government, state government, and federal government that effect the schools.
   E. Notify citizens of opportunities for participation.
2. Get information from and about citizens and community.

    A. Identify parent groups, community organizations, and various sections of the school population or attendance areas.

    B. Identify problems, attitudes, opinions, and objective characteristics of the school district constituents.

    C. Gauge citizen and parent attitudes toward the school and the district as well as local, state, and federal governments.

    D. Generate new ideas and possible alternatives for public action or consideration in respect to the schools and public education.

3. Improve public decisions, programs, projects, and services.

    A. Use information from and about citizens and community (*see* #2 for strategies).

    B. Obtain and use advice from parents, students, educators and community about —

        1. Proposed plans and programs

        2. Policy review (local school and district) and program evaluations

        3. Identification and selection of district program and budget priorities

    C. Enhance program coordination by —

        1. Counter-balancing special interests with general public education interest

        2. Promoting interaction among various educational interest groups to resolve conflicts

    D. Enhance services to students by —

        1. Establishing and using district ombudsmen, student advocates, parent advocates, etc.

        2. Providing special services and resources through other agencies, district office specialists, local universities, and state departments of education

        3. Mounting administrative appeals

        4. Taking legal action

4. Enhance acceptance of state and local school board decisions in regard to programs, projects, services, and budgets.

    A. Seek citizen and parent endorsements of decisions, programs, projects, and services.

    B. Build a supportive public education constituency for programs and budgets.

    C. Minimize opposition by providing full information (*see* #1 for strategies) and supporting reasons behind school board actions.

D. Resolve important and controversial issues (*see* 3-C for strategies).

E. Employ local citizens and community residents in public education programs.

5. Supplement public education system work and efforts.

A. Accept citizen volunteers into existing programs, projects, and services.

B. Accept and use citizen/parent-prepared reports or information on a regular basis.

C. Share report preparation activities with parents, community, educators, and students when applicable.

D. Share policymaking roles with parents and citizens representing community concerns.

E. Encourage voluntary compliance by parents with federal, state, and local rules, regulations, incentives, and initiatives.

F. Encourage complementary citizen action within the school community.

6. Alter political power patterns and resource allocations.

A. Centralize or decentralize programs.

B. Establish citizen/parent control.

C. Oppose school board and state board of education decisions or local, state, or federal government decisions.

D. Change the educational organization and structure through the political process.

7. Protect individual and minority group rights and interests.

A. Take legal action.

B. Mount educational administrative appeals.

C. Stage protests and demonstrations and mount lobbying efforts and letter writing campaigns, etc.

D. Establish and use ombudsmen, parent, student advocates, etc.

E. Provide special services through local educational system, university, state departments of education, etc.

8. Delay or avoid making difficult public decisions.

A. Call for further studies.

B. Take legal action.

C. Mount administrative/legislative appeals.
D. Stage protests and demonstrations and mount lobbying and letter writing efforts, etc.

## THREE STATE MODELS FOR CITIZEN PARTICIPATION IN EDUCATION

There are literally thousands of activities, programs, policies, and mandates that call for or feature strategies to promote citizen participation in education. There are now more people, representing a broader range of interests, involved in various forms of citizen action than at any other time in our nation's history. (Davies, 1976*b*).

This upsurge in activism is more often a result of public discontent and loss of trust in public institutions than simple democratic and patriotic support for governmental programs. Quite simply, public education in the United States is in a state of crisis. The population is shifting away from youth toward older age. Eleven percent of the population in the United States is over sixty-five years old. This represents about 25 million people, a number larger than the total population of our twenty smallest states (Larkin, 1982). There are trends of later marriage, women who choose careers and postpone having children until older or who have one child or no children at all. Life-styles, family structures, and communities have all changed significantly over the past decade, and, while public education has struggled to respond, the public still lacks information and an understanding of school programs, goals, and services.

Approximately four out of five voters are without school-age children ("Parent Involvement in Education: A Powerful Partnership," 1981). With so few taxpayers receiving direct services from public schools, the nation's tax-burdened citizens continue to rebel against education's escalating costs. The rebellion is joined and supported by legislators who read the public mood and join the movement (Jones, 1978).

For public education to continue to thrive and offer quality programs, school officials must be able to demonstrate to the public that education is indispensable. People are demanding that educators be held accountable for the massive amount of tax dollars allocated for public education. The public wants to know what our schools are doing. Most school advocates are calling for efforts to restore the public's confidence in our school. Building and maintaining public confidence in our education system is, therefore, one of education's most important tasks. The tasks must be seen from the citizen's perspective, for confidence in public schools will not improve unless the community's needs, instead of education's needs, become a primary focus of educators (Branch, 1981).

School officials have direct and implied responsibility for promoting educational public relations. Three states have recognized this responsibility and are actively working toward building effective citizen participation programs with an emphasis on school and citizen communication. California, South Carolina, and Florida are all leaders in legislating mandates for participation through school councils.

The council concept is not new to education. Numerous local and district councils have existed for years in many areas in the United States. The focus of this section, however, will feature pertinent information in respect to California's, Florida's and South Carolina's efforts to implement citizen participation through school councils. Positive program benefits, school improvements, and strategies for council effectiveness will also be presented. Each state has taken the initiative to create and legislate policies to illuminate the following concerns:

*Accountability* — Increased state funding and state responsibility to plan and implement programs have placed pressure on state education agencies to monitor local programs in order to assure adherence to state intentions. State legislatures want improved systems of accountability in the monitoring of state funds as well as in the implementation of state programs.

*Equity* — State mandates stem from attempts to equalize expenditures and educational opportunity. State legislatures and executive actions have provided for major school finance reform. Efforts to distribute funds in a more equitable manner provided the impetus for new initiatives in California, South Carolina, and Florida.

*Preservation of Local Control* — Increasing participation efforts in response to increased exercise of state authority in local school affairs is one way of counteracting expansion of state control and preserving local control of education. The legislative notion was "to put the public back into public education" (Zerchyknov, Davies, and Crispeels 1980).

## The California Experience

California's mandate for School Site Councils (SSC) is part of a state incentive program for local school improvement (Zerchyknov et al., 1980). This special program provides state monies in the form of grants for schools that develop and implement locally designed school improvement plans. This School Improvement Program, or SIP, is part of a major school finance reform act, Assembly Bill 65 (AB65), which was signed into law in September 1977. The major provisions of the legislation include (a) fiscal equity by closing the gap between high spending and low spending districts through state aid, (b) education equity by providing additional state aid for special education students, and (c) basic educational improvement through expansion of the Early Childhood Education (ECE) program into a more comprehensive school improvement program for kindergarten through twelfth grade.

### California Mandates for Citizen Participation

California Assembly Bill 65 mandates parental involvement in the following forms:

*Parents in the Classroom*
. . . In elementary schools the School Improvement Plan shall include the active involvement of parents in classrooms activities and in other aspects of the school improvement plan. . . .

*Parent Education for Child Growth and Development*
. . . parent education regarding the growth and development of children shall be an integral part of any funded school improvement plan. . . .

*Parent Roles in Decision-Making*
. . . no school shall recieve funds pursuant to this chapter unless a planning application or school improvement plan has been approved for the school. . . .

*School Site Councils*
. . . A school site council shall be established at each school which participates in the school improvement program. . . .

*Local Options*
. . . Existing schoolwide advisory groups or school district

support groups may be utilized as the school site council if such groups conform to the provisions of this section. . . .

### Council Composition

. . . The council shall be composed of the principal and representatives of teachers selected by teachers at the school; other school personnel selected by other personnel at the school; parents of pupils attending the school selected by such parents and in secondary schools pupils selected by pupils attending the school. . . .

*Parity* — equal distribution of representation between citizens and educators:

. . . At the elementary level the council shall be constituted to ensure parity between: (a) the principal, classroom teachers and other school personnel; and (b) parents and other community members selected by parents. . . . At the secondary level the council shall be constituted to ensure parity between (a) the principal, classroom teachers and other school personnel, and (b) equal number of parents and students.

"Community member" was previously defined as any: . . . person who is neither in the employment of the school district, nor a parent or guardian of a pupil attending the participating school. . . . "Parity" is so defined as to give citizens and teachers a preponderant majority of the Council.

The term and method of selection and replacement must be spelled out in the School Improvement Plan. This means councils determine their own membership and selection procedures.

### Council Roles and Responsibilities

a. Councils will develop a three-year plan based on an assessment of school capabilities to meet the educational needs of each pupil.

b. Councils will specify improvement objectives and indicate steps needed to meet each objective, including outcomes.

c. Councils will monitor the implementation of the School Improvement Plan, which is reviewed by the local school board and funded by the state.

d. Certified school personnel shall design and implement instructional techniques consistent with objectives established by the school site council.

e. The school site council, following approval of a School Improvement Plan by the school board, shall have ongoing responsibility to review with the principal, teachers and other school personnel and pupils the implementation program and assess program effectiveness.

f. No plan shall be approved unless developed and recommended by a School Site Council. If the plan is not approved by the school board, specific reasons for such action will be reported to the council. All modifications will be developed, recommended and approved/disapproved in the same manner.

### State Department of Education Program Reviews

AB 65 also states that the chief state school officer is provided legislative authority to conduct periodic internal and long range external reviews and evaluations of all aspects of local school improvement programs, including the site councils. This is called School Improvement Program Review (Program Review). This review involves a systematic approach to evaluation of all aspects of the program. The Program Review relies upon the process of on-site observation, interview, and documentation to gather information. It is a formative evaluation approach and is not intended to "grade" local councils, but to identify strengths and opportunities for improvement. This review is not punitive. Rather, it establishes eligibility for receiving technical assistance from the state education agency.

California's School Improvement legislation attempts to emphasize the process that builds a program. The review model places primary emphasis on providing positive, helpful, and constructive information to districts and schools. There are four special features of the model:

1. *Peer Group and Self-Assessment* — This approach replaces exclusive reliance on external reviews by visiting state teams.

2. *Program Effects Rather Than Program Processes* — Emphasis is on ends, the effects of processes, rather than mere compliance with means or process for process' sake.

3. *Qualitative Indicators* — The rating scale used in Program Review is anchored on three points that require school-site specific descriptions of high, medium, and low quality.

4. *Practical Utility* — Data generated by these reviews help schools and program planners determine possible next steps and strengths to work from rather than a simple listing of program strengths and weaknesses.

California's approach to citizen participation is grounded in school-site program improvement. The mandates for parent and citizen involvement are linked to findings that report that schools' organizational processes have an impact on students' achievement and that parents should be an integral component in the comprehensive program review/school improvement process. The state has made legislative, fiscal, and administrative commitments to sharing accountability in developing and sustaining a high quality educational program for each student (California SDE, 1980).

## The Florida Experience

The mandate for local school advisory committees was part of Florida's comprehensive school finance reform legislation, which passed in 1973. The Florida Education and Finance Program (FEEP) specifically legislated (1) a more equitable funding formula through a special pupil weighting system, (2) decentralized educational decision-making to the local building level by encouraging (not mandating) local districts to implement* school-based management, (3) and increased citizen participation by requiring local districts to set up either school or district level citizen advisory committees, according to Zerchyknov, Davies, and Crispeel (1980).

### *Florida Mandates for Citizen Participation*

Florida's legislation provides that each council will assist in the preparation and public circulation of annual reports of school progress. The report format allows complete discretion as long as it contains —

---

*School-Based Management (SBM) is a model designed to decentralize authority and promote flexibility in school programs. It embodies four major concepts: (i) *school site budgeting* — lump-sum allocations to individual schools; (ii) *administrative decentralization* — increasing the discretionary authority of the principal; (iii) *accountability* — using statewide criterion-referenced testing and making public those test results via "Annual Performance Reports"; and (iv) *democratized decision-making* — implementing a collaborative and participatory mechanism for planning, policymaking, and program evaluation at the school site.

- Information on how well each school has met program goals and objectives
- Information on the school's budget
- A review and identification of student needs
- Information about the attitudes toward the school from teachers, students, parents, and the community
- Any additional information that would clarify or offer analysis of the current status of education for the school

The school finance reform effort stems from recommendations that were made in a 1972 report from the governor's citizen's study committee entitled *Improving Education In Florida* (cited in Zerchyknov et al., 1980). The final legislation that was passed included the following measures to increase local accountability and citizen participation.

### Florida Annual Report of School Progress

The individual school should be the basic unit of educational accountability. The annual report of school progress will be developed to detail yearly school improvement efforts. The report is a basic performance audit instrument that will help in the achievement of school level improvements and innovations. This "report card" of the school will go to the parents written in a simple, brief style.

### School Advisory Councils

Florida recognized that accountability must be accompanied with citizen involvement. Therefore, each school board will establish a school advisory committee or committees, but such committees will not have any powers reserved by law to the school board. If the school board does not establish advisory committees for each school, it shall establish a district advisory committee.

#### Council Membership
The district school board may establish an advisory committee broadly representative of the community served . . . and composed of teachers, students, parents, and other citizens.
#### Council Functions
Each school advisory committee . . . shall assist in the prepara-

tion of the annual report . . . and shall provide such assistance as the principal may request in preparing the school's annual budget and plan. . . .

## Local Discretion and Financial Support for Advisory Committee Improvement

Amendments in 1978 allowed for further local discretion in regard to councils. Recognized schoolwide support groups that meet all criteria established by law or rule may function as district or school advisory committees. Each district school board, or each principal through the district school board, may submit to the state commissioner of education for approval a proposal for implementing an educational improvement project. Such proposals shall be developed with the assistance of district and school advisory committees and may address any or all of the following areas: school management improvement, district and school advisory committee improvement, school volunteers, and any other educational areas that can be improved through a closer working relationship between school and community . . . for each project approved, the Commissioner shall authorize distribution of a grant, in amount not less than $500 and not more than $5,000. . . .

Florida's 1978 Education Improvements Projects Act initiated a program that allows district or individual school councils to play a key role in planning and implementing small scale school improvement efforts. There now exists a fiscal incentive to encourage networking, collaboration, and resource sharing between councils and other community organizations. Florida's policymakers and citizens are continuing to work toward quality education through a commitment to school improvement through citizen involvement.

## The South Carolina Experience

In 1977, South Carolina adopted a comprehensive and unique piece of legislation called the South Carolina Education Finance Act. The major purpose behind the Act was to provide a more equitable system/formula for financing the public schools in the state (Sovde, 1980).

The Act also listed three other purposes:

. . . (1) To guarantee to each student in the public schools of South Carolina the availability of at least minimum educational programs and services appropriate to his needs, and which are substantially equal to those available to other students with similar needs and reasonably comparable from a program standpoint to those students of all other classifications, notwithstanding geographic differences and varying local economic factors.
(2) To encourage school district initiative in seeking more effective and efficient means of achieving the goals of the various programs.
(3) To ensure that tax dollars spent in public schools are utilized effectively and to ensure that adequate programs serve all children of the State. . . .

Section 6 of the Act outlines the specific aspects of citizen involvement included as part of a cooperative educational planning and evaluation system designed to ensure the three purposes stated above. This new approach to school accountability assigns responsibility to the local school, the district board of trustees, and the state department of education.

## South Carolina Mandates for Citizen Participation

The South Carolina Education Finance Act mandates citizen participation in the following forms.

### School Advisory Councils

Beginning at the school building level, the Act mandates that a school advisory council be established in every school. Specific provisions are excerpted below:

*Councils In Every School*
. . . Each school board shall establish an Advisory Council at each school in the district. . . .

*Membership, Selection, and Composition*
. . . composed of at least two parents, elected by parents of the children enrolled in the school; at least two teachers, elected by the faculty; at least two students in schools with grades 9 and above elected by the students; . . .

*Principal's Discretion To Appoint*
. . . other representatives of the community . . . and persons selected by the principal; provided however, that the elected

members of the committee shall comprise at least a two thirds majority of the membership of the committee. . . .

*Councils Functions*

. . . Each council shall assist in the preparation of the annual school report required in this section. . . . Each school district board of trustees shall cause each school in the district to prepare an annual written report including but not limited to (a) depicting the program being offered in each pupil classification, and (b) recommending program improvements. . . . This report shall present an explicit statement of the needs of students; shall define specific goals and objectives; and propose an identifiable strategy for priorities in the expenditure of funds to achieve the stated objectives . . . [councils] shall provide assistance as the principal may request as well as [carry out] any other duties prescribed by the local school board. . . . However, no council shall have any of the powers reserved by law or regulation to the local school board. . . .

*School Board's Special Authority*

. . . The local school board shall make provisions to allow any council to file a separate report to the local school board if the council deems it necessary.

Further, the Act requires the local Board of Trustees to appraise the reports and to communicate back to the local school as to which goals and objectives included in the report are to be implemented in the coming year. . . .

*District Responsibilities*

In addition, the district's responsibilities are to —

. . . maintain an ongoing systematic evaluation of the educational program needs in the district . . . at a minimum . . . assessing needs and establishing goals and objectives . . . for each of the program classifications specified in the Act; develop a comprehensive annual and long-range plan for meeting these program needs . . . provide a program for staff development for all educational personnel on an annual and long-range basis . . . submit to the State Board of Education, and to the people of the district, that district's fiscal report . . . district's programmatic report including the results of the required testing programs, the annual long-range plan, and the evaluation of program effectiveness.

South Carolina's Education Finance Act clearly lays out a system of educational program development and evaluation that begins at the local school site, involves all constituencies in planning, and moves up to the state department of education. The district board of trustees still retains responsibility for making the final educational and financial decisions, but with the added input from each local school as contained in the annual school report.

South Carolina's approach to citizen participation, like California's and Florida's, emphasizes a formal, viable role for parents and citizens to play in the process of school improvement. The state has further responded to the need for involving the public in education through the formation of the Governor's Task Force on Citizen Participation in Education. This task force works to identify and recognize public schools that have successfully developed procedures for involving citizens in the schools.

## Summary

California, Florida, and South Carolina are all leaders in efforts to implement school improvement through formal citizen participation. These states have expanded citizen participation to include shared decision-making that starts at the school site level. The emphasis is placed on improved accountability, equity, and the preservation of local control. These innovative efforts are not without problems. Unfortunately, legislative mandates are not self-implementing. Potential causes for failure include (1) manipulation by those in power; (2) lack of understanding of the process; (3) lack of awareness/information in respect to the public, particularly those who have no direct ties with the schools; (4) poor organization structures and planning processes; and (5) poor administrative leadership (Robbins and Hutton, 1982).

The opportunity for school improvement through improved citizen participation has yet to be fully realized. Those who are becoming actively involved in the process are finding that the rewards can definitely outweigh the costs.

## CITIZEN PARTICIPATION STRATEGIES THAT WORK

Citizen participation efforts and models are often difficult to replicate across the board due to differences associated with school districts and communities. There are, however, certain conditions or critical factors that are associated with school council and citizen participation effectiveness. The following strategies are presented as promising practices or conditions for success rather than actual blueprints for action.

### Factors Related To Effective School Advisory Councils

School advisory councils can be a bridge between the school and the community. Five critical factors related to effective council functioning have been identified by the School Advisory Council Assistance Project at the University of South Carolina. Educators can make school advisory councils an important part of the education process by addressing these factors.

### Council Training

One commonality among effective councils is that members have received training about their roles and responsibilities. Training can provide the members with the knowledge necessary to make significant contributions to the council's work. Members must understand the council's purpose and duties. The training is most helpful to the council members near the beginning of the school year, but should be an integral component of the year's work. In one school district, all people directly involved with the school advisory council attend an annual workshop. The workshop is held during the second week in September so that the council members can learn their roles and responsibilities at the start of the school year. The annual training is particularly helpful to new council members.

### School and District Policy

Written school district policy concerning school advisory councils is another commonality among effective councils. Written policy provides guidelines for local councils, as well as signifying a district commitment to improved school programs and community relations. Some districts have broadened the scope of the council's involvement by requiring every council to include a senior citizen and a parent of a preschool child in its membership. This approach implies that district policymakers understand the importance of involving members of the community who are not parents of public school students in the education process.

## Formal Exchange of Information

Another characteristic necessary for council effectiveness is the continuous flow of timely and accurate information between the school administrators and the council members. Continuous information allows the council to have the greatest possible impact. Information must flow to the members of the community in order to ensure their support and involvement in the education system. Regularly scheduled information mechanisms, such as discussion meetings and school newsletters, are excellent investments that can assist school officials in gaining increased community support.

## Administrative Leadership

Strong leadership from the school principal is essential to council effectiveness. A supportive principal understands that sharing decision-making enhances his/her authority and increases the likelihood of a responsible council. A positive leader also understands that the council's work can be beneficial to the school only if it is taken seriously and acted upon appropriately. Legislation and policy that provide for citizens to participate in the education process are not enough. The principal must take steps to become involved in and supportive of the council's work and encourage community involvement and improved school communication.

## Two-way Communication

Communication is the key to an effective council. Open and honest communication between the council members and school personnel is essential, and yet only a first step. Two-way communication between the school and the community is vital. Informal means of communication are often insufficient. If teachers and administrators are interested in improving education, a formal assessment, such as a community opinion poll, can serve as a valuable measure of public sentiment. Whatever the system, the council cannot bridge the information gap between the school and the community without improving and expanding existing networks of communication.

It is not enough to simply ask citizens to participate in school advisory councils. Unless the participants see their work as having a worthwhile impact on important school issues, their involvement is likely to be superficial and brief. Councils can become a bridge between the school and community if leadership, training, information, policy, and communication are combined to make the process of citizen involvement effective (Jackson, Kessler, 1982).

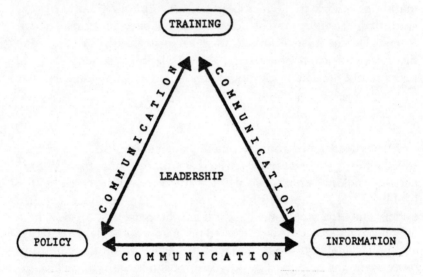

Figure 13-1. Effective Council Model. This model represents the relationship between policy, information, and training that must exist to ensure minimal council effectiveness. Communication is necessary to link policy, information, and training initiatives. Leadership is at the center of council effectiveness as the major support mechanism for the process. Developed by M.C. Jackson and M.H. Kessler, School Advisory Council Assistance Project.

## A LIST OF CRITICAL QUESTIONS
## ON CITIZEN PARTICIPATION

Warden (1977) proposes the following questions that must be answered if the citizen participation effort is to be effective:

1. What are the purposes of the citizen participation effort and who determines such purposes?

2. Who is to be involved and what strategies or procedures are to be employed to ensure effectiveness?
3. What are the limitations, if any, placed on such participation efforts? Who will decide such limitations?
4. What are the personal benefits to be derived by the participants themselves and the community in general? What are the benefits to the school, district, or state?
5. What are the implied criteria of *successful participation* and who determines such criteria? How will such criteria be evaluated?
6. What resources are available to support such efforts (including human, financial and material resources)?
7. How will the roles, responsibilities, and relative functions of both lay citizens and professional educators be decided?
8. If participation is to be linked to other agencies or organizations, how will this affect the organizational structure?
9. To what extent will the participants have access to decision making, information, training, and leadership?
10. What local conditions or factors need to be considered relative to the participation effort?

## FIVE COMPONENTS OF A GOOD SCHOOL

### Summary of a Policy Statement from the Education Commission of the States

- The school places a high value on the uniqueness of the individual student. Teachers believe all children have the ability to learn. Teachers look for and emphasize student strengths.
- Achievement is the school's focus, and instruction time is protected from interruptions and intrusions. Time structures permit a high degree of flexibility, and students are given the time they need on tasks. Attention is given to aesthetic, moral, and social development, as well as intellectual growth. Instruction is monitored and evaluated for quality. The principal is the instructional leader in the school.
- School activities use the resources of the total community. Students, parents, and community members make decisions about school processes.

- The school is realistic in its undertakings, recognizing its limitations. The principal makes major decisions and uses a participatory management style.
- Balance is achieved between differences or opposing forces. Students with diverse backgrounds are brought together. Organization is provided without bureaucracy. The focus is on the needs and goals of students (Tursman, 1981).

## FINAL CONCLUSION

Citizen participation initiatives are only a small part of a grand plan to improve public education systems. Citizen involvement in any form, regardless of its intent and sophistication, does not represent a panacea for school improvement. It does represent a functional strategy to be included in the formal organizational structure of schools that can and will promote a more responsive education system. The notions of improved accountability, equity, and preservation of local control through citizen participation efforts suggest a partnership among parents, educators, school boards, and the community at large. It is not surprising that the paradox of education, the process of learning and teaching, is often most dependent upon the quality of the partnership that exists between citizens and educators.

## RESOURCES

The following organizations provide technical assistance, information, and/or publications regarding citizen participation in education.

California State Department of Education
721 Capitol Mall
Sacramento, California 95814

Center for Early Adolescence
University of North Carolina at Chapel Hill
Suite 223, Carr Mill Mall
Carrboro, North Carolina 27510

Citizen Council for Ohio Schools
545 East Town Street
Columbus, Ohio 43215

Citizen Participation Committee
of the Florida Education Council
Florida Department of Education
1702 Capitol
Tallahassee, Florida 32301

Educational Communication Center
P.O. Box 657
Camp Hill, Pennsylvania 17011.

Information Project on Education-Network
810 Miranda Green
Palo Alto, California 94306

Institute for Responsive Education
Box C, 605 Commonwealth Avenue
Boston, Massachusetts 02215

Local School Budgeting in
Cincinnati Public Schools Project
Coalition of Neighborhoods
6566 Montgomery Road
Cincinnati, Ohio 45213

National Committee for Citizens in Education
Suite 410
Wilde Lake Village Green
Columbia, Maryland 21044

National Community Education Clearinghouse,
Informatics Inc.
6011 Executive Boulevard
Rockville, Maryland 20852

National Parent-Teacher Association
700 North Rush Street
Chicago, Illinois 60611

National School Public Relations Association
1801 North Moore Street
Arlington, Virginia 22209

National School Volunteer Program Inc.
300 North Washington Street
Alexandria, Virginia 22314

School Advisory Council Assistance Project
College of Education
University of South Carolina, Box 51
Columbia, South Carolina 29208

South Carolina Department of Education
Rutledge Building
Columbia, South Carolina 29201

## REFERENCES

Aleshire, R. A.: Planning and citizen participation: Cost, benefits, and approaches. *Urban Affairs Quarterly, 5(4):*369-393, 1970.

Banach, W. J.: Why isn't education's apple shiny? *Journal of Educational Communication, 5(3):*4-7, 1982.

California State Department of Education: *Elementary Program Review Training Manual.* Sacramento, California State Department of Education, 1980.

Clark, P. A.: *Trainers Handbook for Citizen Council Training.* Gainesville, Florida, University of Florida, 1982.

Davies, D.: Making citizen participation work. *National Elementary Principal, 55(4):* 20-29, 1976(*a*).

Davies, D.: Perspectives and future directions. In Davies, D. (Ed.): *Schools Where Parents Make a Difference.* Boston, Institute for Responsive Education, 1976(*b*).

Frank, R.G.: *Planning for Community Education.* Midland, Michigan, Pendell, 1977.

Jackson, M. C., and Kessler, M. H.: School advisory councils: A bridge between school and community. *Journal of Educational Communication, 6(1):*12-14, 1982.

Jones, J.W.: *Building Public Confidence for Your Schools.* Arlington, Virginia, National Public Relations Association, 1978.

Larkin, F.P.: Communicating with senior citizens. *Journal of Educational Communication, 5(3):*4-7, 1982.

Nance, E.: *The Community Council: It's Organization and Function.* Midland, Michigan, Pendell, 1975

Parent involvement in education: A powerful partnership. *Practical Applications of Research: Phi Delta Kappa's Center on Education, Development, and Research, 4(2):*1-4, 1981.

Robbins, W.R., and Hutton, R.: The role of community education in school improvement and citizen participation. *Citizen Action in Education, 9(1):*5, 1982.

Rosenbaum, N.: *Citizen Involvement in Land Use Governance.* Washington, D.C., The Urban Institute, 1976.

Sovde, J. E.: *A Status Report on the Implementation of Section #6 of the Education Finance Act of 1977.* Columbia, South Carolina, Education Finance Review Committee of the South Carolina General Assembly, 1980.

Tursman, C.: *Good Schools: What Makes Them Work.* Arlington, Virginia, National School Public Relations Association, 1981.

Walker D. B.: American traditions of citizen participation. In Walker, D. B. (Ed.): *Citizen Participation in the American Federal System.* Washington, D.C., U. S. Government Printing Office, 1978.

Warden, J. W.: *Citizen Participation: What Others Say . . . What Others Do . . .* Charlottesville, Virginia, University of Virginia, 1977.

Zerchyknov, R., Davies, D., and Crispeels, J.: *Leading the Way: State Mandates for School Advisory Councils in California, Florida, and South Carolina.* Boston, Institute for Responsive Education, 1980.

# APPENDIX

## MODEL FOR SCHOOL ADVISORY COUNCIL REPRESENTATION

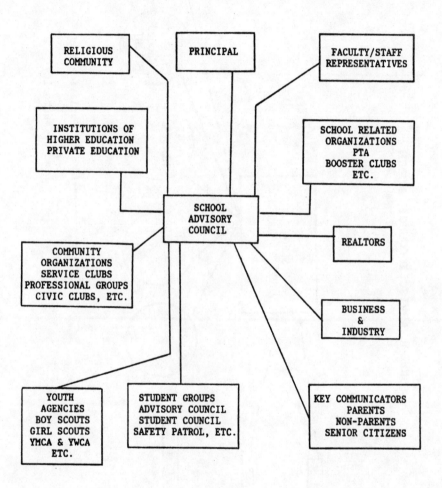

If possible, recruit individuals that can represent more than one of the segments listed in this model. People that can serve a dual role will help keep the council or committee within reasonable working size.

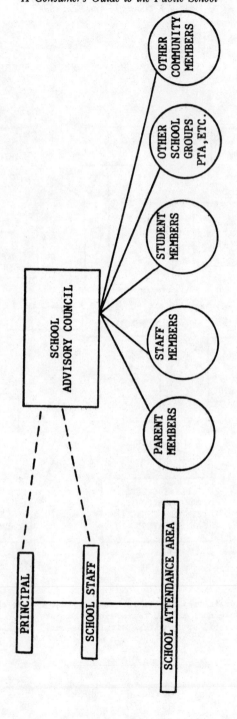

SCHOOL ADVISORY COUNCIL MODEL

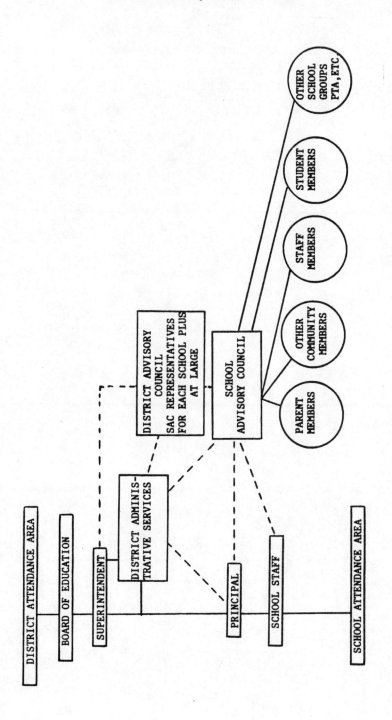

DISTRICT ADVISORY COUNCIL MODEL

# NAME INDEX

## A

Abidin, R.R., 144, 152
Aleshire, R.A., 234, 254
Ames, L.B., 44, 55
Aristotle, 7
Armytage, W.H.G., 12, 37
Artz, F.B., 6, 37
Ashley, M., 13, 37
Aubrey, R.F, 119, 133
Austin, M.C., 186, 187

## B

Baas, A.M., 210, 224
Bader, L.A., 181, 186, 187
Bainton, R.H., 11, 37
Banach, W.J., 254
Bane, M., 65, 70
Barnard, Henry, 25, 26, 27, 32
Barnes, D.R., 5, 37
Baruth, L., 67, 69
Beane, J.A., 97, 102
Bell, Alexander Graham, 156
Benda, H.W., 72, 73, 77, 78, 85
Benton, W., 24, 37
Bergan, J.R., 143, 153
Bernstein, B., 130, 134
Bevan, W., 152, 153
Bindoff, S.T., 11, 37
Binet, 117, 156
Blackham, G.J., 143, 153
Bloom, B.S., 43, 44, 55
Blow, Susan, 57, 58
Bluhm, H.P., 132, 133
Boone, E.J., 224
Borrowman, M.L., 30, 37
Botel, M., 174, 176, 187
Braille, Louis, 156
Branch, 238
Brewer, J.M., 116, 133
Brodinsky, B., 73, 74, 85

Bronfenbrenner, U., 43, 55, 68, 69, 148, 153
Brophy, J.E., 96, 102
Brown, D.T., 140, 153
Bulls, G.E., 44, 55
Butts, R.F., 30, 36, 37

## C

Calhoun, C.C., 201
Calhoun, D., 37
Calvin, 10, 11
Campbell, R.F., 78, 85, 104, 115
Carroll, M.R., 130, 131, 134
Carter, James G., 25, 27
Caspari, F., 11, 38
Cattell, James M., 117
Cawelti, G., 91, 97, 102
Chambliss, J.E., 25, 26, 38
Cicero, 6
Clarizio, H.F., 144, 153
Clark, P.A., 213, 225, 233, 254
Clinton, DeWitt, 23
Colburn, Warren, 24
Coleman, James, 110
Colet, John, 9, 16
Comenius, J.A., 57, 69
Conant, James, 90, 91
Cook, N.C., 209, 210, 213, 224
Cooper, Anthony Ashley, 15
Cremin, L.A., 14, 18, 26, 30, 31, 32, 33, 38
Cressman, R., 72, 73, 77, 78, 85
Crispeels, J., 238, 239, 242, 243, 255
Cubberley, E.P., 19, 23, 26, 57, 69, 71, 72, 73, 85
Cunningham, L., 78, 85, 104, 115
Cutts, N.E., 137, 153

## D

da Feltre, Vittorino, 7
Dave, R.H., 224, 225
Davies, D., 229, 231, 238, 239, 242, 243,

263

254, 255
Decker, L.E., 224
de Mause, L., 41, 55
De Molen, R.L. 6, 10, 11, 38
Dennis, Benjamin, 16
Dewey, John, 30, 31, 38, 57, 58, 211,
  212, 225
Dinkmeyer, D., 50, 55
Dix, Dorothea, 156
Dobbs, R.C., 225
Dolan, R.J., 224
Donley, M.O., 72, 85
Dorris, J., 82, 86
Downs, N., 5, 38
Duff, E., 60, 67, 69, 70
Dupont, H., 44, 55
Durkheim, Emile, 104
Durrell, D.D., 173, 187

**E**

Edelman, M.W., 148, 152, 153
Eisenhower, Dwight, 118
Elson, R.M., 24, 38
Erasmus, 7, 9
Erickson, E.H., 42, 44, 45, 46, 50, 55

**F**

Faunce, R.C., 102
Finch, A.V., 201
Finn, P., 201
Ford, Gerald, 213
Forness, S.R., 155, 172
Forsyth, L.B., 130, 131, 134
Frank, R.G., 232
Franklin, Benjamin, 19, 206
French, W.M., 88, 102
Freud, S., 44, 55, 57, 156
Froebel, F., 29, 57, 58, 69
Fuller, E., 104, 115
Fuhrman, S., 99, 102

**G**

Gallagher, J.J., 154, 172
Gallup, G.H., 79, 85,
Gardner, John, 36
Gates, A.I., 173, 188
Geister, J., 121, 133
Gesell, A., 44, 55, 136

Gilmore, M.P., 9, 38
Goldhammer, K., 201
Goldman, L., 130, 131, 134
Goodlad, J., 77, 86
Goodman, L.V., 157, 172
Gordon, A., 149, 153
Graff, F.A., 130, 131, 134
Greene, J.P., 14, 38
Guthrie, J.W., 96, 102
Gutkin, L.B., 145, 153

**H**

Hadas, M., 6, 38
Hannibal, M.E., 149, 153
Hansen, H., 86
Hansen, L., 178, 188
Hanson, T., 78, 86
Hardy, N., 132, 133
Harris, William T., 29, 35
Havighurst, R.J., 54, 55
Henry VIII, 11, 12
Hesburgh, T.M., 225
Hetherington, M., 148, 153
Hewitt, F., 155, 172
Hickey, H.W., 210, 212, 225
Hobson, C., 62, 70
Hoffman, L.W., 148, 153
Holton, S.M., 89, 102
Horn, A.J., 40, 153
Howe, Samuel, 156
Hoyt, K.B., 196, 199, 201
Hoyt, K.D., 119, 134
Hubbell, V., 65, 66, 69
Hutt, R., 153
Hutton, R., 247, 254
Hymes, J., 58, 69

**I**

Ilg, F.L., 44, 55
Itard, 156

**J**

Jackson, M.C., 250, 254
Jefferson, Thomas, 20, 22, 24, 226,
  227, 229
Johanningmeier, E.V., 25, 29, 38
Johnson, E.N., 5, 39
Jones, J.W., 233, 237, 254

## K

Kameen, M.C., 172
Kaplan, M.H., 213, 225
Katz, M.E., 29, 38
Keller, Helen, 156
Kelly, S.P., 14, 22, 38
Keppel, F., 36
Keppel, F.P., 225
Kessler, M.H., 250, 254
Kilpatrick, W.H., 31, 37, 38
Kinder, R.F., 174, 182, 188
Kirk, S.A., 154, 172
Knight, E.W., 13, 14, 15, 16, 17, 38
Knowles, M., 225
Knox, John, 13
Knox, S., 21, 38
Kohlberg, L., 42, 44, 48, 50, 55
Krug, E.A., 32, 33, 34, 38

## L

Lancaster, Joseph, 23
Larkin, F.P., 237, 254
Lazar, I., 65, 66, 69
Leeper, S., 60, 64, 70
LeFarte, C., 209, 225
Lefrancois, G., 42, 43, 44, 55
Lindstrom, J.P., 140, 153
Lincoln, Abraham, 73
Locke, John, 15, 17
Loveinger, J., 44, 55
Lupton, J.H., 9, 38
Luther, Martin, 7, 10

## M

McGuffey, 24
McIntosh, D.K., 172
McKean, R.C., 102
McMenemy, R.A., 174, 182, 188
McPhee, R.F., 104, 115
Mann, Horace, 25, 27, 32, 36, 73
Marland, S.P., 196, 201
Martin, J.H., 97, 102
Masnick, G., 65, 70
Miller, F.W., 118, 134
Miller, P.A., 225
Monor, J., 130, 134
Minzey, J.D., 209, 225
Monroe, W.S., 27, 38

Montessori, Maria, 58, 156
Morison, S.E., 13, 38
Morrill, Justin, 31, 73, 190
Morse, Jedidiah, 24
Moser, L.E., 120, 134
Moser, R.S., 120, 134
Munshaw, C.L., 102
Muro, J., 130, 131, 134
Muro, J.A., 50, 55
Murray, H., 65, 66, 69

## N

Nance, E., 233, 254
Noll, J.W., 14, 22, 38
Notestein, W., 10, 39
Nye, R.B., 24, 39
Nystrand, R., 78, 85, 104, 115

## O

Ohlinger, J., 225
O'Leary, K.D., 143, 153
O'Leary, S.G., 143, 153
Olsen, E.B., 213, 225
Osborn, D.K., 58, 70
Otto, W., 174, 178, 182, 188

## P

Parsons, Frank, 118
Pavlov, I., 156
Peabody, Elizabeth, 57, 58
Pearson, J.B., 104, 115
Penn, William, 19
Pestalozzi, 24, 26, 27
Piaget, J., 42, 44, 47, 50, 55
Pietrofesa, J.J., 130, 131, 134
Pikulski, J.J., 180, 188
Piper, D.L., 87, 90, 102
Plato, 7
Plumb, J.B., 6, 39
Porter, S., 213, 225

## Q

Quintillian, 7, 8, 9

## R

Raikes, Robert, 23

Raubinger, R.M., 87, 90, 102
Rippa, S.A., 26, 32, 39
Risk, T.M., 102
Robbins, M.P., 149, 153
Robbins, W.R., 247, 254
Robinson, H.A., 174, 177, 188
Rogers, Carl, 118
Rogers, Will, 84
Rosche, M., 65, 66, 69
Rosenbaum, N., 228, 254
Rosenthal, A., 99, 102
Rosenthal, E.L., 225
Ross, E., 180, 188
Rousseau, 57
Rowe, H.G., 87, 90, 102
Royce, J., 65, 66, 69
Rush, Benjamin, 21
Rusk, R.R., 7, 39

**S**

Salvia, J., 141, 153
Sarason, S., 82, 86
Scanlon, Robert, 195
Schumacher, E.F., 202, 225
Seay, M., 212, 225
Seefeldt, C., 59, 64, 66, 70
Sequin, 156
Shane, H., 82, 86
Shane, H.G., 36, 39
Shearon, R.W., 224
Shertzer, B., 118, 119, 130, 134
Silberman, A., 143, 153
Skager, R., 225
Skipper, D., 60, 64, 70
Smith, N.B., 173, 188
Smith, R., 178, 188
Smith, R.J., 174, 182, 188
Smith, W., 18, 19, 20, 21, 23, 24, 39
Sovede, J.E., 244, 254
Stanford, S., 130, 134
Stiles, L., 77, 86
Stone, S.C., 118, 119, 130, 134
Strauss, 156
Stripling, R.O., 131, 134
Sullivan, Anne, 156
Super, D.E., 44, 49, 50
Swick, K., 60, 62, 67, 70

**T**

Taylor, R.E., 201

Terman, L.M., 43, 117, 156
Thompson, C.R., 11, 12, 39
Thompson, J.W., 5, 39
Tieger, A.G., 145, 153
Timar, T.B., 96, 102
Toffler, A., 202, 225
Turiel, P., 55
Tursman, C., 252, 254
Tyler, Ralph, 36

**U**

Ulich, R., 17, 19, 29, 39
Usdan, M., 78, 85

**V**

Van Dyck, N.B., 149, 153
Van Hoose, J., 83, 86
Van Voorhees, C., 210, 212, 225
Vassar, R.E., 21, 39
Vriend, J., 131, 134

**W**

Walker, D.B., 226, 227, 228, 255
Wallace, D.D., 15, 16, 39
Warden, J.W., 250, 255
Webster, Noah, 24
West, C.K., 87, 90, 102
Wharton, C.R., 225
Wheelock, F.M., 7, 39
White, Burton, 62, 66
Wieruszowski, H., 4, 6, 39
Witherspoon, R., 60, 64, 70
Woodward, W.H., 8, 39

**Y**

Yarrington, R., 225
Ysseldyke, J.E., 141, 153

**Z**

Zerchyknov, R., 238, 239, 242, 243, 255
Zwingli, 10

# SUBJECT INDEX

## A

Act, of 1642, 13, 15, 24 (*see also* Community-based education, historical development of)
Act of 1647, 13, 24, 72
Adult Education Act of 1966, 213
Advisory Commission of Intergovernmental Relations, 227
Agricultural education
establishment of, 31-32
Administrators (*see* Public school administration)
American colonial education, 13-19
development of private and parochial schools and, 20
school commissioners and, 16-17
tuition and, 14
*American Journal of Education,* 27
American Personnel and Guidance Association, 131, 132
American Psychological Association (APA), 137, 138, 139, 140, 146, 147, 152
American public education
blacks and
early history of, 27-28
Freedmen's Bureau and, 28
Carter's early views on, 25
early aims of, 22
early curriculum of, 73
establishment of state authority over, 22
first proposals for, 20
government's increasing role in, 33
post-Civil War expansion of, 28
postcolonial history of, 20-30
progressive movement in, 30-34
aim of, 31
slow growth of, 27
South and, 27-28
tax support of
early federal aid to, 73, 91

fair school finance acts, 36
first challange of, 29
first high schools and, 87
reduction in, 91-92
American School Counselor Association
Governing Board, 126, 127, 128, 133
American Youth Commission, 89
Anna Boyd Child Development Center, 60-61
Apprenticeship, mandatory
Act for the Relief of the Poor and, 12-13
Act of 1642 and, 13, 15
Association for Childhood Education, 58
International Kindergarten Union as, 58
Association for Counselor Education and Supervision, 121, 131, 132, 133

## B

*Book of Common Prayer,* 12, 13
Binet-Simon test, 117
*Brown v. Board of Education,* 34

## C

Cambridge, 10, 11, 12
Career education
definition of, 196
models of, 196-199
employer-based, 197
home/community-based, 197
implementation of, 198-199
rural residential-based, 197
school-based, 197
timetable of, 197-198
outcomes of, 199-200
outlook for, 200
professional associations for, 201
Carnegie Commission on Higher Education, 91
Cathedral schools, 3-6

267

church and, 4
curriculum of, 4
evolution into universities of, 5
Charleston Free School, 16-17
Child benefit theory, 35
Child-centered education
  Dewey and, 31
Christ Church College, 11
Civilian Conservation Corps, 89, 212
*Cochran*, 35
College of Philadelphia, 19
Columbia University, 31
Commission on the Reorganization of Sec-
  ondary Education, 88
Committee of Ten, 88
  Seven Cardinal Principles of, 88
Community-based education (*see also* Education, citizen participation in)
availability of, 216
citizen involvement in, 216
community in schools, use of, 215
concept of, 209-210
definition of, 207-208
historical development of, 210-214
  Act of 1642 and, 210-211
  Dewey and, 212
  early legislation and, 211
  first community school and, 211
  first urban model and, 212
  Great Depression and, 212
  Great Society legislation and, 212-213
  international movement and, 214
  1970s legislation and, 213-214
interagency coordination of, 216
major components of, 215
mandate for, 218-224
organization and development of, 215
professional associations for, 224
trends and issues for, 216-218
  public support for, 217, 218
  social change, 217
Community Education Clearinghouse, 213
Community School Development Act, 213
Community Schools and Comprehensive
  Community Education Act, 213
Compensatory education programs
  advantages of, 36
Convents
  curriculum in, 4
  education in, 4
COPE, 224

**D**

Developmental theory
  areas of child development and, 44-45
  characteristics of 5-9-year-olds and, 50-54
  education of children and, 54-55
  Erickson's psychosocial stages and, 45-46
    epigenetic principle and, 45
  Kohlberg's moral stages and, 48, 50
  Lefrancois' principles and, 42-44
  Piaget's cognitive stages and, 47
  Super's vocational stages and, 49, 50

**E**

Early childhood education,
  definition of, 56-57
  Froebel and, 29, 57
  historical overview of, 28-29, 57-59
  historical reasons for, 29, 57, 58
  Great Depression and, 58-59
  issues and trends in, 64-68
    basic skills in, 66
    handicaps and, 66-67
    need for quality programs of, 64-65
    parental role in, 65-66
  professional organizations for, 68-69
  professional preparation for, 59-61
    certification and, 60-61
    curriculum and, 60
    personality prerequisites for, 59
  professional responsibilities for, 61-64
    aims of, 62-64
    comprehensive view of child and, 62
  Quintilian and, 7
Education, citizen participation in,
  checklist for, 234-237
  critical questions for, 250-251
  educational perspectives of, 229-233
    advisory councils and, 233
    community education and, 232-233
    initiatives in, 230
    objectives of, 231
  PTA and, 231
    volunteer programs and, 231-232
  expected outcome of, 251-252
  general purposes of, 233-234
  historical overview of, 226-229
    government growth in, 227-228
    Jefferson and, 226, 227, 229
    social movements in, 227

resource organizations for, 252-254
state models for, 237-247
  California, 239-242
  causes for failure of, 247
  concerns of, 238
  Florida, 242-244
  South Carolina, 244-247
workable strategies for, 247-250
  administrative leadership and, 249
  council training and, 248
  information exchange and, 249
  school/community communication and, 249-250
  school/district policy and, 248-249
Education for All Handicapped Children Act (PL 94-142), 35, 82, 111, 130, 150 157, 158, 161, 162, 165, 166, 168
Education, mandatory
  Act of 1642 and, 13, 210
  Act of 1647 and, 13-14
  Jamestown assembly of 1619 and, 14
  legislation for, 88
  Penn's Second Frame of Government and, 19
Education Professions Development Act, 118
Educational Policies Committee, 89
Eight Year Study, 89
Elementary and Secondary Education Act of 1965 (ESEA), 35, 36, 74, 84, 91, 212-213
Elementary and Secondary Schools Act, 111
Elementary school teacher, role of
  historical overview of, 71-74
    community dictated, 72
    religious instruction in, 71, 72
    regional differences in, 71-72
  law and, 81-84
    accountability of, 83-84
    difficulties imposed by, 81-83
    expanding role of, 81
  organizations for, 84-85
  professional preparation for, 75-76
    curriculum studied in, 75-76
    history of, 75
    pattern of, 76
    student teaching and, 75
  professional responsibility for, 76-79
    1950s, 60s, & 70s profiles of, 76-79
  student behavior and, 79-81

parent-teacher responsibility for, 79-80
school principal and, 80
social influence on, 80-81
Equal opportunity, 34-36
Exceptional children
  catagories of, 155

**F**

Federal Administrative Procedures Act of 1946, 228
Federal aid to education (*see* American public education, tax support of; *see also* specific acts)
Federal Aid to Education Act of 1942, 89
Federal Emergency Relief Administration, 212
Freedom of Information Act of 1966, 228
Free School Act of 1712, 16
Free School Society of the City of New York, 23

**G**

George Peabody College for Teachers, 137
Guidance counselor (*see* Public school guidance counselor)

**H**

Harvard, 14
Head Start, 58
  career ladder and, 61
High school
  early history of, 29
  (*see also* Secondary school teacher, role of)
Home Start, 58

**I**

Individualized Education Plan (IEP), 142, 157, 158, 159, 163, 165, 167
International Reading Association, 175, 176, 182, 184, 185, 187, 188

**J**

Job Corps, 91
Job Service, 129

**K**

Kaiser Center, 58
Kindergarten (*see* Early childhood education)
King's College, 19
  Columbia College as, 19

**L**

Lancaster system, 23-24
Land Grant College Act of 1862, 31-32, 73, 190, 205
Land Ordinance of 1785, 22
Life adjustment education, 33-34, 90
Lifelong education (*see* Community-based education)

**M**

Mann's credo, 26
Mann's reports, 25-26
Manpower Development and Training Act, 212
Massachusetts School Act, 205 (*see also* Act of 1642)
Mechanical arts education
  establishment of, 31-32
Military science education
  establishment of, 31-32
*Murray,* 35

**N**

National Assessment of Educational Progress (NAEP), 36
National Association of School Psychologists (NASP), 137, 138, 139, 146, 153
National Commission on the Reform of Secondary Education, 91
National Committee on Mental Health, 117
National Community Education Association (NCEA), 213, 214
National Community Education Advisory Council, 210, 225
National Community School Education Association, 209 (*see* NCEA)
National Council for Accreditation of Teacher Education (NCATE), 138
National Defense Education Act of 1958 (NDEA), 34, 90, 118

National Defense Education Act of 1964, 91
National Education Association (NEA), 32, 76, 77
National Environmental Policy Act of 1969, 228
National Institute for Mental Health (NIMH), 137
National Institute of Education, 35, 36
National Panel on High Schools and Adolescent Education, 91
National Society for the Promotion of Industrial Education, 190
National Youth Administration, 89
Native Americans,
  education of, 14, 16, 25
*NEA Research Bulletin,* 77, 85, 86
Neighborhood Youth Corps, 91
Normal schools, 25, 26, 29-30, 75

**O**

Occupational and Guidance Services Bureau, 118
Office of Economic Opportunity, 213
Ordinance of 1787, 22
Oxford, 10, 11, 12, 16

**P**

Panel of Youth of President's Science Advisory Committee, 91
*PASE v. Joseph P. Hannon,* 151
Planned Parenthood, 129
Progressive Education Association, 32-33
Project English, 91
PTA, 207, 213, 217, 231
Public school administration
  positions in, 103-109
    assessment unit, 108
    assistant/associate superintendent, superintendent, 106
    assistant principal, principal, 105-106
    attendance officer, 107
    audio-visual services, 107
    business administration, 107
    director, supervisor, coordinator, 106
    food services, 107
    history of, 103-104
    legal officer, 106-107
    personnel officer, 107-108
    prerequisites for, 104-105

professional organizations, 109
public relations officer, 108
state departments of education, 108-109
support services officer, 108
organizations for 111-115
trends in,
  civil rights conflicts, 110
  curriculum changes, 109-110
  federal government's role, 111
  political action, 109
  public/private conflict, 110
  reduced revenue, 110
Public school guidance counselor
developmental perspective and, 120
guidelines for, 119, 120-121
  assessment movement and, 117-118
  behavioral approach and, 119
  career approach and, 119-120
  client-centered approach and, 118
  division of labor and, 116
  evolution of approaches and, 118-121
  federal government and, 118
  growth of technology and, 116-117
  mental health and, 117
  vocational education and, 117
  vocational planning and, 118
issues and trends for, 130-132
professional organizations for, 132-133
professional preparation for, 121-126
  expectations of, 123-126
  general background of, 121-122
  internship for, 122
  laboratory activities and, 122
  practicum and, 122
professional responsibilities of, 126-130
  elementary school and, 126-127
  middle/junior high school and, 127-128
  secondary school and, 128-129
Public school psychologist
historical overview of, 136-138
issues and trends for, 148-152
  American social change, 148-149
  public school changes, 149-150
  school practice changes, 150-152
professional journals for, 147-148
professional organizations for, 146-147
professional preparation for, 138-141
  APA standards, 139-140
  NASP standards, 138-139
  state requirements for, 140-141
professional responsibilities of, 141-146

individuals as, 141-144
groups as, 144-145
organizations as, 145-146
*P. v. Riles.* 151
Public Works Administration, 212

**R**

Reading specialist
professional organizations for, 187
professional preparation for, 182-185
  International Reading Association recommendations, 183-184
professional roles/responsibilities of, 174-182
  Botel's definition of, 177
  International Reading Association's definition of, 175-176
  Pikulski and Ross's definition of, 180-181
  Robinson's definition of, 177-178
  Smith et al.'s definition of, 178-180
trends and issues for, 185-186
  differing certification, 186
  differing job titles, 186
  misleading job descriptions, 186
  varying programs, 186
Reed Act of 1929, 118
Reformation education
classics and, 11
early history of, 10-12
elementary education and, 11-13
Regent's Inquiry, 89
Religion
public schools and
  break between, 35
  nonsectarian Christianity and, 21
Renaissance education
discussion of, 6-10
emphasis of, 6
printing and, 8-9

**S**

*Schempp*, 35
School psychologist (*see* Public school psychologist)
Secondary school teacher, role of
historical perspective of, 87-92
  classroom emphasis in, 88
  purpose and curriculum in, 88-92
issues for, 96-101

constituents as, 97-98
location as, 100-101
methods as, 98-99
personnel as, 99-100
philosophy as, 99
purpose as, 97
preparation for, 93-94
past, 93
present, 93-94
professional organizations for, 101-102
professional responsibilities for, 94-96
to community, 96
to profession, 94-95
to student, 95-96
Segregation
early history of, 28, 72
illegality of, 34-35, 73, 81-82
Slaves
education of, 16, 25
Smith-Hughes Vocational Education Act of
1917, 32, 191, 211
Smith Lever Act of 1914, 211
Society for the Propagation of the Gospel
in Foreign Parts, 16, 18
Special educator, role of
ancillary personnel and, 163-165
psychological services, 163
school guidance counselor, 164
social workers, 164-165
speech and hearing specialists, 164
history of, 155-159
18th & 19th century in, 156
20th century in, 156-159
outside classroom, 161-163
administration, 162-163
aides, 162
consultant, 161-162
professional organizations for, 170-172
professional preparation for, 159-161
resource room teacher, 160
itinerant teacher, 160
self-contained teacher, 160
trends and issues for, 165-169
deinstitutionalization, 167-168
early intervention, 169
handicap prevention, 169
handicap recreation, 169
mainstreaming, 165-167
normalization, 168
rights of handicapped, 168-169
Stanford-Binet test, 156
Sunday school

establishment of
England and, 23
United States and, 23

**T**

Teacher's institutes, 27
establishment of, 73
(*see also* Normal schools)
Tennessee Valley Authority, 212
Textbooks
American principles in, 24
first used in U.S.A., 24
Trinity College, 11
Troy Seminary, 73

**U**

U.S. Department of Commerce, Bureau of
the Census, 148, 153
U.S. Department of Education
early history of, 27, 32
U.S. Office of Community Education, 213
U.S. Office of Education (USOE), 89, 118,
157,196,213
University of Chicago Laboratory School,
30-31

**V**

Vocational education
curriculum/administration of, 192-195
advisory councils in, 194
cooperative programs in, 194
curriculum structure in, 193
service areas in, 191
skill-acquiring courses in, 192-193
staff training in, 194-195
vocational centers, 193-194
definition of, 189-190
future outlook for, 195
historical/legal overview of, 190-191
early history of, 190
20th century and, 191
Vocational Education Act of 1963, 91, 191,
212
Vocational Rehabilitation Act of 1967,
213

**W**

William and Mary College, 15, 21

White House Conference on Children, 58
Women
  education of

early reasons for, 21
first college for, 73
Works Progress Administration, 212

**DATE DUE**